A GENERAL PRACTITIONER'S GUIDE TO INSOLVENCY

A GENERAL PRACTITIONER'S GUIDE TO INSOLVENCY

Paul Finn

Butterworths
London, Dublin and Edinburgh
1993

United Kingdom	Butterworth & Co (Publishers) Ltd, 88 Kingsway, LONDON WC2B 6AB and 4 Hill Street, EDINBURGH EH2 3JZ
Australia	Butterworths, SYDNEY, MELBOURNE, BRISBANE, ADELAIDE, PERTH, CANBERRA and HOBART
Belgium	Butterworth & Co (Publishers) Ltd, BRUSSELS
Canada	Butterworths Canada Ltd, TORONTO and VANCOUVER
Ireland	Butterworth (Ireland) Ltd, DUBLIN
Malaysia	Malayan Law Journal Sdn Bhd, KUALA LUMPUR
New Zealand	Butterworths of New Zealand Ltd, WELLINGTON and AUCKLAND
Puerto Rico	Equity de Puerto Rico, Inc, HATO REY
Singapore	Butterworths Asia, SINGAPORE
USA	Butterworth Legal Publishers, AUSTIN, Texas; BOSTON, Massachusetts; CLEARWATER, Florida (D & S Publishers); ORFORD, New Hampshire (Equity Publishing); ST PAUL, Minnesota; and SEATTLE, Washington

All rights reserved. No part of this publication may be reproduced in any material form (including photocopying or storing it in any medium by electronic means and whether or not transiently or incidentally to some other use of this publication) without the written permission of the copyright owner except in accordance with the provisions of the Copyright, Designs and Patents Act 1988 or under the terms of a licence issued by the Copyright Licensing Agency Ltd, 90 Tottenham Court Road, London, England W1P 9HE. Applications for the copyright owner's written permission to reproduce any part of this publication should be addressed to the publisher.

Warning : The doing of an unauthorised act in relation to a copyright work may result in both a civil claim for damages and criminal prosecution.

© Paul Finn 1993

A CIP Catalogue record for this book is available from the British Library.

ISBN 0 406 02124 4

Printed and bound in Great Britain by Butler & Tanner Ltd, Frome and London

This book is dedicated to the army of unlicensed practitioners of insolvency

PREFACE

> Annual income twenty pounds, annual expenditure nineteen nineteen six, result happiness. Annual income twenty pounds, annual expenditure twenty pounds ought and six, result misery.

In these simple words to young David Copperfield, Mr Micawber defined insolvency and its effects upon an individual's well-being. If only it were so simple in the context of today's insolvency law!

What constitutes 'insolvent' or 'insolvency' depends upon the circumstances under discussion and requires specific statutory tests to be applied to suit those circumstances. Those tests are considered in further detail in Part 1, **1.1**, but the problem in defining the subject itself gives some indication of the difficulties facing general practitioners in attempting to advise a financially troubled client.

This book seeks to make that task a realistic possibility, not by attempting to replace the insolvency practitioner but by taking the general practitioner into his 'world' so that he might be in a position to give both initial advice and continuing comfort to the client through his own understanding of any required formal insolvency procedure.

General practitioners seeking a more subjective reason for strengthening their understanding of the subject need look no further than the remarks of the judge in *Re Produce Marketing Consortium Ltd* who made it perfectly clear that auditors could face claims by their own clients if they failed to give the appropriate advice concerning wrongful trading and the client had a judgment awarded against them as a result.

It is of course true that in most cases the involvement of a licensed practitioner will be essential for the purposes of taking any formal appointment, but the general practitioner could and should play an important role in 'holding the hand' of his client during the early days of financial problems. Thereafter, subject only to the limits of his own insolvency knowledge and experience, he could continue to assist his client either by working with the office-holder or by ensuring that the office-holder carries out his duties and exercises his powers in accordance with the relevant law.

Any text book on insolvency must of necessity devote considerable space to detailing statutory requirements and references. What this book attempts to do is to bring together the various sections of the Insolvency Act 1986 and the Insolvency Rules 1986 within each particular area under discussion so that the general practitioner is afforded an instant 'snap-shot' of what is, should or could be happening at any given time following an insolvency instruction.

The text is divided into three parts, the first dealing with corporate insolvency and the second individual or personal insolvency. The third section is an A to Z of insolvency terminology, written to give the general practitioner the immediate explanation or answers to the more likely phraseology or questions which arise in insolvency-related situations.

The text is cross-referenced; in most instances the fuller definition or explanation will appear in Part 3. Where, however, an important subject such as fraudulent or wrongful trading is encountered within the earlier parts and considered there in full detail, Part 3 will refer the reader to the relevant detail within the earlier text. References to terms found in the Glossary, both in the text (where appropriate) and within the Glossary itself, are printed in small capitals.

I am indebted to my partners Kevin Murphy and Pamela Wade for their invaluable input and to Jill and the boys for their patient support over many months of week-end writing.

My special thanks also to Peter Horrocks and his colleague Joe Bannister of solicitors Lovell White Durrant for reading the text and for their helpful and constructive suggestions.

Notwithstanding all the support received, the responsibility for the text and any mistakes therein, is mine alone.

Paul Finn
Finn Associates
London

August 1993

CONTENTS

Preface vii
Table of statutes xiii
Table of cases xvii
Abbreviations xxi

PART 1 CORPORATE INSOLVENCY

I PRELIMINARY CONSIDERATIONS 3

The definition of insolvency 3
Identifying the client: potential conflicts of interest 4
Avoidance of conflict: separate representation 4

II IMMEDIATE STEPS UPON RECEIPT OF INSTRUCTIONS 5

The insolvency practitioner's approach 5
Ascertaining the exact state of the company's financial position 5
Advantages of a current Statement of Affairs over an historic Balance Sheet 5
Build-up of the figures 6
Format of the Statement of Affairs 6
Pledged assets 6
Bank as a preferential creditor 6
Bank's security under a floating charge 8
Assets subject to hire-purchase or lease agreements 8
Assets caught by a bank's fixed charge: plant and machinery 8
Assets not specifically pledged 9
Preferential creditors 9
Unsecured creditors 9
Inclusion of members in overall deficiency 9
Bases of valuation for Statement of Affairs purposes 10
Need to compare differing bases of valuation 10
Additional claims arising upon insolvency 10
VAT element of creditors' claims 10
Costs of realisation 12
Analysis of the Statements of Affairs 12
Construction of a Surplus and Deficiency Account 12
The available options: the five alternatives to liquidation 16

III GENERAL MORATORIUM 17

Difficulty in achieving creditors' consent 17
Potential benefits to creditors 17
Issues which require to be addressed 18
Advances secured by directors' guarantees/third party collateral 18
Advances secured by a fixed charge 18
Advances secured by a floating charge 18
Need for the involvement of an insolvency practitioner 19
Preparing for meeting with the company's creditors 19
Other considerations 20
Agreement to the scheme 20
Flow chart 20

IV SCHEME UNDER COMPANIES ACT 1985 s 425 ('SECTION 425 SCHEME') 23

Advantage over informal arrangement 23
Need for supervision by an insolvency practitioner 23
Required majorities 23
Implementing the scheme 23
Difficulty in obtaining required majorities 24
The more likely routes 24
Interrelationship between routes 24
Ability to 'reverse' out of liquidation via CVA route 24
Importance of the CVA as a medium for reconstruction 26

V COMPANY VOLUNTARY ARRANGMENT (CVA) 27

Background considerations 27
As a way forward in its own right 27
Position of secured and preferential creditors 27
Need for supervision by an insolvency practitioner 28
Preparing for the CVA – proposals 28
Contents of directors' report to nominee 28
Submission of proposals to court 28
Summoning meetings of members and creditors 29
Required majorities 29
Only creditors receiving formal notice bound by scheme 29
Chairman to prepare and file report 29
Effect of the scheme 30
Comparison of CVA with Section 425 Scheme 30
Risk of winding-up petition 31

VI ADMINISTRATION ORDER 33

Definition 33
Reason for choosing the administration order route 33
Advantages to the directors 34
Advantages to the company 34
Advantages to the unsecured creditors 34
Advantage to the office-holder 35
The position of preferential creditors 35
The position of the holder of a floating charge – right to receive notice of petition 35

Right of floating charge-holder to appoint receiver
    following petition. 35
Effect of the appointment of an administrative receiver – duties of the court 36
Application for the order 36
Reasons for requesting an administration order 36
Independent expert's report 37
Making the application – documentation to be filed with the court 38
The petition 38
Service of the petition 39
Consideration of the application by the court 39
Which proposals to incorporate?; a solution to the problem. 39
Effect of the application 40
Effect of the order 41
Nature of the appointment 42
Powers of the administrator 42
Duties and procedure following appointment 46
Company Voluntary Arrangement (CVA) as an 'exit-route'
    from administration 50
The unintended 'side-effects' of legislation 50
The role of the general practitioner in obtaining an administration order (case
    study) 51
The role of the general practitioner in an administration 53

VII ADMINISTRATIVE RECEIVERSHIP 55

Initial considerations 55
Understanding the bank's perception 55
The significance and importance of the floating charge 56
Definition 56
Registering the charge 57
Reason for choosing the administrative receivership route 57
Advantages to the directors 57
Advantages to the company 57
The position of the preferential creditors 58
Events leading up to the appointment of administrative receivers 59
Nature of the appointment 62
Powers of the administrative receiver 63
Duties and procedure following appointment 66
Powers and responsibilities of directors following appointment of administrative
    receivers 71
The conduct of the receivership 71
Life after receivership (case study) 73

VIII LIQUIDATION 75

The enforced alternative: the creditors' viewpoint 75
Creditors' Voluntary Liquidation as a 'last resort' 75
The choice of liquidator: members v creditors 75
The continuing role of the general practitioner 76

IX WHICH WAY FORWARD? – STRATEGIC PLANNING 77

Anticipating creditors' reactions 77
Considering the position of the bank 77

The next consideration; the reaction of the creditors 79
Matters requiring attention *before* liquidation 79
The personal position of the directors 80
Fraudulent trading 81
Wrongful trading 83
Wrongful trading compared with fraudulent trading 87
Closing observations 87

PART 2   PERSONAL INSOLVENCY

Introduction 91
The need to think positively 91
Personal insolvency: 'individual' or 'collective'? 91
Initial involvement of the general practitioner 92
Informal moratorium 94
Deed of Arrangement 94
Individual Voluntary Arrangement 95
IVAs and the general practitioner 96
Bankruptcy 98
Bankruptcy and the general practitioner 98
Charge taken by trustee on bankrupt's home 101
The general practitioner as adviser to a bankrupt's creditor 103
Partnership Insolvency 105

PART 3   GLOSSARY

Index to Glossary 111

Index 189

TABLE OF STATUTES

References to *Statutes* are to Halsbury's Statutes of England (Fourth Edition) showing the volume and page at which the annotated text of an Act may be found.

	PARA
Agricultural Credits Act 1928 (1 *Statutes* 885)	3.5
Bills of Sale Act 1878 (5 *Statutes* 394)	3.9
Companies Act 1929	
s 145	3.76
Companies Act 1948	
s 208	1.37
293	3.12
Companies Act 1981	
s 106	3.12
Companies Act 1985 (8 *Statutes* 104)	1.84; 3.15, 3.28
s 36A	1.108
368	3.55
369	3.90
371	3.55
375	3.86
378, 379	3.90
395	1.109
405(1)	1.145
425	1.25, 1.36, 1.37, 1.38, 1.42, 1.43, 1.46, 1.59, 1.60, 1.61, 1.74
431–441	3.15
458	1.176
588	3.12
630	1.173
651–653	3.28
Companies Act 1989	95
Company Directors Disqualification Act 1986 (8 *Statutes* 781)	1.178, 1.187; 2.47; 3.41, 3.52
s 2–4, 6	3.15
7	3.15
(3)	1.151
(c)	1.96
(d)	1.151
8–10	3.15
11	2.32; 3.15
13, 15	3.15
16(2)	1.96
22(5)	3.76
Sch 1	3.15
Pt I, II	3.15

	PARA
Deed of Arrangement Act 1914 (4 *Statutes* 672)	2.9; 3.26
Employment Protection (Consolidation) Act 1978 (16 *Statutes* 232)	3.31
Sch 13	3.31
Finance Act 1990	1.21, 1.100, 1.102, 1.148
Income and Corporation Taxes Act 1988 (44 *Statutes* 1)	3.38
s 343	3.37
(4)	3.37
768	3.38
Insolvency Act 1985 (4 *Statutes* 699)	1.43, 1.102, 1.108, 1.173, 1.180
Insolvency Act 1986 (4 *Statutes* 717)	1.1, 1.27, 1.43, 1.47, 1.86, 1.102, 1.115, 1.134, 1.138; 2.10, 2.23, 2.33, 2.34, 2.40, 2.47, 2.48; 3.7, 3.11, 3.12, 3.16, 3.18, 3.20, 3.22, 3.27, 3.28, 3.33, 3.39, 3.40, 3.41, 3.42, 3.44, 3.52, 3.60, 3.62, 3.64, 3.66, 3.79, 3.81, 3.86
s 4(4)	1.55
(6)	1.58
6	1.57
8(2)	1.63
(3)	1.74
(b)	1.48
9(1)	1.73
(3)	1.72, 1.81
10	1.81
11	1.82
(1)(a)	1.82
(b)	1.82, 1.87; 3.66
(2)	1.82
(3)	1.82
(a)–(d)	1.82
(5)	3.66
12	1.94
14	1.87; 3.31
(1), (2)	1.87
15	1.87, 1.132

xiv Table of statutes

	PARA
Insolvency Act 1986—contd	
s 15(a)	1.87
17	1.93
18	1.99
21	1.94
22	1.88
(1)	1.95
(3)	1.95, 1.100, 1.146
(a)–(d)	1.95
(5)	1.95
23	1.91, 1.100
24	1.92, 1.100, 1.103
(5)	1.92
26	3.21
(1)	1.92
29	1.108; 3.3
33, 35	1.32
38	1.29
39	1.136
40	1.113, 1.115, 1.150; 3.66
(2), (3)	1.113
42	1.131
(3)	1.131
43	1.87, 1.132, 1.138
(1)	1.147
(3)	1.132, 1.138
(5)	1.147
44	1.126; 3.31
(1)(a)	1.125
(b), (c)	1.126
46	1.145
47	1.133, 1.146
(1)–(3), (5), (6)	1.146
48	1.149; 3.21
(1), (2), (4)	1.149
49	3.21
84	3.22, 3.90
85	3.22
89	1.1; 3.43, 3.55
91	3.55
93	3.55
94	3.25
96	3.55
98	3.15, 3.21, 3.22, 3.55, 3.67, 3.69, 3.86
99, 100	3.22
101, 103	3.21
106	3.28
108	3.52, 3.55
109	3.22
112	3.30
114	3.22
122	1.1; 3.18
123	1.1; 3.18
(1)(e)	1.1
124, 125, 127, 128, 131, 132	3.18
135	3.59, 3.67
136(5)	3.18
141	3.21
155	3.18
164	3.32, 3.52
166	3.52
(3)	3.12

	PARA
Insolvency Act 1986—contd	
s 167–169	3.52
171	3.52, 3.55
172	3.52
175	1.115
(2)(a)	3.66
176	3.30
177	3.66, 3.77
178	3.27
(5)	3.27
179, 181	3.27
188	3.22
189	3.47, 3.66
201–205	3.28
Pt IV	
Ch X (ss 206–219)	3.53
s 212	1.137
213	1.1, 1.29, 1.34, 1.88, 1.171, 1.172, 1.173, 1.175, 1.179, 1.182; 3.15
(1)	1.175
214	1.1, 1.29, 1.34, 1.88, 1.171, 1.179, 1.83, 1.84, 1.85, 1.86; 3.15, 3.43
(2)–(4)	1.182
216	3.62
218	3.52
233	1.89, 1.134
(1)(c)	1.59
234	1.89, 1.134; 3.49
(1)	3.49
(a)–(d)	3.49
(2)	3.49
235	1.89
(3)	1.89, 1.134
(a)–(e)	1.134
236	1.89, 1.134
(2)	1.89
(a)–(c)	1.89
(3)	1.89
238	1.29, 1.34, 1.72, 1.97, 1.133; 3.7, 3.15
239	1.29, 1.34, 1.88, 1.97, 1.133; 3.7, 3.15, 3.18, 3.64
240	1.72; 3.15, 3.64
241	3.64
242, 243	1.72
244	1.34, 1.97, 1.133; 3.33, 3.47
245	1.72, 1.97; 3.7, 3.8, 3.13
(2), (5)	3.8
246	1.89, 1.157; 3.49
(1)	3.49
(a)–(c)	3.49
(2), (3)	3.49
249	3.7
251	1.84, 1.115; 3.66, 3.76
252	3.39, 3.66
253, 256	3.39

Table of statutes xv

Insolvency Act 1986—contd	PARA
s 258(7)	3.65
260	3.39
264	3.10, 3.39
267, 268	3.10
269	3.39
272	2.19; 3.10
273	3.10, 3.46
275	2.33
276	3.39
278, 279	2.33
281	2.34
(3)–(5)	2.34
282	2.39
283	2.22
(2)	2.22
284, 285	3.10
286	3.10, 3.46, 3.58, 3.66
287	3.10, 3.81
288	3.10
289	3.10
290	2.31
291	2.31; 3.10
293	3.10, 3.82
294	3.82
301	3.21
(2)	3.21
303, 305	3.82
306–308	1.22
313	2.29
314	3.82
315–321	3.27
328	2.39; 3.47
329	2.39
332	2.29
336	2.26, 2.27, 2.28
337	2.27, 2.28
339, 340	3.7, 3.64
341, 342	3.64
343	3.33
344	3.9
350–359	3.11
360	2.32; 3.11
361, 362	3.11
386	3.65, 3.66
(1)	3.66
387(2)(a)	1.69; 3.66
(b)	3.66
(3)(a)	1.69; 3.66
(c)	3.66
(4), (5)	3.66
(6)(a)	3.66
388–390	3.41

Insolvency Act 1986—contd	PARA
s 423	3.15
427	2.32
430	1.146
435	3.7
(1)–(4)	3.7
(5)	3.7
(a), (b)	3.7
(6)	3.7
(a), (b)	3.7
(7)	3.7
(8)	3.7
(a), (b)	3.7
(9)	3.7
(10)	3.7
(a), (b)	3.7
(11)	3.7
436	2.22
Sch 1	1.85, 1.86, 1.130, 1.131
para 1–23	1.86
Sch 4	3.52
Sch 5	3.82
Sch 6	1.15, 1.29, 2.39; 3.31, 3.66
Sch 10	1.146
Sch 11 para 1	1.71
Judgments Act 1838 (22 *Statutes* 302)	
s 17	3.47
Law of Distress Amendment Act 1888 (13 *Statutes* 623)	143
Law of Property Act 1925 (37 *Statutes* 72)	1.31, 1.82; 3.48, 3.70, 3.71
s 30	2.26, 2.27
101, 109	3.71
Magistrates' Courts Act 1980 (27 *Statutes* 143)	2.34
Matrimonial and Family Proceedings Act 1984 (27 *Statutes* 857)	2.34
Matrimonial Homes Act 1983 (27 *Statutes* 614)	2.27
Mental Health Act 1983 (28 *Statutes* 632)	3.41
Partnerships Act 1890 (32 *Statutes* 636)	
s 33	2.47
Sale of Goods Act 1979 (39 *Statutes* 106):	3.72
Taxation of Chargeable Gains Act 1992 (43 *Statutes* 1439)	
s 66	3.81
Value Added Tax Act 1983 (48 *Statutes* 598)	
s 22(3)	1.148

TABLE OF CASES

PARA

A

Alabaster and Alabaster Automobiles Ltd v S P J Wadstead & P H Finn (1990) unreported . 1.21
Alliance Acceptances Co Ltd v Graham (1974) 10 SASR 220 . . . . . 1.138
Aluminium Industrie Vaassen BV v Romalpa Aluminium Ltd [1976] 2 All ER 552, [1976]
 1 WLR 676, 119 Sol Jo 318; affd [1976] 2 All ER 552, [1976] 1 WLR 676, 120 Sol Jo
 95, [1976] 1 Lloyd's Rep 443, CA 3.72
American Express International Banking Corpn v Hurley [1985] 3 All ER 564, [1986]
 BCLC 52, 2 BCC 98, 993, [1985] NLJ Rep 1034, 1985 FLR 350 . . . . 1.127
Atlantic Computer Systems plc, Re [1992] Ch 505, [1992] 1 All ER 476, [1992] 2 WLR
 367, [1991] BCLC 606, [1990] BCC 859, CA 1.167

B

Bacon (M C) Ltd, Re [1990] BCLC 324, [1990] BCC 78 . . . . . . 3.76
Banbury Foods Pty Ltd v National Bank of Australasia Ltd (1984) 58 ALJR 199 . . 1.21
Bank of Baroda v Panessar [1987] Ch 335, [1986] 3 All ER 751, [1987] 2 WLR 208, 131
 Sol Jo 21, [1986] BCLC 497, 2 BCC 99, 288, [1986] NLJ Rep 963, [1987] LS Gaz R
 339 . . . . 1.121
Borden (UK) Ltd v Scottish Timber Products Ltd [1981] Ch 25, [1979] 3 All ER 961,
 [1979] 3 WLR 672, 123 Sol Jo 688, [1980] 1 Lloyd's Rep 160, CA . . . 3.72
Brightlife Ltd, Re [1987] Ch 200, [1986] 3 All ER 673, [1987] 2 WLR 197, 131 Sol Jo
 132, [1986] BCLC 418, 2 BCC 99, 359, [1987] LS Gaz R 653 . . . . 1.115
Bristol Airport plc v Powdrill [1990] Ch 744, [1990] 2 All ER 493, [1990] 2 WLR 1362,
 [1990] BCLC 585, [1990] BCC 130, [1990] 17 LS Gaz R 28, 1 S & B AvR IV/121,
 CA 3.49

C

Centrebind Ltd, Re [1966] 3 All ER 889, [1967] 1 WLR 377, 110 Sol Jo 905 . . . 3.12
Clarks of Hove Ltd v Bakers' Union [1979] 1 All ER 152, [1978] 1 WLR 1207, [1978]
 ICR 1076, 13 ITR 356, sub nom Bakers' Union v Clarks of Hove Ltd [1978] IRLR
 366, 122 Sol Jo 643, CA 3.31
Clayton's Case. See Devaynes v Noble, Clayton's Case
Company, a (No 001418 of 1988), Re [1991] BCLC 197, [1990] BCC 526 . . 1.173
Condon, Re, ex p James (1874) 9 Ch App 609, [1874-80] All ER Rep 388, 43 LJ Bcy 107,
 30 LT 773, 22 WR 937 . . . . 1.83
Contract Corpn, Re, Gooch's Case (1872) 7 Ch App 207, 41 LJ Ch 338, 26 LT 177, 20 WR
 345 . . . . 1.83
Cretanor Maritime Co Ltd v Irish Marine Management Ltd, The Cretan Harmony [1978] 3
 All ER 164, [1978] 1 WLR 966, 122 Sol Jo 298, [1978] 1 Lloyd's Rep 425, CA . 3.54
Cuckmere Brick Co Ltd v Mutual Finance Ltd [1971] Ch 949, [1971] 2 All ER 633, [1971]
 2 WLR 1207, 115 Sol Jo 288, 22 P & CR 624, [1971] RVR 126, CA . . . 1.137
Cyona Distributors Ltd, Re [1967] Ch 889, [1967] 1 All ER 281, [1967] 2 WLR 369, 110
 Sol Jo 943, CA 1.173

D

DMG Realisations Ltd, Re (1990) unreported 3.31
Devaynes v Noble, Clayton's Case (1816) 1 Mer 529, 572, [1814-23] All ER Rep 1, 8 LJ Ch
 256, 35 ER 767 . . . . 3.13

xviii Table of cases

PARA

Downsview Nominees Ltd v First City Corpn Ltd [1993] AC 295, [1993] 2 WLR 86, 136
Sol Jo LB 324, [1992] 45 LS Gaz R 26, PC 1.137

G

Gooch's Case, Re. See Contract Corpn, Re, Gooch's Case
Griffiths v Secretary of State for Social Services [1974] QB 468, [1973] 3 All ER 1184,
[1973] 3 WLR 831, 117 Sol Jo 873 . . . . 3.31

H

Harris Simons Construction Ltd, Re [1989] 1 WLR 368, 133 Sol Jo 122, [1989] BCLC 202,
5 BCC 11, [1989] 8 LS Gaz R 43 . . . . 1.79, 1.132
Hendy Lennox (Industrial Engines) Ltd v Grahame Puttick Ltd [1984] 2 All ER 152, [1984]
1 WLR 485, 128 Sol Jo 220, [1984] 2 Lloyd's Rep 422, [1984] BCLC 285, [1984] LS
Gaz R 585 . . . . 3.72
Hurley v American Express International Banking Corpn [1985] 3 All ER 564, [1986]
BCLC 52, [1985] NLJ Rep 1034, 1985 FLR 350 . . . . . . 1.139

I

Imperial Motors (UK) Ltd, Re [1990] BCLC 29, 5 BCC 214 . . . . 1.79
IRC v Goldblatt [1972] Ch 498, [1972] 2 All ER 202, [1972] 2 WLR 953, 116 Sol Jo 332,
47 TC 483 . . . . 3.66
IRC v Olive Mill Ltd [1963] 2 All ER 130, [1963] 1 WLR 712, 107 Sol Jo 476, 41 TC 77,
[1963] TR 59, 42 ATC 74 . . . . 3.38
IRC v Olive Mill Spinners Ltd [1963] 2 All ER 130, [1963] 1 WLR 712, 107 Sol Jo 476,
41 TC 77, [1963] TR 59, 42 ATC 74 . . . . 3.81

J

Johnson (B) & Co (Builders) Ltd, Re [1955] Ch 634, [1955] 2 All ER 775, [1955] 3 WLR
269, 99 Sol Jo 490, CA 1.136

L

Leitch (William C) Bros Ltd, Re [1932] 2 Ch 71, [1932] All ER Rep 892, 101 LJ Ch 380,
148 LT 106 . . . . 1.174
Levy v Abercorris Slate and Slab Co (1887) 37 Ch D 260, [1886-90] All ER Rep 509, 57
LJ Ch 202, 58 LT 218, 36 WR 411, 4 TLR 34 . . . . . . 3.24
Lewis Merthyr Consolidated Collieries Ltd, Re, Lloyds Bank v Lewis Merthyr Consolidated
Collieries Ltd [1929] 1 Ch 498, 98 LJ Ch 353, 140 LT 321, 73 Sol Jo 27, 22 BWCC
20, CA 3.66
Litster v Forth Dry Dock and Engineering Co Ltd [1990] 1 AC 546, [1989] 1 All ER 1134,
[1989] 2 WLR 634, [1989] ICR 341, [1989] IRLR 161, 133 Sol Jo 455, [1989] NLJR
400, HL 3.31

M

Maidstone Buildings Provisions Ltd, Re [1971] 3 All ER 363, [1971] 1 WLR 1085, 115 Sol
Jo 464 . . . . 1.177
Mareva Cia Naviera SA v International Bulkcarriers SA, The Mareva [1980] 1 All ER
213n, 119 Sol Jo 660, [1975] 2 Lloyd's Rep 509, CA 3.54
Midland Bank Ltd v Joliman Finance Ltd (1967) 203 Estates Gazette 1039 . . 1.138

N

New Bullas Trading Ltd, Re [1993] BCC 251 . . . . . . 3.34
Newhart Developments Ltd v Co-operative Commercial Bank Ltd [1978] QB 814, [1978] 2
All ER 896, [1978] 2 WLR 636, 121 Sol Jo 847, CA 1.154

O

Oriental Bank Corpn, Re, ex p Guillemin (1884) 28 Ch D 634, 54 LJ Ch 322, 52 LT 167,
1 TLR 9 . . . . 3.31

PARA

P

Paramount Airways Ltd, Re. See Bristol Airport plc v Powdrill
Peck (Polly) International plc, Re [1992] BCLC 1025, [1991] BCC 503 . . . 3.21
Piller (Anton) KG v Manufacturing Processes Ltd [1976] Ch 55, [1976] 1 All ER 779,
 [1976] 2 WLR 162, 120 Sol Jo 63, [1976] RPC 719, CA 3.6
Portbase Clothing Ltd, Re [1993] 3 All ER 829, [1993] 3 WLR 14, [1993] BCLC 796,
 BCC 96 . . . . 1.115, 1.150
Power v Sharp Investments Ltd & Chandru Mahtani [1993] BCC 609 . . . 3.8
Purpoint Ltd, Re [1991] BCLC 491, [1991] BCC 121 . . . . . 1.173

R

R v Grantham [1984] QB 675, [1984] 3 All ER 166, [1984] 2 WLR 815, 128 Sol Jo 331,
 79 Cr App Rep 86, [1984] BCLC 270, [1984] LS Gaz R 1437, [1984] Crim LR 492,
 CA 1.174
Rowbotham Baxter Ltd, Re [1990] BCLC 397, [1990] BCC 113 . . . 1.74

S

SEIL Trade Finance Ltd, Re [1992] BCC 538 . . . . . . 3.49
Saunders (G L) Ltd, Re [1986] 1 WLR 215, 130 Sol Jo 166, [1986] BCLC 40, [1986] LS
 Gaz R 779 . . . . 3.66
Scotlane Ltd, Re (1986) unreported 3.66
Secretary of State for Employment v Spence [1987] QB 179, [1986] 3 All ER 616, [1986] 3
 WLR 380, [1986] 3 CMLR 647, [1986] ICR 651, [1986] IRLR 248, 130 Sol Jo 407,
 [1986] LS Gaz R 2084, CA 3.31
Sewell v DMG Realisations Case Nos 15486/89 - 15506/89; 13227/89 - 13254/89 and
 13681/89 . . . . 3.31
Siebe Gorman & Co Ltd v Barclays Bank Ltd [1979] 2 Lloyd's Rep 142 . . 3.33
Standard Chartered Bank Ltd v Walker [1982] 3 All ER 938, [1982] 1 WLR 1410, 126 Sol
 Jo 479, 264 Estates Gazette 345, [1982] LS Gaz R 1137, [1982] Com LR 233, CA . 1.139

W

Warnford Investments Ltd v Duckworth [1979] Ch 127, [1978] 2 All ER 517, [1978] 2
 WLR 741, 76 P & CR 295, 122 Sol Jo 63 . . . . . . 3.60
Watts v Midland Bank plc [1986] BCLC 15, 2 BCC 98, 961 . . . 1.137, 1.154
Westminster Corpn v Haste [1950] Ch 442, [1950] 2 All ER 65, 114 JP 340, 66 (pt 1) TLR
 1083, 49 LGR 67 . . . . 1.156
White and Osmond (Parkstone) Ltd, Re (30 June 1960, unreported) . . . 1.174
Wood Preservation v Prior [1969] 1 WLR 1077 . . . . . . 3.38

ABBREVIATIONS

Unless otherwise stated, all references are to the Insolvency Act 1986.

CA 1929	Companies Act 1929
CA 1948	Companies Act 1948
CA 1985	Companies Act 1985
CDDA 1986	Company Directors Disqualification Act 1986
CVA	Company Voluntary Arrangement
CVL	Creditors' Voluntary Liquidation
DOA	Deed of Arrangement
EPA 1978	Employment Protection (Consolidation) Act 1978
FA	Finance Act
FA 1990	Finance Act 1990
IA 1985	Insolvency Act 1985
IA 1986	Insolvency Act 1986
ICAEW	Institute of Chartered Accountants in England and Wales
IPO	Insolvent Partnerships Order
IR 1986	Insolvency Rules 1986
IVA	Individual Voluntary Arrangement
JIEB	Joint Insolvency Examination Board
LPA 1925	Law of Property Act 1925
MHA 1983	Matrimonial Homes Act 1983
MVL	Members' Voluntary Liquidation
Newco	Newly formed subsidiary
OR	Official Receiver
ROT	Retention of Title
SPI	Society of Practitioners of Insolvency
TUPER 1981	Transfer of Undertakings (Protection of Employment) Regulations 1981

PART 1

CORPORATE INSOLVENCY

I PRELIMINARY CONSIDERATIONS

The definition of insolvency

1.1 Up to the implementation of the Insolvency Act 1986 most insolvency practitioners would have agreed that the 'standard' definition of insolvency was 'the inability to meet one's debts as and when they fell due'.

Since the Insolvency Act 1986 came into effect on 29 December 1986 we have a further definition placing the test onto an 'asset and liability basis'. Section 122 lists the circumstances in which a company may be wound up by the court, one of which being:

> (f) the company is unable to pay its debts.

Section 123 then gives a definition of inability to pay debts which includes the wording:

> A company is also deemed unable to pay its debts if it is proved to the satisfaction of the court that the value of the company's assets is less than the amount of its liabilities, taking into account its contingent and prospective liabilities.

This second 'definition' is in addition to the original 'test' of insolvency, itself restated in s123(1)(e):

> (a company is deemed unable to pay its debts) if it is proved to the satisfaction of the court that the company is unable to pay its debts as they fall due.

When assessing the solvency or otherwise of a company any practitioner should ensure that it passes *both* tests as otherwise problems could ensue if trading were continued on the strength of passing one but not both criteria and the company proceeded ultimately into insolvent liquidation. (see below for the definition of insolvent liquidation).

Other 'definitions' of or tests to determine insolvency *in the specific instances identified* include:

- MEMBERS' VOLUNTARY LIQUIDATION. If in the opinion of the directors the company will be able to pay its debts in full, together with statutory interest within 12 months from the date of winding up, then the company is deemed *solvent* for the purpose of s89.
- FRAUDULENT TRADING (s213). The test of whether a director could be guilty of a charge under this section is whether he was knowingly a party to the company incurring liabilities at a time when he knew that there was no reasonable prospect of those liabilities being discharged as they fell due or shortly thereafter (see **1.174**).
- WRONGFUL TRADING (s214). A company is deemed to have gone into insolvent liquidation if it goes into liquidation at a time when its assets are insufficient for the payment of its debts and other liabilities and the expenses of the winding up.

The preparation of a Statement of Affairs (discussed in paragraphs **1.4–1.23**) adjusted as necessary to include contingent and prospective liabilities will determine a position of solvency or insolvency on the 'assets and liabilities' criteria. On the basis of 'cash flow' it should not be difficult to assess the ability of the company to meet its liabilities as and when they fall due. One unmistakable sign which is often present and will usually establish a position of insolvency beyond doubt, is evidence of dishonoured cheques within the last few weeks of trading.

Identifying the client: potential conflicts of interest

1.2 The first thing to remember if a client company is in financial difficulties, is that your client cannot, of itself, consult with you (or for that matter with anyone else) for advice. Your client is a company, without the ability to speak or write; in practice it will be a director who seeks your help. This could bring about an immediate conflict of interest, for the interests of the individual could well clash with those of the company.

Consider for example a director who is a guarantor to the company's overdrawn bank account. He may well see his duty to his family as paramount and require advice on how he can best set about reducing the company's indebtedness and consequently his personal liability under the guarantee. This in itself is unlikely to have anything to do with the interests of the company and its creditors which may well call for a continuation of trade with bank borrowings at current if not increased levels.

A general practitioner could find himself in a position of conflict where he is asked to advise the board of a company how it should proceed and where the interests of individual members of the board are at variance; eg where some but not all of the directors are guarantors of the company's indebtedness.

The conflict becomes apparent in the case of a general practitioner being asked to advise a client company in financial difficulties where he is already acting for another client owed money by the financially troubled client company. Yet the potential conflict between a director in his individual position with his position as an officer of the company or that between the director and the company itself if anything calls for even greater care, simply *because* it is not quite so obvious and therefore likely to be overlooked until too late.

There are other situations, perhaps not all quite so obvious, which could lead to similar conflict. The point to remember however is that there must inevitably be a *potential* conflict situation whenever the client is a company.

Avoidance of conflict: separate representation

1.3 If you are to avoid the danger of being accused of acting for both company and director in a conflict situation, you should ensure separate representation for the director. Any insolvency practitioner introduced at this early stage would almost always advise the company, leaving you to look after the interests of the director. Where however there is to be some time elapse before an insolvency practitioner is consulted, the director's or company's solicitor could be approached. Remember however that you are going to be called upon to prepare accounting information upon which decisions will turn as to the 'way forward'. The solicitor would therefore inevitably adopt the role of advising the director and one of his first recommendations may well be that the company enlist the assistance of an insolvency practitioner.

II IMMEDIATE STEPS UPON RECEIPT OF INSTRUCTIONS

The insolvency practitioner's approach

1.4 What then should *you* be doing that an insolvency practitioner would do immediately following appointment? The answer is to:
1. Ascertain the *exact* state of the company's financial position.
2. Consider what options are available.
3. Plan a way forward in the light of your findings.

Let us consider these steps in further detail.

Ascertaining the exact state of the company's financial position

1.5 Here, at the very beginning, we arrive at the fundamental difference in approach which distinguishes the insolvency practitioner from the general practitioner, for whereas the former prepare up to date Statements of Affairs (preferably supported by Surplus and Deficiency Accounts) the latter tend to rely upon historic accounts (which were they consumables would be way past their 'use by' date) occasionally supported by unaudited 'management accounts' themselves two or three months old at best and often of doubtful accuracy.

What we need to do now is to follow the insolvency practitioner's lead and prepare an up to date Statement of (the company's) Affairs.

Advantages of a current Statement of Affairs over an historic Balance Sheet

1.6 The preparation of a Statement of Affairs brings with it distinct advantages, namely:
1. It shows the *current* financial position of the company; and
2. It groups the various assets with corresponding attaching liabilities, thereby establishing the financial position of each class of creditor, namely:
   - secured (by a fixed charge);
   - preferential;
   - covered by a floating charge;
   - unsecured.

The two things that every creditor wants to know when being asked to go along with any proposal which falls short of immediate payment in full, are 'how much?' and 'when?'

As we shall see it is the ability to identify the current position as it affects each class of creditor that enables us to answer the first question, with the answer to the second question following a consideration of available options.

Build-up of the figures

1.7 In preparing your figures, you may well find computerisation a mixed blessing. On the one hand, given proper organisation, the figures should already be available at least up to the end of the previous month. On the other hand it is not unusual to find a multitude of anomalies that for one reason or another have crept into the figures over a period of time which for no apparent reason have never been corrected. Thus, the time you 'gain on the swings', you tend to 'lose on the roundabouts'.

However the records are maintained, any general practitioner who has received a thorough training in preparing accounts from incomplete records should, with a little practice, have no difficulty in preparing an accurate Statement of Affairs. It affords the opportunity for the general practitioner to exercise his skills in the art of single-entry accounting, which has little in common with the science of double-entry bookkeeping. Indeed, you will find it not just helpful, but far simpler to prepare each component part of the Statement of Affairs in isolation, as it were, so that you end up with individual totals for each category of asset and liability which are then set-out in their own 'pigeon-holes' within the predetermined structure of the Statement.

Format of the Statement of Affairs

1.8 The format of a typical Statement of Affairs is set out in diagram 1.

In this 'pro-forma' Statement of Affairs, certain assumptions have been made which are identified by reference to notes 1–7. These notes are now explained as follows:

Pledged assets

1.9 Note 1. We start by grouping together those assets which have been 'pledged' against specific borrowings and relate the borrowings to the value of the assets.

In the example, the bank has advanced monies against a DEBENTURE granting fixed charges over the company's freehold property and book debts and a floating charge over the remaining assets.

Note 2. As the Statement of Affairs suggests, there is insufficient value in the freehold property and book debts to settle the bank in full, so that the estimated shortfall to the bank at this stage will be carried down to the next level of its security.

Bank as a preferential creditor

1.10 As will be further explained within the text, it is the preferential creditors who are first entitled to the proceeds of realisation of the 'unpledged' assets which are caught by a floating charge (subject to the costs of realisation). Thus, it is only after the preferential creditors have been paid in full that any surplus from realisations of unpledged assets caught by the bank's floating charge will be available to the bank.

It is precisely because the preferential creditors rank before the bank under its floating charge, that where a bank is facing a shortfall under its fixed charge it will

Diagram 1
Estimated ('Pro-Forma') Statement of Affairs

	Note		Book Value £	£
Secured	1	*Assets Specifically Pledged*		
		Freehold Property	x	
		Book debts	x	
		Less: Due to Bank	x	
	2	Shortfall to contra	x	
	3	Motor Vehicles	x	
		Less: Due on Hire Purchase	x	
		Surplus		x
		Shortfall to contra	x	
Preferential	4	*Assets Not Specifically Pledged*		
		Plant & Machinery		x
		Fixtures & Fittings		x
		Motor Vehicles (free of charge)		x
		Stock and Work in Progress		x
		Estimated Total Assets		x
	5	*Preferential Creditors*		
		PAYE & NI	x	
		VAT	x	
		Employees' claims	x	
	2	Bank for Wages paid	x	x
Floating charge		*Estimated surplus for bank under floating charge*		x
	2	Shortfall to Bank per contra		x
		Estimated surplus available for Unsecured Creditors		x
Unsecured	6	*Unsecured Creditors*		
		Trade & Expense	x	
		PAYE & NI	x	
		Hire Purchase per contra	x	
		Directors' Loans	x	x
		Estimated Deficiency as regards Unsecured Creditors		x
	7	Share Capital		x
		Estimated Overall Deficiency		x

seek to maximise any claim it might have which will rank pari passu with the other preferential creditors thereby 'lifting it up' into the 'preferential section'.

Where the bank has paid wages within the preferential period it is entitled to 'stand in the shoes' of the employees and claim the appropriate part of its lending as preferential. Note however how '*Clayton's Case*' can act against the bank and reduce, if not completely wipe out any claim and how banks frequently attempt to counter this problem through the medium of opening a 'wages account' (see **1.119**).

Bank's security under a floating charge

1.11 Once the preferential creditors have been paid in full, any surplus will next be available to meet any remaining shortfall to the bank under its floating charge. If, at this point there is a surplus after the bank has been paid in full, then this surplus will be available for division among the unsecured creditors.

In order to follow the payments to the bank under its various charges, culminating in the final balance being met from the assets caught by its floating charge, it has been necessary to temporarily leave the 'secured' assets; it is to those assets that we now return.

Assets subject to hire-purchase or lease agreements

1.12 Note 3. Where motor vehicles are subject to hire purchase agreements they will be grouped in the 'secured' section. If there are a number of individual agreements with the same company, it is usual to find a 'consolidation clause' included within the terms of each agreement. This in itself could have a significant impact where, for example, there is substantial equity in one agreement and large shortfalls in others. It is therefore worth spending a little time looking carefully at the hire-purchase assets and considering whether, in advance of some formal scheme, it might be advisable to attempt to settle a specific agreement in order to release funds which would otherwise be absorbed within a consolidation.

Where there is more than one hire purchase company involved it is possible that both surpluses and shortfalls could arise, as contemplated in the pro-forma Statement of Affairs. In such instance the surplus will not be aggregated with the shortfall, the latter ranking with the other unsecured creditors.

For many years, hire purchase companies were content for liquidators and receivers to sell goods subject to their hire purchase, paying off the settlement figure and retaining any surplus for the benefit of creditors. Then came the recession in the late 1980s and with it some of the worst losses the hire purchase companies had ever sustained. Almost all of them reverted to the strict letter of their agreements and many an insolvency practitioner saw estimated surpluses disappear as the hire companies insisted on repossessing their assets, selling them and retaining the entire surplus. It remains to be seen whether we will see a return to the old routine but, here again, it may be worthwhile considering paying off any individual agreement where it would release a large potential equity.

Assets caught by a bank's fixed charge: plant and machinery

1.13 Freehold and leasehold property and book debts are the main assets to be found included in any bank's fixed charge under the terms of its debenture. Banks like to sweep as many assets as possible into their fixed charge security and, additionally, will often register charges covering fixed plant and machinery, goodwill and uncalled share capital. Of these, fixed plant and machinery is probably the only one that requires further comment.

Solicitors have been known to give conflicting advice where plant and machinery is concerned; suffice it to say that, by and large, for plant and machinery to be safely regarded as fixed, it needs to become an integral part of the building itself (eg a central heating system). The problem is perhaps best put into perspective by an appreciation that plant and machinery does not necessarily become 'fixed' simply by virtue of its being bolted to the floor or walls of a building. In most instances, plant and machinery will be treated as 'not specifically pledged' assets.

Assets not specifically pledged

1.14 Note 4. Assets not specifically pledged will first be available to pay the preferential creditors with any surplus being caught by the bank's floating charge.

Preferential creditors

1.15 Note 5. The preferential creditors in most instances will comprise:
- the Inland Revenue, for up to 12 month's arrears of PAYE;
- DSS for up to 12 month's arrears of NI;
- HM Customs & Excise for up to 6 month's arrears of VAT;
- employees, for arrears of holiday pay and, to a maximum per employee – currently £800 – up to 4 months' arrears of wages.

(but see IA 1986 Sch 6 for full list)

In addition, as indicated by the pro-forma Statement of Affairs as discussed above, it is common to see the bank claim a preferential element in connection with wages paid during the preferential (last) 16 week period.

Unsecured creditors

1.16 Note 6. Creditors who can claim neither to be secured nor preferential will inevitably rank as unsecured. It is usual to see the vast majority of trade and expense creditors ranking unsecured (subject to any RETENTION OF TITLE claims) but additionally, any 'preferential' creditor whose claim exceeds the time limits imposed (or, in the case of employees, the maximum allowable) will rank unsecured for the relevant part of that claim.

So too will any secured creditor whose claim exceeds the value of their security, except to the extent that, as in the case of a bank with a 'standard' debenture, any shortfall is caught by a floating charge.

Inclusion of members in overall deficiency

1.17 Note 7. Once the deficiency as regards unsecured creditors has been established, all that remains at this stage of the operation is to add to it the book value of the issued share capital, to arrive at the estimated overall deficiency. Although it might appear academic to bring in the shareholders on the basis that if the unsecured creditors are not to be paid in full then there will be nothing for them in any event, we need to include them when, in due course, we prepare our estimated Surplus and Deficiency Account.

Bases of valuation for Statement of Affairs purposes

1.18 It can be seen that the pro-forma Statement of Affairs sets out the various assets and liabilities at book values. If done correctly, what this would produce is a Balance Sheet in a different format. What we now need to do is incorporate the estimated realisable values of the assets and include any further claims which might arise upon a cessation.

To the purist there are not two but three bases upon which Statement of Affairs either can or should be prepared, namely:
1 book values;
2 going concern;
3 cessation.
At this stage the general practitioner should regard 1 and 2 as being one and the same thing ignoring the subtle differences between them.

Need to compare differing bases of valuation

1.19 There are two important reasons for preparing 'side by side' Statements of Affairs for purpose of comparison.

Firstly, creditors themselves will require to know their likely position in the event of a cessation so that you will need that information should it be necessary to confer with creditors as to the route forward.

Secondly, it is simpler for the general practitioner to start with book values, which themselves form the basis of the information required to complete the Surplus and Deficiency Account.

Only when this comparative information is available will it be possible to move on to the next stage of considering the available options.

WORKED EXAMPLE

> In diagram 2 the Statement of Affairs is re-stated with the addition of actual figures, firstly at book value, and then, alongside, on the basis of cessation.

Additional claims arising upon insolvency

1.20 Where there are employees, cessation will inevitably create additional claims, with unpaid holiday pay and arrears of pay ranking preferentially and claims for redundancy and pay in lieu of notice ranking unsecured.

VAT element of creditors' claims

1.21 Up to 1 April 1991 it was customary for suppliers to claim 'VAT BAD DEBT RELIEF' in such form as entailed reducing their claims for dividend purposes within

Diagram 2
Estimated Statement of Affairs

	Book Value		Cessation	
	£000s	£000s	£000s	£000s
Assets Specifically Pledged				
Freehold Property	380		265	
Book debts	185		150	
	565		415	
Less: due to bank	580		580	
Shortfall to contra	15		165	
Motor vehicles	60		46	
Less: due on hire purchase	48		48	
Surplus		12		2
Shortfall to contra	–		4	
Assets Not Specifically Pledged				
Plant & Machinery		35		65
Fixtures & Fittings		11		5
Motor Vehicles (free of charge)		10		7
Stock and Work in Progress		45		10
Estimated Total Assets		113		89
Preferential Creditors				
PAYE & NI	32		32	
VAT	18		18	
Bank for wages paid	15		15	
Holiday pay and Arrears of Pay	–	65	8	73
Estimated Surplus available for bank under floating charge		48		16
Shortfall to Bank per contra (165 – 15)		–		150
Shortfall to bank carried to unsecured creditors				134
Estimated Surplus available for unsecured creditors		48		–
Unsecured Creditors				
Bank	–		134	
Trade & Expense	160		160	
PAYE & NI	28		28	
Hire Purchase per contra	–		4	
Directors' Loans	50		50	
Redundancy and Pay in Lieu of Notice	–	238	14	390
Estimated Deficiency as regards Unsecured Creditors		190		390
Share Capital				
10,000 Ordinary £1 shares		10		10
Estimated Overall Deficiency		200		400

the insolvency. The provisions of the Finance Act 1990 which came into effect on that date have altered the whole basis in which claims are now made. Creditors' claims should now all be included to rank for the *gross* amount (ie including any VAT element).

Costs of realisation

1.22 Although it is normal to prepare Statements of Affairs and note them as being subject to the costs of realisation etc these costs may be substantial and it may be necessary to carry out a separate exercise to evaluate the likely costs and consider any impact they might have upon each individual class of creditor.

Analysis of the Statements of Affairs

1.23 What these particular Statements of Affairs disclose is that even on book values, the company is clearly insolvent. This will almost certainly mean that cessation is inevitable unless fresh working capital can be introduced.

Compare however the anticipated outcome in a cessation with the picture depicted by the 'book value' statement. The most significant difference must be the position of the bank. On the one hand the books would seem to say that the bank will receive payment in full. On the other hand, those same books tell us that the company is insolvent and, unless the directors are to risk personal liability in any continuation, must find fresh capital or cease to trade forthwith.

Therefore it is essential we construct the second Statement of Affairs, for if cessation is inevitable, any Statement of Affairs based solely on book values is dangerous for the purpose of being used as a base upon which to make crucial decisions.

Construction of a Surplus and Deficiency Account

1.24 Having prepared the Statements of Affairs, the next stage is the construction of the estimated Surplus and Deficiency Account, for it is this exercise that provides the trading result for the period since accounts were last prepared and also acts as an arithmetic 'check' to ensure that the Statement of Affairs is not obviously incorrect.

Every accountant knows that the difference between the 'Profit and Loss Account' figure in two Balance Sheets of the same company represents the profit or loss of that company earned or sustained within the period between the Balance Sheet dates. It is this simple fact which a Surplus and Deficiency Account utilises to disclose what in effect has happened to the company since its last Balance Sheet date.

From a comparison of the two Statements of Affairs, we can summarise the information (see diagram 3).

Diagram 3
Reconciliation of the two Statements of Affairs

	Book Value £000s	Value at Cessation £000s	(Surplus)/ Deficiency £000s
Freehold Property	380	265	115
Book Debts	185	150	35
Motor Vehicles	70	53	17
Plant & Machinery	35	65	(30)
Fixtures & Fittings	11	5	6
Stock and Work in Progress	45	10	35
Overall reduction in values			178

Additionally, the following amounts arise upon insolvency

Holiday Pay and Arrears of Pay	8
Redundancy and Pay in Lieu of Notice	14
	22

Let us assume that the abridged Balance Sheet of the company at a date 10 months previously read as shown in diagram 4.

Diagram 4
Balance Sheet at commencement of the trading period

Fixed Assets		525
Current Assets	265	
Current Liabilities		
Bank overdraft	230	
Trade & Expense	140	
PAYE, NI & VAT	60	
Hire Purchase	18	
Directors' Loans	50	
	498	
		(233)
Bank Loan	300	
Hire Purchase	30	
		(330)
		(38)
represented by:		
Share Capital		10
Profit & Loss Account (debit balance)		(48)
		(38)

With this information we can now complete the Estimated Surplus and Deficiency Account as shown in diagram 5:

Diagram 5
Estimated Surplus and Deficiency Account

	£000s	£000s
Excess of capital and liabilities over assets as at (10 months previously)		48
Amounts written-off for the purpose of the Statement of Affairs		
Freehold Property	115	
Book Debts	35	
Motor Vehicles	17	
Plant & Machinery	(30)	
Fixtures & Fittings	6	
Stock and Work in Progress	35	
		178
Amounts arising upon insolvency:		
Holiday Pay & Arrears of Pay	8	
Redundancy & Pay in Lieu of Notice	14	
		22
		248
Balance, being estimated trading loss for the (10 months) period		152
Total Estimated Deficiency per Statement of Affairs		400

The available options: the five alternatives to liquidation

1.25 Having determined the exact state of the company's current financial position, the next step is to consider the options available to an insolvent company.

Liquidation may be regarded as the ultimate solution resulting, as it usually does, in the demise of the company. It is the alternatives we need to consider and utilise whenever possible in the hopes of achieving some form of reconstruction and financial re-establishment. Even where this proves unattainable, it is often possible to improve the financial position of the company's creditors by following some route other than liquidation.

There are five possible routes forward which we will first of all identify, thereafter considering each in turn.

They are:
- a general informal moratorium;
- scheme under CA 1985 s425;
- company voluntary arrangement;
- administration order;
- administrative receivership.

III GENERAL MORATORIUM

1.26 We start with the option that has always been available; a general moratorium granted by the company's creditors. This 'informal' arrangement, where possible to achieve, has the advantages of simplicity and being relatively inexpensive to administer. There are no mandatory formal reporting or regulatory disciplines and, in theory at least, anyone may be appointed to administer the scheme.

Under such an arrangement, the creditors agree not to pursue their outstanding claims, instead allowing the company to continue to trade, usually under the supervision of the company's auditor or an independent accountant, with future supplies of goods or services being paid for on a cash basis or agreed strict credit terms.

The 'supervisor' realises the assets that are to form the basis of the available funds and distributes them among the creditors, in accordance with the agreed formula in full satisfaction of all claims, leaving the company free to continue to trade. In this way the company is restored to solvency by virtue of the compromise by creditors of their claims.

Difficulty in achieving creditors' consent

1.27 If such a scheme sounds attractive it must be remembered that, in practice, an informal moratorium is usually very difficult to achieve. Indeed, it was precisely *because* of the difficulty in saving companies through this route that an alternative was contemplated by way of formal legislation, now incorporated within IA 1986.

The problem with an informal scheme is that there is nothing to stop any individual creditor from taking immediate action to pursue a claim, if necessary by petitioning for the (compulsory) winding-up of the company. It has to be realised that some creditors conclude understandably that if they press their own individual claim, there is always a chance the company might pay them, just to 'get rid of them' and allow the proposed scheme to go forward.

It was inevitably such action that was the occasion of the failure of the majority of attempts to achieve a moratorium in years past, as the scheme requires the agreement of *all* creditors before it can commence.

Potential benefits to creditors

1.28 Notwithstanding the difficulties involved, an informal moratorium may represent the best route forward for creditors in certain specific instances. Invariably this will be when there are only a handful of creditors with whom to negotiate, all of whom continue to believe in the integrity of the directors, probably where they are hopeful of enjoying future profitable trade with the company and where there are indications of substantial dividend prospects payable within a reasonable period of time.

Issues which require to be addressed

1.29 Given these criteria, the proposals to creditors will need to recognise the rights of each individual class of creditor, treating all creditors pari passu within each class. Thus, creditors who would enjoy preferential status (s386 and Sch 6) in a formal insolvency, will almost certainly require that their claims be recognised in preference to the claims of the general body of unsecured creditors.

Care must also be taken to ensure creditors do not give up valuable rights that, for example, could be pursued if a liquidator was appointed. The obvious examples are the right to bring actions against the directors for:
- wrongful trading (s214)
- fraudulent trading (s213)
- preferences (s239)
- transactions at under-value (s238)

Advances secured by directors' guarantees/third party collateral

1.30 Where a bank or other lender is involved, its co-operation in any proposed scheme will depend entirely upon the circumstances surrounding the case and, in particular, the nature of the security, amount of the outstanding advance and question of personal guarantees. If we are talking about an overdraft of a few thousand pounds, with a director's guarantee supported by a collateral charge over his private residence, the bank is unlikely to become particularly excited at any proposed informal arrangement with creditors. In such instances, it would be usual for the bank to convert the overdraft into a personal loan to the director, with the director then 'standing in the bank's shoes' for dividend purposes within the moratorium.

Advances secured by a fixed charge

1.31 Where the bank also holds security over an asset of the company, for example a fixed charge over a specific property, it must inevitably come down to negotiation. The bank may be perfectly content to allow the director to organise a sale, awaiting repayment out of the sale proceeds. Alternatively, it could adopt a more formal approach and either:
- sell as mortgagee in possession; or
- appoint its own receiver under the Law of Property Act 1925 to dispose of the charged asset.

In either case the company could still pursue an informal moratorium with the rest of its creditors, as the bank's interest would be restricted to the property over which it held its charge.

Advances secured by a floating charge

1.32 The situation would be different where the bank holds a debenture which also grants a floating charge. Here, the bank would be entitled to appoint an administrative receiver (ss33ff) to recover its indebtedness and would need to be persuaded that both its rights and prospects of recovery would in no way be jeopardised by allowing an informal arrangement to proceed.

Again, it will probably, although not necessarily, be the level of the bank's borrowings that determines its decision. Where, however, the director *is* able to persuade the bank to transfer the borrowings from the company into a personal advance, he would be wise in his proposals to creditors *not* to attempt to assume for himself the benefit of the bank's floating charge, thereby taking a charge over the assets in priority to the creditors whose support he seeks!

Need for the involvement of an insolvency practitioner

1.33 Although there is no formal requirement for an insolvency practitioner to supervise or otherwise be involved in monitoring an informal general moratorium, whether or not any creditor raises the question of supervision by an insolvency practitioner will depend very much upon the luck of the draw. The greater the issues, the more likelihood of an insolvency practitioner negotiating on behalf of one of the creditors. Where a bank is involved however and particularly where it holds a floating charge, it will almost certainly insist upon the involvement of an insolvency practitioner if it is not to enforce its security and appoint an administrative receiver.

Preparing for meeting with the company's creditors

1.34 If, having surmounted all other obstacles, you are successful in reaching the stage where you are able to meet with the creditors to put to them your proposals, you will need to be armed with answers to the following questions:
- How did the insolvency arise?
- Are the directors in any way to blame and have they any proposals to contribute personally to the available fund?
- *Where the directors are also creditors*: are the directors prepared to waive their claims or defer them in favour of other creditors?
- Who is to be the supervisor of the proposed scheme?
- What is the proposed level of the supervisor's fees?
- *Where there are bank borrowings*: has the bank agreed to participate in the proposed scheme and if so, under what terms?
- What proposals are there to maintain the status of the 'preferential' creditors?
- Have investigations been made to ensure there have been no
  (a) preferences (s239),
  (b) transactions at an undervalue (s238),
  (c) extortionate credit transactions (s244),
  (d) wrongful trading (s214),
  (e) fraudulent trading (s213)?
- If the scheme is approved and the supervisor becomes aware of potential claims under (a)–(e) above, will the director give his irrevocable undertaking to petition immediately for the winding-up of the company?; and for which purpose?
- Will the supervisor confirm sufficient funds will at all times be maintained within the estate?
- Has a cash flow been prepared detailing anticipated income and expenditure?
- How long is the scheme proposed to last?
- What level of dividend is anticipated for unsecured creditors and when will the dividend(s) be paid?

Other considerations

1.35 There will almost certainly be other questions to consider – for example the absence of any available VAT bad debt relief on creditors' claims – but the above need addressing in *every* instance. Just how you go about approaching the creditors must be a matter of judgment. Where the director has a good relationship with creditors, it is often sensible that as a first step he makes a personal approach to each individual creditor, starting with the largest, to 'test the water'. Speed is, however, vital. All information should be to hand *before* making the initial approach; even bad news is more palatable when coupled with prospects of some improvement and the recipient has a measure of confidence in the proposed solution.

Agreement to the scheme

1.36 Once agreed, each individual creditor should sign a formal agreement setting out the terms of the moratorium; only once this has been done by *every* creditor may the scheme go forward. In reality each creditor enters into a new contract with the company incorporating terms not to take any (further) action as regards the existing debt. Only then is the company safe from the threat of a winding-up petition.

Flow chart

A flow-chart summarising the various stages in attempting to effect a successful moratorium is set out in diagram 6.

Diagram 6

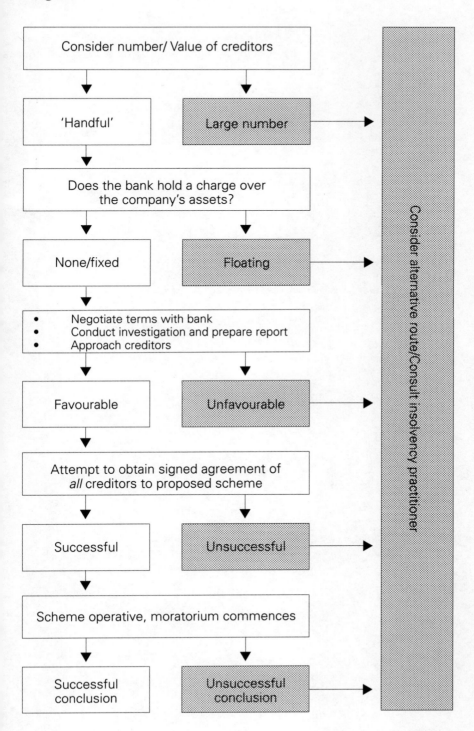

IV SCHEME UNDER COMPANIES ACT 1985 s425 ('SECTION 425 SCHEME')

1.37 The opportunity to reconstruct a company with the consent of the *majority* of its creditors with the sanction of the court, has been available for many years. CA 1985 s425 (and before that CA 1948 s206) provides a formal framework within which a company may seek a scheme of reconstruction with its creditors, which, if approved by the required majorities and the court becomes binding upon any dissenting minority. (Such a scheme of reconstruction may also either be extended to alter the share structure of the company or, alternatively, used solely for that purpose. Note however that this section is not intended as a mechanism for either attacking or defending the position of minority shareholders.)

Advantage over informal arrangement

1.38 The advantage of pursuing a moratorium or reconstruction with creditors through a Section 425 Scheme over attempting an informal arrangement, is that the agreement of every creditor is not necessary; provided the majorities required are attained, the court will bind any dissenting minority to the scheme.

Need for supervision by an insolvency practitioner

1.39 The scheme must be supervised by an insolvency practitioner.

Required majorities

1.40 To achieve success, it is necessary to obtain the assent of a simple majority – that is more than 50% – of creditors, present or represented by proxy, at a meeting convened for voting purposes, whose combined claims in value must amount to at least 75% of the total claims of *all* creditors (whether present or not).

Implementing the scheme

1.41 Having formulated a scheme, the next step is to seek the court's consent by way of an order to summon a meeting of creditors for the purpose of considering and voting upon the scheme. Here we meet our first logistical problem; before a meeting may be held to vote upon the scheme, the court must order that such a meeting be held and to enable the court to judge upon the issues it will require full information both as to the proposals and of the background leading to the financial problem. The court is also likely to be influenced by the initial reaction of creditors to the proposals and the chance of the scheme obtaining the required majorities.

Difficulty in obtaining required majorities

1.42 If the time (and expense) in reaching the stage where a formal meeting is convened for voting purposes is the first logistical problem, the second has to be obtaining the approval of 75% by value of all creditors, who must vote in favour (either in person or by proxy) *at that meeting*. Over the years, as insolvencies have become almost commonplace, attendances at creditors' meetings have dropped considerably, thereby adding to the difficulties involved.

It is for these reasons that Section 425 Schemes tend to be restricted to reconstructions of share capital, which are not subjected to the same pressures as when the rights of creditors are involved.

The more likely routes

1.43 Having considered the preferred if unlikely possibility of an informal moratorium and the even unlikelier route via a scheme under CA 1985 s425, let us look at the remaining three available options as a way forward, one (or as we shall see, perhaps a combination of two) of which will almost certainly provide the answer. Those options are:
- to seek the creditors' approval to a Company Voluntary Arrangement (often referred to by the abbreviation 'CVA').
- to petition the court for the grant of an Administration Order.
- to request (often as an alternative to having imposed) the appointment of Administrative Receivers.

Of these three routes, the first and second became available following the implementation of IA 1986, the third appointment being the inevitable alternative or precursor to liquidation ever since lenders took out debentures granting floating charges as part of their security. (Up to the introduction of the IA 1985 the equivalent title of the appointee was 'Receiver and Manager'.)

Interrelationship between routes

1.44 Set out as diagram 7 is a chart which identifies the interrelationship of these routes in the context of an insolvent company attempting to avoid outright liquidation.

Ability to 'reverse' out of liquidation via CVA route

1.45 Note particularly that even when a company is in liquidation, it is now possible for it to be restored to solvency, by compromise with its creditors, via the route

Scheme under Companies Act 1985 s425 ('Section 425 Scheme') 25

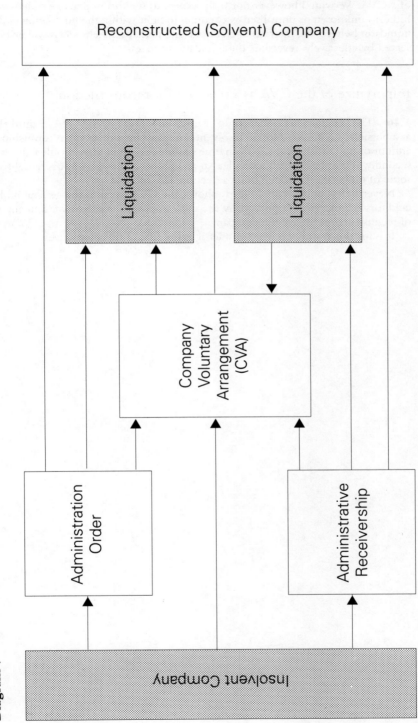

Diagram 7

of a CVA. We would however normally expect to see this in practice only when a hitherto unknown or unrealised asset comes to light within the liquidation and the liquidator believes the interests of creditors (and perhaps shareholders) will be better served by effectively 'reversing' the liquidation process.

Importance of the CVA as a medium for reconstruction

1.46 The general practitioner could be forgiven for placing the CVA in 'third place' as a possible way forward for an insolvent company. First of all the receivership and administration order routes do from time to time feature in high-profile failures and secondly, as we shall shortly consider, an attempt to achieve a CVA is fraught with some of the problems which beset a Section 425 Scheme.

Nevertheless, as diagram 7 clearly shows, the CVA so far as the general body of creditors is concerned, is potentially the most important route forward in any plan of reconstruction to save the company.

It is for this reason we will consider it as the first of the alternatives.

V COMPANY VOLUNTARY ARRANGMENT (CVA)

1.47 When IA 1986 was implemented, it contained parallel proposals for the financial reconstruction of the affairs of companies and individuals, the former through the medium of a Company Voluntary Arrangement (or CVA) the latter through an Individual Voluntary Arrangement (or IVA).

Background considerations

1.48 There were however two distinct difference between them. Firstly, VAT BAD-DEBT RELIEF was available in the case of an IVA but not a CVA and secondly, in the case of the IVA, an approach could be made to the court for the grant of an 'interim order' which had the effect of halting any further legal action by any creditor, thereby enabling creditors' approval to be sought to the scheme without the threat of a bankruptcy order pre-empting the outcome.

Subsequent overall changes in VAT bad debt relief legislation have removed the first anomaly, but the second, the lack of ability to obtain an interim order in the case of a CVA, remains.

It could be that these inherent differences, coupled with the legislation contained within the section dealing with the reasons for seeking the grant of an administration order (s8(3)(b)), namely:

> The purposes for whose achievement an administration order may be made are –
> (b) the approval of a voluntary arrangement.

provide an insight into the intentions of the draughtsmen; namely that they perceived the CVA as a 'second-stage' in any reconstruction process and particularly following on from an administration order.

As a way forward in its own right

1.49 Nevertheless (for the moment leaving aside the position of *secured* creditors), provided the problems of keeping the creditors 'at bay' and managing to fund the operation of the company up to the time that the creditors meet to vote upon the proposed CVA, it remains very much a potential route forward in its own right despite being available as an 'exit route' from an administration order and a route by which to 'reverse' out of a liquidation.

Position of secured and preferential creditors

1.50 In fact, one class of creditor that *cannot* be ignored in any proposed CVA is the secured creditor, be it a hire-purchase or leasing company, a bank, or any other lender who, for whatever reasons, has been granted a valid charge over any asset of the company. The reason is straightforward; it is not possible to bind any secured creditor to a proposed CVA without that creditor's consent.

Note also however that neither is it possible to bind any preferential creditor without that creditor's consent and that s4(4) prohibits any proposal which seeks to dilute the rights of preferential creditors.

The first step of any proposed CVA must, therefore, be to consider the position of any secured or preferential creditor and seek his agreement to the scheme; only then is the way open to proceed.

Need for supervision by an insolvency practitioner

1.51 As the CVA must be supervised by an insolvency practitioner, whose input is required *before* the scheme can be approved, it will be necessary from the outset to identify an insolvency practitioner and obtain his agreement to act.

Preparing for the CVA – proposals

1.52 The proposals for the CVA will be put forward by the directors, usually with the direct help of the insolvency practitioner, who, at this stage, is referred to as the 'nominee'. (Liquidators and administrators may also put forward proposals for CVAs with regard to those companies in which they hold office.)

Contents of directors' report to nominee

1.53 The proposals will be incorporated within a report to be delivered to the nominee. It is usual for a full statement of the company's affairs to be included, but, if not, such a statement must be delivered to the nominee within seven days of delivering the proposals. The statement, duly certified as correct, must be made up to a date not earlier than two weeks before the date of the notice to the nominee.

If the statement of affairs is not incorporated within the initial report, then the report must contain details of the company's assets, liabilities and charges. It must also give full details of any transactions which are capable of being challenged or set aside by a liquidator, eg transaction at an undervalue, preferences, extortionate credit transactions or invalid floating charges, together with the director's proposals for rectification. (Without satisfactory proposals the nominee would be obliged to report that the company ought more properly to be placed into liquidation.) A full list of all matters to be included within the proposals is set out in IR 1986 r 1.3.

Submission of proposals to court

1.54 Within 28 days, (or such longer period as the court may allow) the nominee must submit both the directors' report and his own observations thereon to the court stating whether in his opinion (separate) meetings of the company's shareholders and creditors should be convened for the purpose of voting upon the proposals.

If the nominee concludes that the proposed scheme should go ahead, he reports accordingly to the court and must himself fix the date, time and place at which the meetings are to take place.

Summoning meetings of members and creditors

1.55 Once the nominee has made a favourable report to the court it becomes his duty to summon the meetings in accordance with his own proposals. The court itself will not make any order nor is there any other formal requirement, for although the conduct of the CVA is under the aegis of the court, the court itself is not involved in a judicial capacity (except to the extent its guidance might be sought by way of direction or it is called upon to make a ruling in case of any disagreement).

The meetings must be convened not less than 14 days and no more than 28 days from that on which the nominee's report is filed in court. At least 14 days' notice of the meetings should be given the venue of which should be chosen for the convenience of creditors. The meetings should be held on the same day and at the same venue; the creditors' meeting should be held first and both meetings should be commenced between the hours of 10am and 4pm.

The meetings will decide whether or not to approve the scheme with or without modifications. Given that the status of the preferential creditors is specifically protected, to the extent that s4(4) prohibits any proposal or modification which seeks to dilute their rights, it will be necessary to obtain approval to the scheme from all preferential (and secured) creditors.

Required majorities

1.56 The scheme requires the approval of a simple majority (ie more than 50% in value) of the members of the company either personally present or voting by proxy at the meeting and over 75% in value of the (non-secured) creditors of which over 50% must represent the votes of 'non-connected' parties (see ASSOCIATED AND CONNECTED PERSONS)

The scheme only becomes effective if approved in identical terms by both creditors and members. It is usual, but not necessary, that the nominee will be appointed as supervisor of the scheme, his appointment taking effect following approval by the creditors (but only if the scheme is also approved at the subsequent meeting of members).

Only creditors receiving formal notice bound by scheme

1.57 There are provisions for any member or creditor to challenge the decisions of the meeting (s6) but, subject to this, if the required majorities are obtained, any dissenting member or creditor *who received formal notice of the meeting convened for the purpose of voting on the scheme* is bound by the majority decision.

It is therefore of the utmost importance to ensure that *all* creditors receive due notice; failure to inform a creditor of the meeting will place that creditor outside any scheme and could well result in his debt having subsequently to be paid in full.

Chairman to prepare and file report

1.58 Once the meetings have been held, the chairman must prepare a report on the outcome which must be filed with the court within four days.

In practice, one would anticipate the nominee would act as chairman, as IR 1986 r 1.14(1) requires that:

> ... at both the creditors' meeting and the company meeting, and at any combined meeting, the convener shall be the chairman.

However, given that r 1.24 requires that it is the chairman rather than the nominee who is charged with filing the report on the meetings at court, within four days, it allows the nominee the opportunity to take advantage of r 1.14.(2) which states,

> If for any reason he is unable to attend, he may nominate another person to act as chairman in his place.
>
> But a person so nominated must be either –
> (a) a person qualified to act as an insolvency practitioner in relation to the company, or
> (b) an employee of the convener or his firm who is experienced in insolvency matters.

Thus, if the nominee knows he will be personally unable to deal with the requirement to report (under s4(6)) and for whatever reason unable to sign the report, he may arrange to nominate the chairman under the provisions contain in r 1.14(2).

Effect of the scheme

1.59 Once the scheme is approved, creditors are bound by its terms. In this connection, it is worth noting that s233(1)(c) restricts suppliers of gas, electricity etc, from imposing separate terms as to payment of outstanding debts as a condition for making a supply available.

One of the most attractive features of the CVA route is the flexibility it offers the proposers. Within the framework of the legislation, it is possible to use great imagination in proposing a scheme of reconstruction. A simple example would be the treatment of unsecured creditors where it is not necessary to treat all claims as ranking pari passu for dividends. Thus, it might be proposed that the first dividend pay off all creditors below £1,000 in full, a move which could remove the majority of creditors at a single stroke, thereafter making the CVA both less cumbersome and less expensive to operate.

Comparison of CVA with Section 425 Scheme

1.60 A comparison of the CVA route with a Section 425 Scheme identifies the main advantage in favour of the CVA as being the ability to obtain a decision at the meeting of creditors. Whereas the Section 425 Scheme requires the agreement of only a simple majority in number voting in favour, the combined value of those in favour must represent at least 75% of the total of *all* creditors *whether present or not at the meeting*.

The CVA requirement is far simpler and much more readily attainable – a vote in value only, irrespective of the actual *number* of creditors in favour, in excess of 75% of the total claims of creditors actually present or represented by proxy at the meeting convened for the purpose of voting on the proposals. Thus, where for whatever reason the majority of creditors opt not to attend or be represented at the meeting, it is quite feasible that a relatively small minority of creditors, both in number and value, could bind all other creditors to the scheme.

Risk of winding-up petition

1.61 So much for the advantages of the CVA route, but what of the disadvantages? As is the case where an informal general moratorium and a Section 425 Scheme are being formulated there is nothing to stop any creditor from petitioning to wind up the company prior to the approval of CVA (cf an IVA where the court can make an 'interim order' which has the effect of halting all legal proceedings).

From time to time voices are heard calling for an amendment to the law to enable the court to grant an interim order (as in the case of an IVA) thus affording complete protection from the possibility of a winding-up petition. Although it is possible the law might be amended to accommodate these requests, initial reaction seems to be for leaving the legislation as it is, on the grounds that if such protection is required in a specific case, it can be achieved effectively by first petitioning the court for the grant of an administration order. Nevertheless, many insolvency practitioners believe that the costs of interposing an administration order, particularly in smaller cases, increases substantially the expense involved and thus renders reconstruction less attractive.

The interposing of an administration order as a first step to achieving a CVA is something we will consider in the following section.

VI ADMINISTRATION ORDER

1.62 If directors of insolvent companies were asked to choose their own route forward they would surely choose the least formal route; an informal moratorium.

Their second choice would have to be the CVA route and, for all but those who simply wished to walk away from the whole financial nightmare, their next likely choice would be via an administration order.

It is difficult to appreciate fully the potential advantage to a company, its creditors and members which could follow an administration order (as opposed to an administrative receivership) from a simple 'textbook' understanding of the relevant law. Naturally all cases are different and what works in one instance will not necessarily work in another. More particularly there is the perfectly natural reluctance of banks to allow an administrator to be appointed when they hold floating charges and could appoint their own administrative receiver. (This is further explained within the text.)

In order to obtain a real 'feel' for the potential to reconstruct and save a business within the framework of an administration, it is necessary to consider a 'case study' which reveals everything by reference not simply to a hypothesis but to real-life achievement.

In the ensuing text, the relevant law is set out with appropriate explanation. At the end of the text (**1.103**) is a story demonstrating what actually happened when, with the bank's agreement, an administration order was granted and administrative receivership avoided.

Definition

1.63 The IA 1986 s8(2) defines an administration order as:

> an order directing that, during the period for which the order is in force, the affairs, business and property of the company shall be managed by a person ("the administrator") appointed for the purpose by the court.

Reason for choosing the administration order route

1.64 There could be a number of reasons for seeking an administration order. An example of a 'negative' reason would be because a company had not granted any floating charge as security to a lender (see FIXED AND FLOATING CHARGES) the lender could not appoint an administrative receiver and administration provided the only acceptable alternative.

It is however far more likely it will be one or more of a number of positive reasons which dictate the choice of administration the precise reasons depending upon the relevant circumstances.

In each instance, the reason will be that it offers some underlying advantage and that advantage could be to the:
1   directors;
2   company;

3   unsecured creditors; and
4   office holder (who following appointment, will be the administrator).

Advantages to the directors

1.65 There are a number of reasons which could appeal to directors, all of which are understandably subjective, ie:
- It enables them to choose their 'own man' to act as administrator.
- It often affords better opportunity for them to have 'more say' in the day-to-day management notwithstanding the ultimate responsibility lies with the administrator.
- It enables them to present 'their side of the story' to creditors and (either contemporaneously with the petition for the grant of the order or subsequently by working with the administrator) allows their own proposals for possible reconstruction under a CVA to be put forward.
- It carries less 'stigma' than inevitably accompanies a receivership.

Advantages to the company

1.66 Leaving aside any personal benefits which the directors might perceive as being reason enough for the seeking of an administration order, there are occasions when there could be significant benefits for the company in seeking an administration order as opposed to the appointment of administrative receivers.

Specific instances would be:
- where it was essential to prevent a lessor of plant and machinery seeking immediate recovery of its equipment;
- to prevent a distraint;
- following grant of the order, to prevent any attempts by a creditor to obtain a winding-up order against the company.

Although these are positive reasons, the end result is to *stop* something from happening, so to that extent they appear almost negative. There is, however, a very positive additional advantage in that the very nature of the appointment allows the officeholder far more scope to seek out opportunities for maximising realisations and reconstructing and saving the company. Other potential advantages follow the administrator's duties as an officer of the court (see **1.83**)

Advantages to the unsecured creditors

1.67 Section 9 allows for an application for an administration order to be made '… or by a creditor or creditors (including any contingent or prospective creditors)…'.

Given that creditors have no say whatsoever in the appointment of an administrative receiver, the opportunity of petitioning the court and requesting the appointee of their own choice as administrator has to be of significant benefit to creditors.

Even where an order is granted following the petition of the directors or the company (ie by the petition of *all* the individual directors or by the company following a resolution passed by a majority of the board) there remain potential benefits to creditors following the administrator's duties as a court appointee (see **1.83**).

Another area of advantage to creditors is the opportunity afforded to the administrator to use his imaginative powers to create the opportunity of maximising realisations and perhaps saving the company and the whole or part of the business.

Advantage to the office-holder

1.68 Again, the advantage to the office-holder to act as an administrator rather than an administrative receiver is subjective in that it flows entirely from the opportunity afforded to use his powers of inventiveness with the result that his professional skills meet a greater challenge. Thus even more so than in an administrative receivership, he is able to concentrate on the 'constructive' side of insolvency, his ultimate goal, wherever possible, being the saving of the company and the whole or part of its business.

The position of preferential creditors

1.69 If the directors and unsecured creditors perceive the administration route as holding potential advantages, there are others who will not see things in quite the same light.

First of all there are the creditors who would rank as preferential in an administrative receivership or a liquidation. There are no preferential creditors within an administration although preferential rights will be restored as at the date of the administration order provided the company ultimately proceeds to *compulsory* liquidation (s387(3)(a)) or the administration order is discharged following the agreement by creditors to a Company Voluntary Arrangement (s387(2)(a)).

The position of the holder of a floating charge – right to receive notice of petition

1.70 Where the company has given a floating charge to a bank or some other creditor, the charge-holder is put at an immediate disadvantage following the making of an administration order in that the charge will be subordinated against all debts subsequently incurred. It is to avoid this sort of unfair advantage that any holder of a floating charge must be given notice of and provided with a copy of the petition and supporting affidavit and documents not less than five days before the hearing of the petition.

Right of floating charge-holder to appoint receiver following petition.

1.71 Upon receiving notice of a petition for the grant of an administration order, the holder of a floating charge who has power to appoint a receiver over the whole or substantially the whole of the company's property and which provided for this power to be exercised under such circumstances, may appoint an administrative receiver. For debentures created before the IA came into force, ie 29 December 1986,

Sch 11 para 1 deems such a provision to be included. Debentures created after that date must contain express provision in any floating charge drawn up

Effect of the appointment of an administrative receiver – duties of the court

1.72 Section 9(3) spells out the effect upon the petition, thus:

> Where the court is satisfied that there is an administrative receiver of the company, the court shall dismiss the petition unless it is satisfied either
> (a) that the person by whom or on whose behalf the receiver was appointed has consented to the making of the order, or
> (b) that, if an administration order were made, any security by virtue of which the receiver was appointed would –
>   (i) be liable to be released or discharged under sections 238 to 240 in Part VI (transactions at an undervalue and preferences),
>   (ii) be avoided under section 245 in that Part (avoidance of floating charges), or
>   (iii) be challengeable under section 242 (gratuitous alienations) or 243 (unfair preferences) in that Part, or under any rule of law in Scotland.

In practical terms, the holder of a (well drawn) valid floating charge will be able to block the application for an administration order by appointing an administrative receiver before the petition is heard by the court.

Application for the order

1.73 The application itself is to the court by petition which will usually be presented by the directors, although s9(1) allows for other parties to present a petition, including a creditor(s) to include contingent or prospective creditors. Application by the directors is by the board following a proper resolution (notwithstanding that a minority of the board may have voted against the resolution) or, if done 'informally' must be an application by all the directors. (As we are concerned here with considering a route available to the company – as opposed to its creditors – the text is written accordingly.)

There is no requirement to advertise the petition.

Unlike a CVA, it is a requirement that the company is, or is likely to become insolvent.

Reasons for requesting an administration order

1.74 It is necessary for the petitioner(s) to identify to the court at least one of four purposes specified as expected to be achieved by the making of an administration order. These are set out in s8(3) as follows:

> (a) the survival of the company, and the whole or any part of its undertaking as a going concern;

(b) the approval of a voluntary arrangement under Part 1 (CVA).
(c) the sanctioning under Section 425 of the Companies Act of a compromise or arrangement between the company and any such persons as are mentioned in that section; and
(d) a more advantageous realisation of the company's assets than would be effected on a winding-up.

It is worthwhile pausing a moment to reflect upon the wording of (a) which is interpreted strictly by the court. The survival of the whole or part of the business is *additional* and not an alternative to the survival of the *company*. Thus, a proposal to sell a 'hived-down' company, formed specifically to take over part of the company's business could not fall within (a) (*Re Rowbotham Baxter Ltd* [1990] BCC 113) although there would seem to be no reason why it could not be included within (d)

Purposes (b) and (c) are alternative parallel routes; we have already considered each of these in detail in the aforegoing sections and it is clear that the CVA route, (b), will be the chosen option in the majority of administrations.

It is understandable that in practice, directors usually seek to incorporate (a), (b) and (d) within their petition to the court, for not only does this have the effect of presenting the state of the company in the 'best light' but it also (perhaps tendentiously) sets the scene for some form of ultimate survival and places the spectre of liquidation to the back of, if not outside of, everyone's mind.

In the first applications to the court in 1987, this was usually what happened, even though the evidence presented to the court might not have fully supported what was often nothing more than wishful thinking. Judges rapidly became skilled at reading both 'in between' and 'behind' the written lines and their degree of sophistication has been the occasion of the embarrassment of more than one advising insolvency practitioner.

Rapid re-appraisal has resulted in far more detailed information being supplied to the court usually in support of only one or two of the four stated purposes.

The general practitioner should take care to avoid recommending any application for an administration order which the court might regard as spurious.

Independent expert's report

1.75 The one purpose most directors are reluctant to omit from their application is (b), the approval of a Voluntary Arrangement. However, also to be filed at court before the hearing of the petition for the administration order is an 'independent' report on the company's affairs (r 2.2). The Insolvency Rules state:

> ... There may be prepared with a view to its being exhibited to the affidavit in support of the petition, a report by an independent person to the effect that the appointment of an administrator for the company is expedient ... The report may be by the person proposed as administrator or by any other person having adequate knowledge of the company's affairs, not being a director, secretary, manager, member or employee of the company.

These Rules set the scene for the entry of an insolvency practitioner for almost without exception there will be an independent report filed and inevitably it will have been prepared by the licensed practitioner proposed as administrator. (The absence of a report must be explained.) Moreover, it will be this report that tempers the aspirations of the directors and which will eventually form the basis for their own affidavit so that a reasoned and realistic argument is placed before the court for its consideration.

The absence of a report will require careful explanation to the court and may be fatal to the application for administration. Over the years judges have displayed an increasing tendency to rely upon the views of the licensed practitioner when evaluating the strength or otherwise of the case for administration. For this reason, careful attention should be paid to the report's drafting and content.

Making the application – documentation to be filed with the court

1.76 The documentation placed before the court should contain the following information:

Directors' affidavit

- a statement that the deponents believe the company is, or is likely to become unable to pay its debts, together with the grounds for that belief;
- which of the (4) purposes specified in s8(3) is expected to be achieved by the making of an administration order;
- an up-to-date Statement of Affairs of the company to include contingent and preferential liabilities;
- details of any security held by creditors of the company, whether any floating charges have been granted and, if so, whether an administrative receiver has been appointed;
- whether any petition has been presented for the winding-up of the company;
- whether there are any other known relevant matters which will assist the court in deciding whether to make such an order;
- whether an independent expert's report has been prepared and if not, an explanation therefor.

The petition

1.77 (Remember we are dealing here with a petition presented by the directors.)
- a statement that it is presented by the directors (but which following presentation is thereafter treated as a petition of the company).
- the name and address of the person proposed to be appointed as administrator with a statement that to the best of the petitioner's knowledge and belief, that person is qualified to act as an insolvency practitioner in relation to the company.

The petition must be exhibited to the supporting affidavit as must also be annexed:
- a written consent by the proposed administrator to accept appointment if an administration order is made; and
- a copy of the independent expert's report (if any).

Once the petition has been filed, it becomes the duty of the petitioner to notify the court in writing as soon as he becomes aware of any subsequent winding-up petition.

Service of the petition

1.78 In addition to filing the petition with the court, copies must also be served:
- on any such person who has appointed or is entitled to appoint an administrative receiver; or
- upon an administrative receiver if already appointed;
- on any petitioner for the winding-up of the company and any provisional liquidator if so appointed; and
- on the person proposed as administrator.

It is not proposed to deal with the actual detailed procedure involved in effecting service, but it is useful to further consider the factors that the court will take into account in considering whether or not the order should be granted and to look at the effects of the application upon individual parties.

Consideration of the application by the court

1.79 In considering the petition, the court must:
1. be satisfied that the company is, or is likely to become, unable to pay its debts; and
2. consider that an administration order would be more likely to achieve one or more of the proposals specified in s8(3) (as fully considered above).

The first of these two prerequisites is relatively straightforward, the test of insolvency (at least in the first instance) being the company's ability to pay its current debts as and when they fall due (*Re Imperial Motors (UK) Ltd* [1989] 5 BCC 214).

It is the second consideration that has given rise to the greater difficulty as no guidance is to be found within IA 1986 as to the nature of the evidence upon which the ruling is sought. Current view following the decision of Hoffman J. in *Re Harris Simons Construction Ltd* [1989] 1 WLR 368, 5 BCC 11 wherein he concluded the requirements of s8(3) would be satisfied if the court considered that there was a 'real prospect' that one or more of the statutory purposes might be achieved.

It is in assisting the court to arrive at this conclusion that the independent expert's report assumes a high degree of importance and where there is any doubt in the mind of the expert as to whether or not there is a real prospect that a specific purpose is achievable, it is now usual for the matter to be considered within the report, but the issue then left in abeyance to be re-addressed if circumstances dictate.

Take by way of example, the situation where the directors believe that:
- although it might not be possible to save the company as opposed to the business, creditors will undoubtedly fare better via the administration order route than they would in outright liquidation; and
- under an administration order it would be possible to obtain creditors' approval of a CVA.

When the independent expert comes to review the overall position although he may have no difficulty in proving a case for the former purpose, it may prove far harder 'hand on heart' to set out a convincing argument for the latter.

Which proposals to incorporate?; a solution to the problem.

1.80 The problem is not difficult to understand. The directors will look understandably to the CVA route as an opportunity to preserve at least part of the business in restructured form, free from the former burden of debt but without the introduction of further working capital. This will mean inevitably retaining assets or cash within the restructured company as necessary working capital, which would otherise have been available for dividend purposes had the company simply closed down once the better realisation has been achieved.

It is true, as we will discuss later within the text, that it is quite possible to advocate the approval of a CVA, not for the purpose of allowing a restructured company to continue to trade, but, having effected the most beneficial realisation of the assets, to distribute the proceeds via a CVA rather than within a liquidation in order to keep costs down to a minimum.

This however is an aspect which is unlikely to win support from the directors at the time of drafting the initial proposals and neither would any administrator elect wish to see proposals incorporated, the very basis of which it is intended then be changed 'to suit' within the administration itself.

The way forward, which has won the court's approval is for the expert's report to consider the relevant facts with regard to the approval of a CVA and 'leave the door open' for a return to court to seek an extension to the order to include the approval of a CVA.

It is then, quite usual for an administration order to be granted for only one of the four stated purposes and for that purpose to be (d) ie, 'a more advantageous realisation of the company's assets than would be effected on a winding up'.

Effect of the application

1.81 The immediate result of the petition for an administration order is to effectively stay all actions against the company until such time as an order is made or the petition itself dismissed.

Section 10 spells out the effect in these words:

(a) no resolution may be passed or order made for the winding-up of the company;
(b) no steps may be taken to enforce any security over the company's property, or to repossess goods in the company's possession under any hire-purchase agreement, except with the leave of the court and subject to such terms as the court may impose; and
(c) no other proceedings and no execution or other legal process may be commenced or continued and no distress may be levied against the company or its property except with the leave of the court and subject to such terms as aforesaid.

Thus, if there is already a petition on file for the winding-up of the company, that petition cannot be heard until the application for the administration order has itself been heard. In such circumstances it is open to the court to continue the hearing of the two petitions and indeed, such a step would make obvious sense. If the court found in favour of the application for the administration order, then the petition for the winding up would be dismissed. If however the court decided that liquidation was to be the ultimate order it would first be necessary to dismiss the application for the administration order.

What the application does then is to impose an official and automatic moratorium upon creditors. Except with the leave of the court, no creditor (including a landlord) may distrain against the company's assets and no hire-purchase or leasing company may repossess its goods.

What the application does *not* do is prevent:

1. the holder of a floating charge from appointing an administrative receiver (in which event – subject to the provisions of s9(3) – discharge of the application for the administration order will follow automatically); or
2. any creditor from *presenting* a petition for the winding-up of the company, in which event the court will have to decide whether to make an order in favour of one of the petitioners, with the other being discharged. Alternatively, the court may decide not to make any order at all and dismiss both petitions.

Given that at the hearing of the application for the administration order the court makes the order as requested, the company will now be under the control of one or more duly appointed administrators.

Effect of the order

1.82 Section 11 sets out the effects of the order as follows:

(1) ...
    (a) any petition for the winding up of the company shall be dismissed, and
    (b) any administrative receiver of the company shall vacate office.

(2) Where an administration order has been made, any receiver of part of the company's property shall vacate office on being required to do so by the administrator.

(3) During the period for which an administration order is in force.
    (a) no resolution may be passed or order made for the winding up of the company;
    (b) no administrative receiver of the company may be appointed;
    (c) no other steps may be taken to enforce any security over the company's property, or to repossess goods in the company's possession under any hire-purchase agreement, except with the consent of the administrator or the leave of the court and subject (where the court gives leave) to such terms as the court may impose; and
    (d) no other proceedings and no execution or other legal process may be commenced or continued, and no distress may be levied, against the company or its property except with the consent of the administrator or the leave of the court and subject (where the court gives leave) to such terms as aforesaid.

Once the order has been granted, the statutory moratorium imposed on creditors is effectively both reinforced and extended. Section 11(2) is of particular interest to holders of fixed charges especially where that charge is incorporated into a debenture granting a 'limited' floating charge. An example would be where a lender takes a fixed charge over land together with buildings to be erected thereon and a floating charge over plant and equipment on the site.

Such a floating charge is not a charge over 'the whole (or substantially the whole) of a company's property' (see ADMINISTRATIVE RECEIVER) and does not allow the holder of the charge to appoint an administrative receiver. What it does allow is the appointment of a 'fixed charge' receiver under the Law of Property Act 1925 (see

RECEIVERSHIP UNDER THE LAW OF PROPERTY ACT (1925)) who is subject to the provision of s11(2), ie:

> ... any receiver of part of the company's property shall vacate office on being required to do so by the administrator.

This ability for an administrator to remove a fixed charge-holder has obvious implications for lenders who are contemplating taking fixed charges over assets within a company where no floating charge has been taken over substantially the whole of the company's property.

Nature of the appointment

(a) Officer of the court

1.83 Although often perceived as an administrative receiver appointed by a route other than via a floating charge, an administrator is a court appointee and his powers are more akin to those of a liquidator in a compulsory liquidation or a court appointed receiver.

As an officer of the court he must be impartial as to the various competing interests in his administration, owing a duty both to the creditors and the shareholders to make himself fully conversant with the company's business and affairs and must not suppress relevant information (*Gooch's Case* (1872) 7 Ch App 207).

It should, however, be noted that, in common with a liquidator, it would seem an administrator does not owe duties to the creditors or members of the company as such. He is an agent of the company to which he owes a duty of care in his management of its affairs.

As an officer of the court he is subject to the principle known as 'the rule in *ex parte James*' (*Re Condon, ex p James* (1874) 9 Ch App 609) which means that he must not take advantage of third parties who act in good faith, notwithstanding that legally he may be so entitled.

(b) Officer of the company

1.84 By virtue of s251 an administrator (as a 'manager') is also an officer of the company, as a consequence of which:
1. He may be fined for failing to ensure the company fulfils its various statutory duties under CA 1985.
2. He is subject to such other statutory regulations as may affect officers of the company.
3. He owes fiduciary duties to the company.
4. He must exercise due care and skill in the performance of his duties to a level of competence higher than that of an ordinary director.

Powers of the administrator

1.85 Once appointed the administrator is given considerable powers to enable him to fulfil his function.

(a) Powers granted under IA 1986 Sch 1

1.86 IA 1986 grants a long list of statutory powers both to administrators and administrative receivers, so that they both share certain common powers. Those powers are set out in to IA 1986 Sch 1 and are reproduced as follows:

Schedule 1 – Powers of Administrator or Administrative Receiver

1 Power to take possession of, collect and get in the property of the company and, for that purpose, to take such proceedings as may seem to him expedient.

2 Power to sell or otherwise dispose of the property of the company by public auction or private auction or private contract or, in Scotland, to sell, feu, hire out or otherwise dispose of the property of the company by public roup or private bargain.

3 Power to raise or borrow money and grant security therefor over the property of the company.

4 Power to appoint a solicitor or accountant or other professionally qualified person to assist him in the performance of his functions.

5 Power to bring or defend any action or other legal proceedings in the name and on behalf of the company.

6 Power to refer to arbitration any question affecting the company.

7 Power to effect and maintain insurances in respect of the business and property of the company.

8 Power to use the company's seal.

9 Power to do all acts and to execute in the name and on behalf of the company any deed, receipt or other document.

10 Power to draw, accept, make and endorse any bill of exchange or promissory note in the name and on behalf of the company.

11 Power to appoint any agent to do any business which he is unable to do himself or which can more conveniently be done by an agent and power to employ and dismiss employees.

12 Power to do all such things (including the carrying out of works) as may be necessary for the realisation of the property of the company.

13 Power to make any payment which is necessary or incidental to the performance of his functions.

14 Power to carry on the business of the company.

15 Power to establish subsidiaries of the company.

16 Power to transfer to subsidiaries of the company the whole or any part of the business and property of the company.

17 Power to grant or accept a surrender of a lease or tenancy of any of the property of the company, and to take a lease or tenancy of any property required or convenient for the business of the company.

18 Power to make any arrangement or compromise on behalf of the company.

19 Power to call up any uncalled capital of the company.

20 Power to rank and claim in the bankruptcy, insolvency, sequestration or liquidation of any person indebted to the company and to receive dividends, and to accede to trust deeds for the creditors of any such person.

21 Power to present or defend a petition for the winding up of the company.

22 Power to change the situation of the company's registered office.

23 Power to do all other things incidental to the exercise of the foregoing powers.

(b) Other powers

1.87 Section 11(1)(b) gives an administrator the power to require a 'fixed charge' receiver to vacate office.

Section 14 grants an administrator further general powers. Sub-section 14(1) enables him to:

> do all such things as may be necessary for the management of the affairs, business and property of the company

Sub-section 14(2) gives the power for an administrator to remove or appoint directors and to call meetings of the members or creditors of the company.

Section 15 gives the administrator power to sell property of the company charged to a lender, or property held by the company under a hire-purchase or similar agreement without the consent of the chargee or owner of the property. Unless the charge is (or was originally) a floating charge, the consent of the court will be required and the monies realised must be used firstly to discharge the sums secured by the security or payable under the hire-purchase agreement. Note that for the purpose of this section references to hire-purchase agreements include conditional sale agreements, chattel leasing agreements and retention of title agreements (s15(9)).

This power can be particularly useful to an administrator where he wishes to dispose of the company as a going concern and a security-holder is refusing to co-operate (s43 grants a similar more restricted power to an administrative receiver which does not extend to property subject to reservation of title).

(c) Powers which follow a duty

1.88 Once appointed, an administrator has a duty under s22 to call for a Statement of Affairs. He has other duties, one of which is to challenge any preferences under s239. Although duties of his office, it nevertheless follows that an administrator has the power vested in him to require the preparation of a Statement of Affairs and to challenge preferences. This power and duty to challenge preferences places the administrator on the same footing as a liquidator who possess similar powers. It should however be noted that unlike a liquidator, an administrator's powers do not extend to bringing claims under s213 and s214 for fraudulent and wrongful trading.

(d) Powers as an 'office holder'

1.89

- Section 233 enables an administrator to require the (public) supply of gas, electricity, water or telephone without the requirement to discharge any outstanding account as at the date of his appointment (although he will almost certainly be required to accept personal liability for any supply during the administration).
- Section 234 enables an administrator to request that the court orders property of the company to be delivered to him.
- Section 235 empowers him to require the co-operation of any officer or former officer of the company (and a number of other stiplulated parties – see s235(3) for further details).
- Section 236 enables him, through the court, to carry out an enquiry into the affairs of the company. These are wide powers and it is worthwhile setting out the relevant section in full so as to obtain a full appreciation of the importance of this power. This section states that:

> (2) The court may, on the application of the office-holder, summon to appear before it –
> (a) any officer of the company.
> (b) any person known or suspected to have in his possession any property of the company or supposed to be indebted to the company, or
> (c) any person whom the court thinks capable of giving information concerning the promotion, formation, business dealings, affairs or property of the company.
>
> (3) The court may require any such person as is mentioned in subsection (2)(a) to (c) to submit an affidavit to the court containing an account of his dealings with the company or to produce any books, papers or other records in his possession or under his control relating to the company or the matters mentioned in paragraph (c) of the subsection.

It should be appreciated that none of the above powers as 'office-holder' is unique to an administrator. Sections 234, 235 and 236 grant identical powers to an administrative receiver, liquidator and provisional liquidator appointed by the court.

Section 233 similarly applies to the above office holders and in addition to a supervisor under a Company Voluntary Arrangement (CVA).

Section 246 provides an administrator with a most important power (shared only with a liquidator or provisional liquidator) to claim books, papers or other records of the company which, but for the section could be held by way of lien against unpaid fees.

This could be of some importance to a general practitioner holding any of the above documents at the time the administration order was granted as his ability to 'bargain' with the office-holder against return of the documents is lost if the company proceeds to administration (or liquidation). Note, however, that this section does not apply in the case of administrative receivership or Company Voluntary Arrangement.

Duties and procedure following appointment

(a) Principal duty

1.90 It is an administrator's principal duty to fulfil the purpose of the administration which itself will fall into two separate phases or sections, namely before and after the administrator meets with the creditors to consider his proposals.

(b) Duty to call a meeting of the company's creditors

1.91 The requirement to meet with the company's creditors and put to them his proposals (or in other words his 'plan') designed to achieve the purpose for which the administration order was made, is contained in s23. This requires that the administrator, within three months (or such longer period as the court may allow) after the making of the order sends to the registrar of companies and to all creditors and members of the company a statement of his proposals which must be laid before the creditors at a meeting summoned for that purpose of which not less than 14 days' notice has been given. The meeting itself must be held within the three months' period.

(c) Procedure at the creditors' meeting

1.92 The conduct of the creditors' meeting is governed by the requirement of s24 and r 2.18 – 2.30

In short terms:
1. It must be held at a venue convenient for creditors between the hours of 10am and 4pm on a business day.
2. Notice of the meeting must be given in the newspaper in which the administration order was advertised.
3. The administrator's proposals may be modified by the creditors, but only if the administrator consents to each modification.
4. A resolution to accept the administrator's proposals (with or without modification) is passed when a majority (in value) of those present and voting, in person or by proxy, have voted in favour of it (r 2.28(i)). However, r 2.28 (1A) renders invalid any resolution.

    if those voting against it include more than half in value of the creditors to whom notice of the meeting was sent and who are not, to the best of the chairman's belief, persons connected with the company.

    In other words, a resolution cannot be carried against the wish of a majority of 'unconnected' creditors (see ASSOCIATED AND CONNECTED PERSONS).
5. The meeting may, 'if it thinks fit, establish a committee ('the creditors' committee') to exercise the functions conferred on it by or under this Act' (s26(1)) (For further explanation of the construction and functions of a creditors committee within an administration, see **3.21** in the Glossary).
6. If the meeting has declined to approve the administrator's proposals (with or without modifications) the court may by order discharge the administration order and make such consequential provision as it thinks fit, or adjourn the hearing

conditionally or unconditionally, or make an interim order or any other order that it thinks fit (s24(5)).

If the administrator's proposals (with or without modifications) are approved then the administration moves into its second phase. Meanwhile, we need to consider the position over the intervening period between the making of the administration order and the date of the creditors' meeting convened under s23.

(d) General Duties

1.93 An administrator's 'general duties' are defined in s17 which require him to:
- take control of the company's property;
- manage the affairs and business of the company; and
- summon meetings of the company's creditors if so requested by creditors who represent collectively not less than one-tenth in value of the company's creditors, or if so directed by the court.

An administrator owes a duty of care to the company in his management of its business affairs and property. This duty is demonstrable in the context of a sale of a company's property. Whereas an administrative receiver must exercise reasonable care to obtain a true market value at the time of sale, he may nevertheless effect an immediate sale whether or not this was identified as being likely to obtain the best price. An administrator, on the other hand, is under a duty to take reasonable care to obtain the best price as circumstances permit and he must therefore exercise reasonable care in choosing the 'right' time to sell the property.

(e) Information to be given by administrator following making of administration order

1.94 Section 21 requires an administrator to notify all creditors of the company of the order within 28 days and to send notice 'forthwith' (as soon as practicable) to the company and publish details of the order as prescribed (in r 2.10).

In addition, s12 requires that notification of the order be brought to the attention of third parties with whom the company transacts business; with the words

> Every invoice, order for goods or business letter which, at a time when an administration order is in force relating to a company, is issued by or on behalf of the company or the administrator, being a document on or in which the company's name appears, shall also contain the administrator's name and a statement that the affairs, business and property of the company are being managed by the administrator.

(f) Duty to call for a Statement of Affairs

1.95 Section 22(1) imposes a duty on an administrator to require 'forthwith' some or all of the persons mentioned (in s22(3)) to make out and submit to him a statement in the prescribed form as to the affairs of the company.

Section 22(3) list those persons as:

(a) those who are or have been officers of the company;

(b) those who have taken part in the company's formation at any time within one year before the date of the administration order;
(c) those who are in the company's employment or have been in its employment within that year, and are in the administrator's opinion capable of giving the information required;
(d) those who are or have been within that year officers of or in the employment of a company which is, or within that year was, an officer of the company.
In this subsection 'employment' includes employment under a contract for service.

Although this section imposes a duty on an administrator to require a statement of affairs, s22(5) somewhat paradoxically allows him 'if he thinks fit', at any time to release a person from the obligation of providing a statement of affairs or to extend the period for its submission.

Rule 2.15 enables an administrative receiver to pay the reasonable expenses incurred in the preparation of the statement of affairs. This is an aspect covered in further detail in the next section which deals with administrative receiverships where a similar situation subsists, for it represents an opportunity for the general practitioner to work with the insolvency practitioner on a fee basis. The provisions referred to in that section are identical in their effect to those applying in administration.

(g) Duty to report on the conduct of unfit directors

1.96 CDDA 1986 s7(3) imposes a duty on an office holder (which under CDDA 1986 s7(3)(c) includes an administrator) to submit a report to the Secretary of State where he suspects unfitness in a director or former director, to include a SHADOW DIRECTOR. The Rules which reinforce this requirement are to be found within The Insolvent Companies (Reports on Conduct of Directors) No 2 Rules 1986 (SI 1986/2134).

For certain offences the Secretary of State or the official receiver acting on his behalf alone has the authority to apply to court for an order disqualifying an individual from acting as a company director and the information required to found an application will in most instances have been submitted by an office holder in the course of his duties. In other instances application may be made by the liquidator or any past or present member or creditor of the companies concerned (CDDA 1986 s16(2)).

Application to the court must be made within two years of the insolvency and because of the strict time scale, office-holders are required to submit a conduct report (or at least an interim report) within six months of their appointment.

(h) Duty to investigate prior transactions

1.97 In order to allow an administrator to fulfil his function in gathering in all the assets of the company for the benefit of all creditors, he is given powers corresponding to those of a liquidator (who shares the same common function). Those powers enable him to investigate

- Transactions at an undervalue (s238)
- Preferences (s239)

- Extortionate credit transactions (s244)
- Certain floating charges (s245)

all of which are dealt with in individual detail in the Glossary.

(i) Duties following acceptance of the administrator's proposals

1.98 Once the creditors have approved the administrator's proposals it is his duty to act in accordance therewith in the fulfilment of the purposes of the order.

(j) Duty to make application to the court for discharge or variation of administration order

1.99 Section 18 requires an administrator to apply for a discharge or variation of the administration order if either the purpose of the order has been achieved or he deems it incapable of achievement, or if so required by the company's creditors.

(k) Duty to report to creditors

1.100 Apart from the requirement to advise creditors within 14 days of the result of the statutory meeting convened to consider the administrator's proposals (convened under s23 to consider the proposals under s24 and commonly referred to by insolvency practitioners as a 'Section 24 meeting') the administrator must also keep creditors informed upon the progress of the administration.

Rule 2.30(2) requires that 'within 14 days of the end of every period of 6 months beginning with the date of approval of the administrator's proposals or revised proposals, the administrator shall send to all creditors of the company a report on the progress of the administration'.

Rule 2.52 requires that the administrator shall:

(a) within 2 months after the end of 6 months from the date of his appointment, and of every subsequent period of 6 months, and
(b) within 2 months after he ceases to act as administrator,
send to the court, and to the registrar of companies, and to each member of the creditors' committee, the requisite accounts of the receipts and payments of the company.

Rule 2.56 requires an administrator to issue a 'certificate of insolvency', which will enable creditors to recover any VAT element of their claims, in accordance with s22(3) of the Value Added Tax Act 1983. The certificate is not to be circulated to creditors but retained by the administrator. Creditors should however be advised of its issue. (Note however that since the provisions of the FA 1990, creditors have been able to claim VAT bad debt relief automatically.) (Administrators are liable to a fine if they make default in complying with this rule.)

Finally, under this heading, r 2.30(3) requires that upon vacating office the administrator sends to creditors a report on the administration up to that time. (This requirement is waived where the administration is immediately followed by the company going into liquidation.)

Company Voluntary Arrangement (CVA) as an 'exit-route' from administration

1.101 We left the subject of CVAs with the statement that 'The interposing of an administration order as a first step to achieving a CVA is something we will consider in the following section'.

It is first of all necessary to have an appreciation of the fundamental differences between the two 'routes'; ie between administration and CVA

Although the two 'routes' share the common theme of representing a 'way forward' for an insolvent company there are a number of important and fundamental differences.

Firstly, an administration order is made by the court and the administrator becomes not only an officer of the company but a servant of the court for the purpose of his office. Although a CVA is approved under the aegis of the court, the court plays no part in the scheme and the supervisor (the 'equivalent' of the administrator) is neither an officer of the company nor a servant of the court.

Secondly, whereas a CVA is a 'complete' way forward (in the context as an alternative to liquidation) an administration order can only ever be a 'half-way house' in that it is only meant to allow the company a relatively short-term respite or 'breathing space' in which to formulate proposals to creditors following which an early discharge of the administration order will be expected. This is necessary because the administrator has no authority to pay out funds held under a floating charge or discharge the preferential creditors. An 'exit route' is therefore required from an administration order and a CVA will usually be the chosen alternative to liquidation.

On the other hand, what the administration order lacks 'at the end' (in that it must be discharged in favour of yet some other formal route) it gains 'at the beginning'. From the moment the petition is lodged with the court, all actions against the company are stayed until such time as the petition, or subsequent order, is discharged. Compare this with a CVA where there is no such protection and it is possible a winding up order could be given against the company before the scheme for a CVA obtained the creditors' approval.

It is because of these 'weaknesses' at the end of an administration order and the 'beginning' of a CVA that in practice we often see them combined with an administration order being sought initially to be replaced by a CVA once the necessary protection is in place.

The unintended 'side-effects' of legislation

1.102 There are times when the very way in which legislation is drafted provides an incentive for following one route rather than another. Although currently no longer relevant – because for the time being at least, the anomaly has disappeared with a change in the law – such was the situation which faced insolvency practitioners when the new laws under IAs 1985 and 1986 came into effect.

Initially, creditors could not obtain VAT bad debt relief on their claims in a CVA (cf the position in an IVA where relief was available) whereas they could obtain the relief within an administration. Once apprised of that information it was not unnatural for all concerned to consider the desirability of firstly seeking an administration order, with a CVA exit route incorporated as one of the administrator's proposals to creditors! As explained at **3.85** in the Glosasary this anomaly has now been addressed by the provisions of FA 1990 enabling creditors to claim VAT bad debt relief automatically, whether or not the CVA is preceded by administration.

The role of the general practitioner in obtaining an administration order (case study)

1.103 At the beginning of this chapter on administration orders (**1.62**) reference was made to the difficulty in understanding the full potential afforded by the administration procedure. The following story is true. It is based on actual facts adapted only to allow those concerned therein to retain their anonymity. It should serve to illustrate the role that the general practitioner can play in helping to save his client company.

CASE STUDY

> Fred Long walked into his office on Monday morning, having just returned from a fortnight's holiday to find an urgent message on his desk to contact his old friend and client Titus Jay. Fred was a general practitioner whose firm had for many generations looked after the affairs of the Jay family textile company Crabbe Engineers Ltd whose business had started well over a hundred years ago but which in common with virtually every company within the textile industry was now feeling the full impact of the seemingly never-ending recession.
>
> When Fred reached the factory, matters were far worse than he could have imagined. It seemed he had hardly departed on holiday when the bank telephoned Titus Jay to insist that independent investigating accountants be instructed to carry out an appraisal of the company. Cash flow was tight; the company had sustained a number of bad debts where customers had 'gone bust' on them and the bank overdraft was at its limit. Titus had no option but to accede to the bank's request if cheques were not to be dishonoured.
>
> The investigating accountants arrived, obtained a print-off from the computer of the last management accounts made up to a date two months previously, asked questions for an hour then disappeared back to their office. They had not looked round the factory. Two days later they issued a report which demonstrated that the company was insolvent and recommended receivership. The bank was now pressing the directors to agree to the appointment of administrative receivers.
>
> There was more to come. In Fred Long's absence, desperate to talk to a 'friendly face', Titus had discussed the problem with one of Fred's former partners with whom (and with Fred Long's agreement) he had kept in touch over the years. Still in general practice he had looked at the report and recommended immediate liquidation. Titus had an appointment to see him that afternoon. Fred asked Titus to show him the report which disclosed a marginal deficiency to unsecured creditors on the basis of an estimated realisable value of £20,000 for plant and machinery. Upon questioning Titus he learned that the reporting accountants had not inspected the plant, let alone had a professional valuation and that the figure of £20,000 was their own estimate based on personal experience that machinery with a book

value of £80,000 would be unlikely to realise more than 25% of that value. Fred also noticed by pure chance that, unbelievably, the Statement of Affairs contained an addition mistake which meant that the assets as mentioned were understated by £20,000 meaning that in effect no value whatsoever had been placed upon the plant!

Fred Long telephoned to speak to the bank. The manager faced with the mistake in the report and after conferring with the bank's 'recovery department' agreed to allow the company two days' 'breathing space' in which to formulate proposals for repayment failing which they were determined to go ahead with their intention to appoint receivers.

Titus Jay kept his appointment with the other general practitioner. On being shown into his office he was introduced to another gentleman, a licensed practitioner who had just 'happened to drop in for a cup of coffee' as he was in the area at the time. Titus apprised both gentleman of Fred Long's return and immediate discoveries and the meeting was effectively 'adjourned sine die'.

Meanwhile Fred Long had contacted a professional colleague, a licensed practitioner with whom he had worked over the years; together they had shared a number of interesting cases. The practitioner was out of town on business for the remainder of the week but offered to send along one of his managers to assist with the figures, content to leave Fred to mastermind the situation, secure in the knowledge of his friend's abilities.

Within 24 hours Fred had instructed agents specialising in plant and machinery valuations and received their written report following immediate attendence at the factory. One hundred and fifty thousand pounds! The bank appeared to remain unimpressed. The preferential creditors were almost £90,000 and any realisations from a sale of plant and machinery within a formal insolvency would first of all go to discharge the preferential claims. The bank was content to look to recover its £250,000 advance from the book debts.

Fred Long brought in a solicitor experienced in dealing with insolvency matters who himself held an insolvency licence. Forty-eight hours later Titus Jay went round to see the bank with a banker's draft for £60,000 from the sale of plant and machinery surplus to requirements. With the help of Fred Long, the bank was persuaded that it would not be prejudiced if an administrator was appointed and by the time the insolvency practitioner returned to his office, everything was ready for an application to court.

The court granted the order for the purposes of:
1   seeking to achieve the survival of the company and the whole or any part of its undertaking as a going concern;
2   seeking the approval of a Voluntary Arrangement; and
3   effecting a more advantageous realisation of the company's assets.

Fred Long worked closely with the administrator. Under their guidance the work-force was cut by two thirds, creating a liability for redundancy pay in excess of £100,000. The sales director was also made redundant and the remaining work-force re-grouped within a small section of the factory building. The now vacant part of the building was refurbished and divided into smaller units which, despite a continuing recession were all quickly let on tenancies which produced a rental income in excess of £50,000 pa.

Meanwhile the administrator negotiated with a number of finance companies who in a receivership could and in this instance almost certainly would have repossessed their equipment essential to a continuation of trade. Deals were struck and production continued uninterrupted.

Within two weeks the bank had been repaid in full. Within a month further plant surplus to requirements had been disposed of and by the time the administrator held the 'Section 24' meeting of creditors the company was trading with suppliers on a cash basis and £125,000 was held on deposit with the bank.

With profitability re-established, creditors voted unanimously for a Company Voluntary Arrangement and the underlying value of the company's freehold premises, now uncharged ensured that they would eventually receive 100p in the pound. Only the depressed property market occasioned a delay in raising immediate funds for the purpose.

Through the availability of the administration route and the insolvency skills of the *general practitioner* involved, jobs were saved, the company was saved, the creditors repaid and the general practitioner retained a grateful client.

The role of the general practitioner in an administration

1.104 Of all the formal routes, administration must surely offer the general practitioner the best opportunity for some form of significant ongoing relationship with his client company, particularly where a continuation of trade forms part of the administrator's proposals. Given that the statutory obligation to file audited accounts continues coupled with the probability that it is the general practitioner who influenced the directors' choice of office holder there are many potential areas where the general practitioner not only may but also can continue an ongoing involvement.

Inevitably there will be occasions when the administrator forms the view that the general practitioner has little or nothing to contribute. Occasionally, there may be the perception, however unjustified, that the company's difficulties have arisen as a result of previous poor advice. At the end of the day it will inevitably be the general practitioner's own knowledge and experience of insolvency law and procedures which will prove to be the limiting factor.

VII ADMINISTRATIVE RECEIVERSHIP

Initial considerations

1.105 The two questions any practitioner advising an insolvent company must ask, are:
- is a bank (or other secured lender) involved, holding a debenture granting a floating charge over assets of the company?; and if so,
- can it be persuaded not to enforce those powers and refrain from appointing administrative receivers?

(where there is talk of 'receivership' or 'receivers being appointed', it is usually, but not necessarily, an appointment by a bank of administrative receivers. For the sake of simplicity within the text of this section this will henceforth be assumed, as will be the normal preference to appoint two receivers (from the same firm) notwithstanding a sole appointment is all that is required).

Contrary to the adverse press that appears from time to time, banks are not heartless machines that simply close down businesses and put people out of work through the receivership process for no good reason other than they want their money back.

It is true all banks incorporate a clause within their lending that the overdraft is repayable on demand, but in practice this will not happen unless the bank feels it has just cause. Indeed, many is the time a bank could have been criticised for having supported for too long in an attempt to save a business!

Understanding the bank's perception

1.106 It would be wrong to assume that care and understanding is not called for in negotiating with a bank at a financially critical stage in a client company's 'lifetime'.

Great care is required if the bank is not to be frightened into trying to protect its position through an early receivership appointment.

Great understanding is required if the bank is to feel comfortable with the ability of the adviser to address the relevant issues and produce a reasoned and balanced survival plan which fully protects the bank's position outside of a receivership.

The first thing to understand is how the bank operates and 'thinks' under a given set of circumstances. In very broad terms the bank divides its operations into two parts; those who lend the money (the bank managers) and those who recover it (by whatever name 'the recovery departments'). Linking the two are the Regional Head Offices.

Thus, in its own way the division within the banking profession can be compared with the accountancy profession's own division between general and insolvency practitioners and it will be the bank's own 'insolvency practitioners' who decide what action the bank will take to protect its interests.

When someone wishes to borrow money from a bank, it is usual to provide the local manager with a business plan at a personal interview. In all but the simplest and smallest of cases, the manager will seek approval from the Regional Head Office. Through this modus operandi, an unseen customer has an application discussed by a faceless banker on the recommendation of an intermediary who knows them both, namely the local branch manager.

Conversely, when the manager suspects or is advised of financial problems, he is obliged to report to Regional Head Office, where a decision will be taken whether or not to refer the matter to the bank's recovery department.

You will then in effect be dealing with the bank's own 'insolvency practitioners' and must yourself be able to plan with a complete understanding of the bank's requirements. You will need to look at the position through the eyes of the bank and resist all temptation to draw up proposals in any other light. Of one thing you may be certain; any attempt to unduly pressurise the bank other than on constructive lines which fully protect its interests at all times will inevitably lead to an early appointment of receivers.

The significance and importance of the floating charge

1.107 Although banks will look to take as much security as possible under a fixed charge the floating charge offers the possibility of further cover subject to the prior interest of the preferental creditors (see PREFERENTIAL DEBTS).

More importantly, however, it is the floating charge under which a lender is able to appoint an administrative receiver (a fixed charge allows the appointment of a 'fixed charge' receiver only) (see **3.71** in the Glossary) and enables the lender to block the appointment of an administrator (see **1.71**).

Definition

1.108 The term 'administrative receiver' was first introduced by IA 1985, replacing the 'receiver and manager' appointed under the provisions of the Companies Acts.

An administrative receiver is a licensed insolvency practitioner appointed by a bank to recover its outstanding loan to a company pursuant to an authority contained within a debenture, duly registered by the lender, granting the lender a floating charge over the assets of the company.

Up to the 31 July 1990, the debenture would have required to be executed under the Common Seal of the company. Since that date, under the provisions of Companies Act 1985, s36A a company no longer needs to have a Common Seal and documents signed by two directors, or by a director and the company secretary and expressed to be executed (in whatever form of words) have the same effect as if executed under the Common Seal of the company.

The legal definition of an administrative receiver is to be found in s29:

> "administrative receiver" means
>
> > (a) a receiver or manager of the whole (or substantially the whole) of a company's property appointed by or on behalf of the holders of any debentures of the company secured by a charge which as created, was a floating charge, or by such a charge and one or more other securities, or
> >
> > (b) a person who would be such a receiver or manager but for the appointment of some other person as the receiver of part of the company's property.

Registering the charge

1.109 For the security to be valid it must be registered at Companies House as required by CA 1985 s395 failing which, although valid against the company itself it is void against the company's creditors or a liquidator. Note however, that the charge will be deemed to be valid, *even if registered out of time,* following the issue by the Registrar of a certificate of registration.

Following the introduction of CA 1989 Part IV the Registrar will cease to issue certificates and care will need to be taken to ensure that the registration formalities have been properly observed

Reason for choosing the administrative receivership route

1.110 In the majority of cases it will not be so much a question of the directors 'choosing' the receivership route, as having the decision made for them by the bank. Nevertheless, true to the old saw 'it is an ill wind that blows nobody good' receivership brings with it certain advantages.

Advantages to the directors

1.111 Although given the choice most directors would choose administration over administrative receivership, they would undoubtedly perceive receivership as far preferable to outright liquidation.

In most instances receivership will have followed a period of intense creditor pressure and the daily burden of attempting to teem and lade with cash flow in order to maintain essential supplies while fending off irate creditors threatening distraint or winding up petitions is brought to an immediate end. Many directors suffer serious health problems connected with these business pressures, and handing over the company for someone else to deal with all its future financial problems, has been known to be accompanied by a rapid and welcome improvement in a director's health!

In common with all formal insolvency appointments, administrative receivership crystallises directors' potential liabilities with regard to bank guarantees or future claims by a liquidator for fraudulent or wrongful trading (see **1.172** and **1.180**). Given however that *only* a liquidator can bring a claim for fraudulent or wrongful trading, receivership could have the unintended effect of providing a shield against claims under these headings. (This is simply because creditors frequently abandon any intention of petitioning for the winding-up of a company following the appointment of administrative receivers.)

Advantages to the company

1.112 The major advantages to the company follow from its ability to continue to trade given the support of the bank. There is a touch of irony to be found in the concept of a bank making additional funds available to receivers which it denied the directors, but then of course the circumstances change immediately following the receivers' appointment, with the bank secure in the knowledge that the advance of those new monies cannot be attacked by creditors.

Thus, with funding in place the receivers are in a position to continue to trade with the hopes and intentions of achieving a more advantageous price for the business and its assets as a going concern, than could be effected in a break-up on a cessation.

This in itself will often preserve continuing employment for at least certain of the employees which, all moral and social aspects aside means that claims by employees following redundancy are minimised, thereby eliminating additional creditor claims which would otherwise compete for dividend purposes.

One other potential area of benefit follows the ability of the receivers to continue to trade so that there is no automatic cessation for tax purposes, with trading losses in the current accounting period being preserved and available for offset against any capital gain realised by the receivers within the same period. Although offering perhaps only limited application following the collapse in property prices in the late 1980s the principle remains intact and will be useful in certain instances.

The position of the preferential creditors

(a) Company not in liquidation

1.113 The 'preferential periods' (see **3.66** in the Glossary) are triggered as at the date of appointment of the administrative receivers. Section 40(2) states '... (the preferential debts) shall be paid out of the assets coming into the hands of the receiver in priority to any claims for principal or interest in respect of the debentures.'

Under s40(3) 'payments made under this section shall be recouped, as far as may be, out of the assets of the company available for payment of general creditors'.

In simple terms the preferential creditors have priority over a lender secured by a floating charge (to receive the benefit from realisation of those assets caught under the floating charge) with the costs of meeting the claims of preferential creditors being met from any available 'free' assets and thereby falling on the unsecured creditors.

It is the administrative receivers' responsibility and duty to deal with and pay the claims of the preferential creditors (s40).

(b) Company in liquidation

1.114 Where administrative receivers are appointed to a company already in liquidation (and this can and does infrequently happen where for whatever reason the bank prefers to see its interests 'looked after' by a chosen receiver rather than the creditors' chosen liquidator) the 'preferential period' will have already commenced by reference to the liquidation itself and payment of the preferential claims will be the responsibility of the liquidator.

(c) Liquidation following receivership

Konkursverwaltung

1.115 The IA 1986 introduced a new wording with regard to floating charges to close an earlier loophole. Previous legislation provided that payment should be made to preferential creditors out of assets caught by a floating charge, including a charge that crystallised on the appointment of a receiver. With considerable initiative, ap-

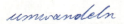

proved by the Court in *Re Brightlife Ltd* [1987] Ch 200, 2 BCC 99, 359 floating charges were crystallised *prior* to the appointment of a receiver, so that it became a fixed charge at the time of appointment, thereby neatly side-stepping the requirement to pay preferential creditors out of those assets.

Section 251 defines a floating charge as '... a charge which, as created, was a floating charge ...'

Section 40 'payment of debts out of assets subject to floating charge' again uses the same wording:

> The following applies, in the case of a company, where a receiver is appointed on behalf of the holders of any debentures of the company which, *as created*, was a floating charge (emphasis supplied).

This new wording, coupled with the wording of s175 (preferential debts in a winding up) gave immediate rise for concern that where a company in receivership was subsequently wound up prior to the payment of floating charge realisations to the debenture holder, the receiver would then have to pay the *liquidation* preferential creditors. These fears were realised following the decision in *Re Portbase Clothing Ltd* [1993] 3 All ER 829, BCC 96 so that, whether or not the original intention of the legislation, where liquidation occurs during a receivership the liquidation preferential creditors and the costs and expenses of the liquidation rank ahead of the debenture holder.

(d) The effect of *Re GL Saunders Ltd*

1.116 The effect of the decision in this case is considered in further detail at **3.66** in the Glossary.

In short terms, payment in full to a debenture holder out of fixed-charge monies not only redeems the fixed charge but also simultaneously redeems the floating charge with the effect that under such circumstances any surplus fixed-charge realisation is not caught by the floating charge (and therefore available for distribution among the preferential creditors) but must be paid to the company or (if in liquidation) its liquidator.

Events leading up to the appointment of administrative receivers

(a) Reason for appointment

1.117 The prospect of a bank appointing receivers 'out of the blue' without any sort of warning or indication of its intention to the directors of the company is a virtual impossibility. Something has to have happened to persuade the bank to commence action to recover its advances and that 'something' will be that the bank:

1. has lost faith in the integrity of the directors;
2. believes its security to be inadequate or at risk;
3. will be placed at risk should the company continue to trade;
4. some combination of the above.

Whatever the reason, it is virtually certain that one or more things will happen before receivers walk in to take over the control or running of the company.

(b) The 'warning signs'

(i) Call for additional security

1.118 One of the first warning signs will be a request by the bank for additional security, more particularly when this is in support of existing levels of borrowing and not to facilitate a further advance.

Where the bank already holds a debenture granting fixed and floating charges its request is likely to be for third party, or collateral security which often takes the form of directors' guarantees supported by second-charges on their family homes. Whether it is worth placing their families' financial future in jeopardy in an attempt to save the company must, on proper advice, be a decision for the directors. Realistically however a demise of the company will often cut off the families' only source of income so that a refusal to give personal guarantees might only serve to delay the inevitable (see also GUARANTOR—acting as).

Legal advice should always be sought where the bank faces an existing shortfall on an immediate receivership and the additional security requested would simply cover that shortfall.

(ii) Request to open a 'wages account'

1.119 The subject of a wages account is also considered at **3.13** in the Glossary.

A bank will sometimes request that the current account overdraft facility be 'split', with wages and salaries being paid out of a separate account which is then reduced from time to time by transfer from current account in accordance with a pre-determined formula.

The reason for dealing with matters in this way is to preserve the bank's preferential claim for wages paid in any ensuing insolvency (see **1.10**). Therefore the very fact that the bank is requesting the operation of a wages account has to mean that it is looking at the company as a potential receivership candidate.

(iii) Request for independent investigating accountant's report

1.120 The third and unmistakable sign that the company is now under the scrutiny of the bank's own 'insolvency department' is the request for an independent report. When this is called for, the bank will choose accountants who have had no previous connection with the company or its directors (but see **1.123** below) and request that, usually at the company's expense, they carry out an appraisal of the current state of the company and its future viability. They will be asked to report their findings directly to the bank, (with copies of their report forwarded to the company) to include recommendations as to how the bank should proceed in the light of the company's financial problems. In preparing their report, the independent accountants will almost certainly be required to accept a duty of care to the bank.

Although a request by the bank for the preparation of such a report can never be good news for the company, it by no means necessarily signals the 'end of the road', particularly when called for before financial deterioration has eroded the company's resources too deeply. Somewhat paradoxically, the more detailed and painstaking the scope and depth of the investigation the better the chance of future survival. It is what insolvency practitioners are often heard to refer to whimsically as a 'quick and dirty' – usually an hour or two's look at the company followed by a two- or three-page report – that acts as a precursor to receivership. (This because the bank has concluded there is little chance of saving the situation and elects to balance its preference to act upon written professional independent advice against further unnecessary expenditure which in the final analysis it might well have to fund.)

(iv)   Formal demand for repayment

1.121   Although included among the 'warning signs', receipt of a formal demand for repayment is almost invariably (although not necessarily; see *Colin James Alabaster & Colin Alabaster Automobiles Ltd v SPJ Wadstead & PH Finn* [CH 1990] A 2319 (Unreported)) as good as a promise by the bank that receivers will be taking over in a matter of days if not hours.

The law concerning demands for repayment is probably of little more than academic interest to general practitioners. For those interested in further researching this area, in addition to the case cited above, other recent cases include *Banbury Foods Pty Ltd v National Bank of Australasia Ltd* (1984) 58 ALJR 199 and *Bank of Baroda v Panessar* [1986] 3 All ER 751, 2 BCC 99, 288.

(c)   Agreement of borrower to appointment of administrative receivers

1.122   Notwithstanding the bank's right to appoint under the terms of its debenture, it is customary for banks to seek the co-operation of the directors when it comes to requesting an appointment.

It is the practice of banks to so organise matters that the directors write to them and request the bank appoint receivers. The request itself will be in a simple form for which the bank will supply a draft. The rationale behind this is fairly obvious; it is difficult for directors to challenge the bank's decision to appoint subsequently if they have written and requested that appointment in the first instance!

Should the directors refuse to provide written request for the appointment, this in itself will not deter the bank from appointing if it has already decided upon that route; it will simply mean that the bank has to accept the inevitability of a 'hostile appointment' which in the end is unlikely to have any bearing on the receivership one way or the other (although challenges by directors to the appointment of receivers have become more commonplace of recent years).

(d)   Choice of appointees

1.123   Faced with the inevitability of a receivership it is understandable that in many instances directors and their advisers seek to introduce their own choice of appointees to the bank.

Just as understandable is the bank's negative reaction. Total independence is always essential and the bank will not appoint any individual as an administrative receiver simply because he is a licensed practitioner. Where a company's business is of a specialised nature, the bank will usually seek to appoint receivers who have experience within that industry.

All banks maintain their own 'panel' of receivers and it is of course possible that individuals put forward by the directors regularly accept appointment from the company's bank. This in itself is no guarantee that they would be appointed; in the majority of instances, the bank's choice will prevail.

Where the directors have given personal guarantees to the bank and there is a potential shortfall under the debenture, this creates an additional factor which the bank will always weigh carefully before making any final decision. It could however only ever influence that decision if the bank was happy with the actual individuals proposed and the guarantee became the deciding factor in arriving at a decision.

(e) Timing of the appointment

1.124 The serving of a formal demand for repayment is a requirement before appointment. Although in most cases demand will not be served until the bank has reached the decision to appoint, there are occasions when demand is made by the bank to 'keep open its options'.

Once a final decision has been made, with the formal written demand duly served, events will move quite rapidly. How long the bank will wait between serving formal demand and appointing the receivers will depend upon the circumstances surrounding the case. Where for example there is a realistic hope that alternative bank facilities might be forthcoming the bank would almost certainly be prepared to wait a reasonable period of time, perhaps a number of days if not weeks to allow the company the opportunity of reorganising its finances. In most instances however this will not be the case, with appointment following within hours of demand and usually within the same working day or the day following.

Over the years there have been a number of attempts by directors to have appointments declared invalid on the grounds that either insufficient or alternatively too much time has elapsed between demand and appointment. Although every case would be looked at on its own merits, as with any other area of law, the court will look back to earlier decisions. In that regard it is worth noting that in the case of the former, a time of less than one hour was held to be reasonable and in the case of the latter appointment was held to be valid even though made several months after service of a written formal demand for repayment (see *Bank of Baroda v Panessar* and *Alabaster v Wadstead & Finn*).

Nature of the appointment

(a) Agent of the company

1.125 Provided the company is not in liquidation at the time of his appointment, an administrative receiver is deemed by statute to be the agent of the company (s44(1)(a)).

(b) Contracting as principal

1.126 It is customary for most administrative receivers to overstamp all receivership correspondence and documents with the words that '... the receivers contract as agents of the company and without personal liability'.

At first sight this might appear something of an 'over-kill'; after all, given that they act as agents under s44, why the need to spell it out in this manner?

The reason is because a receiver's agency differs from a normal agency in that under certain circumstances he may act as principal with personal liability. Thus he will be personally liable on contracts entered into by him as receiver unless liability is expressly excluded under the terms of the contract.

He could also find himself deemed to have 'adopted' contracts of employment in fulfilling his duties and accepting personal liability thereon (s 44(1)(b)). In order to avoid this liability most receivers will ensure that within 14 days of appointment they:
1. make redundant such staff as will not be required; and
2. write in the clearest of terms to all other employees advising that they will not personally be adopting the contracts of employment but attempting to arrange funding for the company to allow it to continue to employ the retained workforce.

Other situations in which the receiver could find himself acting with personal liability are:
1. in the discharge of those statutory duties which fall upon him personally;
2. when instructing professional advisers; and
3. in borrowing monies for the purpose of the receivership.

Where an administrative receiver does incur personal liability on contracts, he is entitled to an indemnity out of the assets of the company (s44(1)(c)).

(c) The effect of liquidation

1.127 Following liquidation, the administrative receiver will effectively no longer act as agent of the company, but depending upon the circumstances continue to fulfil his function either as principal or, in exceptional instances, as agent for his appointor (see *American Express International Banking Corpn v Hurley* [1985] 3 All ER 564).

Where a receiver is negligent in his capacity as agent for the debenture holder resulting in loss to his appointor, the debenture holder will have an implied right of indemnity against him.

(d) Contrast with position of an administrator

1.128 In contrast to the position of an administrator who must, as an officer of the court be impartial as to the various competing interests in his administration (see **1.83**) an administrative receiver is the 'bank's man' and it is to the debenture holder that he owes his primary duty. This he fulfils through the realisation of the assets of the company in reduction of the secured debt of his appointor.

Directors are sometimes heard to complain that receivers do not have sufficient regard to the saving of companies and are too quick to close down businesses simply so as to pay off the bank. It is this very complaint that highlights the difference between the two appointments for whereas an administrator will act in accordance with the terms of the administration order and, following approval by creditors, his own proposals which will often include a continuation of trade, an administrative receiver has no duty to trade on. What he does possess are the *powers* of management, but those powers are ancillary to his duty to his appointor.

Powers of the administrative receiver

1.129 A receiver's powers are both:
1. contractual; and
2. statutory.

(a) Contractual powers

1.130 Such powers as an administrative receiver may enjoy and exercise will derive from the charges or debenture which specify those powers. It is customary to draft the relevant clauses to allow the receiver as much scope as possible within the context of the overriding understanding that such powers do not extend beyond the powers which the company could grant to a third party as a matter of contract.

(b) Statutory powers

(i) Insolvency Act 1986 Sch 1

1.131 In common with an administrator, an administrative receiver has the powers specified in IA 1986 Sch 1 conferred upon him. In the case of an administrative receiver these powers are conferred by virtue of s42 which states:

> The powers conferred on the administrative receiver of a company by the debenture by virtue of which he was appointed are deemed to include (except in so far as they are inconsistent with the provisions of those debentures) the powers specified in Schedule 1 to this Act.

In this manner the administrative receiver is given statutory powers as if by contract; in other words as if they were written into the debenture under which he was appointed. This contrasts with the manner in which identical powers contained within the schedule are given to an administrator (see s14.1). The end result is however identical; they share the same powers.

IA 1986 Sch 1 is reproduced in full at **1.86**.

It is worth noting that under s42(3) anyone dealing with an administrative receiver in good faith and for value need not be concerned to enquire whether the receiver is acting within his powers.

(ii) Other powers

1.132 Under s35 an administrative receiver has power to seek the directions of the court in relation to any particular matter arising in connection with the performance of the functions of the receiver.

This is a useful power which allows the receiver (or his appointor) to apply to the court for directions where the legal procedure is in doubt.

Section 43 which also involves an application to the court, gives an administrative receiver the power to make an application to dispose of property subject to a security (normally a fixed charge) as if it were not subject to the security.

Here, we are talking about security not held by the receiver's appointor. The court must be satisfied that there was a reasonable prospect the disposal would promote a more advantageous realisation of the company's assets (*Re Harris Simons Construction Ltd* [1989] 1 WLR 368, 5 BCC 11).

If the court makes such an order, then by virtue of s43(3) it will be a condition of the order that:

1   the net proceeds of the disposal, and
2   where those proceeds are less than such amount as may be determined by the court to be the net amount which would be realised on the sale of the property in the open market by a willing vendor, such sums as may be required to make good the deficiency,

shall be applied towards discharging the sums secured by the security.

What the section is saying is that if the court decides that a sale proved to be at an undervalue, then the deficiency must be made good.

This section corresponds with the power granted to an administrator under s15. Note however that unlike that section, s43 does not extend to cover goods covered by retention of title.

(c) Powers which follow a duty

1.133 An administrative receiver shares the same power as an administrator following a duty to call for a statement of affairs to be submitted to him in the prescribed form (s47).

What an administrative receiver does *not* share with an administrator is the power (and duty) to challenge transactions at undervalue (s238), preferences (s239) extortionate credit transactions (s244) and certain floating charges (s245). These may be challenged only by a liquidator or administrator.

(d) Powers as an 'office-holder'

1.134 One of the problems which used to face receivers immediately following appointment was the insistence of gas and electricity boards and water and telephone authorities that (unsecured) outstanding accounts and accrued but unbilled charges as at the date of appointment be met in full by the receiver as a condition for granting an ongoing supply.

In reality their demands, viewed by many insolvency practitioners as little short of blackmail, were no different from the demands of an unsecured creditor whose co-operation was needed in continuing to supply the receiver with an essential product, unavailable elsewhere. It has always been perfectly lawful to pay a past debt against fresh consideration and payment of an otherwise unsecured debt to procure a continuity of supply otherwise unavailable does not constitute a preference.

Nevertheless, following the implementation of IA 1986, under the provisions of s 233 an administrative receiver can now require the supply of gas, electricity, water or telephone without the requirement to discharge any outstanding account. He will however almost certainly be required to accept personal liability for any supply made to him during the course of the receivership.

Section 234 entitled 'Getting in the company's property', enables an administrative receiver to apply to the court for an order that any property, books, papers or records to which the company appears to be entitled be surrendered to him. Note however that this section should not be confused with s 246 which deals with liens and which does not apply in an administrative receivership. (It applies in an administration or liquidation.) This could be important to a general practitioner owed fees at the time of appointment of administrative receivers who may well be able to agree some payment with the receiver in return for handing over any of the company's accounting records in his possession.

Section 235(3), imposes a duty to co-operate with the office-holder on:

(a) those who are or have at any time been officers of the company;
(b) those who have taken part in the formation of the company at any time within one year before the effective date;
(c) those who are in the employment of the company, or have been in its employment (including employment under a contract for services) within that year, and are in the office-holder's opinion capable of giving information which he requires;

(d) those who are, or have within that year, been officers of, or in the employment (including employment under a contract of services) of, another company which is, or within that year was, an officer of the company in question; and

(e) in the case of a company being wound up by the court, any person who has acted as administrator, administrative receiver or liquidator of the company.

Under this section an administrative receiver may seek such information as he might reasonably require.

Section 236 enables him, through the court, to carry out an enquiry into the affairs of the company.

Duties and procedure following appointment

(a) Principal duty

1.135 An administrative receiver's primary duty is to realise the assets of the company in the interests of his appointor. If through his negligence he fails to repay the debt secured to the debenture holder or recovers less than he should have done, the debenture holder has the right to sue him for damages.

(b) Duty of care

(i) To his appointor

1.136 The first duty of an administrative receiver is owed to his appointor, his powers of management being ancilliary to that duty (*Re B Johnson & Co (Builders) Ltd* [1955] Ch 634).

(ii) To the company

1.137 The duty which is first and foremost in the minds of all parties is that specific duty to obtain a proper price for the assets. Up to 1993 administrative receivers have been able to assess that duty by reference to a number of cases which identified the relevant parameters based in negligence. Now, in a Privy Council decision, *Downsview Nominees Ltd v First City Corpn Ltd* [1993] AC 295 the liability of administrative receivers was held to be based not in negligence but in equity.

In *Watts v Midland Bank plc* [1986] BCLC 15 it was held that an administrative receiver owes a duty of care when acting as agent of the company and must use reasonable skill to ensure that a proper price is obtained for its assets. If he fails in that duty the company, through its directors, may bring proceedings against him.

After liquidation, the receiver's agency terminates and any action against the receiver for breach of duty to the company would be brought by the liquidator under s212. Moreover, whether he acts as principal or agent for the debenture holder, he will still owe a duty to sell the mortgaged property for a proper price (*Cuckmere Brick Co Ltd v Mutual Finance Ltd* [1971] Ch 949).

Note however that whereas it was held an administrative receiver must exercise reasonable care to obtain a true market value at the time of sale, he may nevertheless effect an immediate sale whether or not this was identified as being likely to obtain the best price (cf the duty of an administrative receiver to choose the 'right' time to sell the property (see **1.93**)).

The *Cuckmere Brick Co Ltd v Mutual Finance Ltd* [1971] Ch 949 decision limited the receiver's liability to 'the proposition that, if the mortgagee decides to sell, he must take reasonable care to obtain a proper price but is no authority for any wider proposition'. In *Downsview Nominees Ltd v First City Corpn Ltd* [1993] AC 295 the court held that 'the general duty of a receiver manager ... leaves no room for the imposition of a general duty to use reasonable care in dealing with the assets of the company'.

It would seem therefore that subject to a requirement that he takes reasonable care to obtain a proper price, he may exercise his powers of sale even though the outcome places the borrower at a disadvantage.

(iii) To other secured creditors

1.138 At **1.132** we identified an administrative receiver's power under s43 to seek the court's approval to allow him to sell property charged to a lender other than his appointor. Section 43(3) may be interpreted as saying that an administrative receiver must make good any deficiency if it proved he has sold at an undervalue.

In *Midland Bank Ltd v Joliman Finance Ltd* (1967) 203 Estates Gazette 1039 it was held that in negotiating a sale an administrative receiver owes a duty of care to a second mortgagee when selling property subject to their security. In *Alliance Acceptances Co Ltd v Graham* (1974) 10 SASR 220 this was extended to include a third mortgagee.

Now however we have the *Downsview Nominees Ltd v First City Corpn Ltd* [1993] AC 295 decision in which the court held that the mortgagee or receiver is not under any duty of care to the mortgagor or subsequent encumbrances. It remains to be seen to what extent the English courts will follow that approach in relation to receivership under IA 1986.

(iv) To guarantors

1.139 Where the debt owing by the company to the debenture holder has been personally guaranteed (which in most circumstances will be by one or more of the company's directors) the administrative receiver owes a duty of care to each and every guarantor in disposing of the company's assets. (*Standard Chartered Bank Ltd v Walker* [1982] 1 WLR 1410 and *American Express International Banking Corpn v Hurley* [1985] 3 All ER 564.)

(v) To preferential and unsecured creditors

1.140 Although an administrative receiver has a duty to pay the preferential creditors (see s40) he owes no duty of care either to them or the unsecured creditors (although it is worth noting that a number of authorities believe the law should be amended to extend the scope of an administrative receiver's duty to cover all creditors).

(vi) To retention of title holders

1.141 An administrative receiver will often find himself in a position of selling goods which prove to be subject to a valid retention of title claim. Whether or not the company is in liquidation, the receiver cannot claim to act as agent of the company without personal liability, and any claim (in conversion) will be against the receiver in his personal capacity.

(vii) As constructive trustee

1.142 If an administrative receiver accepts funds as a constructive trustee (other than in accordance with the directions of the beneficial owner) he may incur personal liability as trustee.

(c) Statutory duties

1.143 An administrative receiver has a number of statutory duties with which he must comply following appointment.

(i) Duty to accept appointment in writing

1.144 Rule 3.1 required him to accept his appointment in writing or confirm acceptance in writing within seven days.

(ii) Duty to give notice of appointment

1.145 Section 46 requires him to give notice of his appointment 'forthwith' to the company. It also requires him to publish notice of his appointment and, within 28 days, unless the court otherwise directs, send such a notice to all creditors of the company so far as he is aware of their addresses.

Rule 3.2(2) details the matters which must be stated in the notice, thus:

(a) the registered name of the company, as at the date of the appointment, and its registered number;
(b) any other name with which the company has been registered in the 12 months preceeding that date;
(c) any name under which the company has traded at any time in those 12 months, if substantially different from its then registered name;
(d) the name and address of the administrative receiver, and the date of his appointment;
(e) the name of the person by whom the appointment was made;
(f) the date of the instrument conferring the power under which the appointment was made;
(g) a brief description of the assets of the company (if any) in respect of which the person appointed is not made the receiver.

Rule 3.2(3) stipulates the manner in which the requirement under s46 to publish notice of the administrative receiver's appointment is to be carried out. One notice of appointment must be placed in the *London Gazette*, and one other in whichever newspaper the receiver thinks most appropriate for ensuring that it comes to the notice of the company's creditors.

Section 39 requires that every invoice, order for goods or business letter issued after his appointment must identify that an administrative receiver has been appointed.

The requirement to give notice of the appointment of an administrative receiver to the registrar of companies is contained within CA 1985 s405(1) and falls upon his appointor, who must give such notice within seven days.

(iii) Duty to call for a Statement of Affairs

1.146 Section 47(1) imposes a duty upon an administrative receiver to 'forthwith' require some or all of the persons mentioned (in s47(3)) to make out and submit to him a statement in the prescribed form as to the affairs of the company.

It is with respect to the preparation of the Statement of Affairs that the general practitioner is uniquely placed to assist his client company and, at the same time perhaps gain some modest financial compensation for the loss of an audit client. This follows the ability of the administrative receiver under r 3.7 to pay out of his receipts the reasonable expenses incurred by 'a deponent making the statement of affairs and affidavit'. Very few directors will have the technical ability to complete a statement of affairs 'in the prescribed form' and the general practitioner, with all his background knowledge of the company and some guidance as to the formal requirements should be able to complete the exercise with an efficiency that enables financially rewarding charge-out rates to be achieved. For this reason, the relevant authorities are now considered in further detail.

Section 47(2) lists the detail required to be included within the statement of affairs, ie:

(a) particulars of the company's assets, debts and liabilities;
(b) the names and addresses of the creditors;
(c) the securities held by them respectively;
(d) the date when the securities were respectively given; and
(e) such further or other information as may be prescribed.

The statement must be verified by affidavit.

Section 47(3) details the list of persons some or all of whom may be required by the administrative receiver to submit a statement of affairs. This list compares exactly with the list required under s22(3) in an administration order which is to be found detailed at **1.95**.

The receiver may if he wishes give releases from the obligation to submit a statement of affairs (s47(5)) and if the receiver refuses to exercise his power under this section, the individual may apply to the court. Section 47 calls for the statement of affairs to be submitted within 21 days but the receiver may extend this period to allow further time for completion (s47(5)(6) and r 3.6). Criminal sanctions (s430 Sch 10) are imposed on defaulters who fail without reasonable excuse to comply with their obligations to produce statements of affairs.

Under r 3.4(6) the receiver must retain the verified copy of the statement of affairs as part of the receivership records.

(iv) Duty to give notice to secured creditors

1.147 Rule 3.31 requires an administrative receiver who has applied to the court under s43(1) for authority to dispose of property which is subject to security to give notice of the order to the secured creditor.

More importantly perhaps from the receiver's point of view, s43(5) requires him to file a copy of the order with the registrar of companies within 14 days of the making of the order. Failure to comply with this section exposes the receiver to criminal sanctions.

(v) Duty to issue a 'Certificate of Insolvency'

1.148 Rule 3.36 requires an administrative receiver to issue a 'certificate of insolvency', which will enable creditors to recover any VAT element of their claims, in accordance with Value Added Tax Act 1983 s22(3). The certificate is not to be circulated to creditors but retained by the administrative receiver. Creditors should however be advised of its issue.

(Note however that since the provisions of the FA 1990 which were brought in with effect from 25 July 1990, creditors have been able to claim VAT bad debt relief automatically.)

(vi) Duty to report and convene a meeting of unsecured creditors

1.149 Section 48(1) Imposes a duty upon an administrative receiver to report within three months (or such longer period as the court may allow) to:
- the registrar of companies
- any trustee for secured creditors; and
- all known secured creditors of the company.

The report must detail:
1. the events leading up to his appointment, so far as he is aware of them;
2. the disposal or proposed disposal by him of any property of the company and the carrying on or proposed carrying on by him of any business of the company;
3. the amounts of principal and interest payable to the debenture holders by whom or on whose behalf he was appointed and the amounts payable to the preferential creditors; and
4. the amount (if any) likely to be available for the payment of other creditors.

Section 48(2) and r 3.8 require that within the same timescale the administrative receiver must either:
- send a copy of the report to all known unsecured creditors; or
- publish in the same newspaper in which he advertises his appointment a notice giving an address to which unsecured creditors should write for copies of the report to be sent to them free of charge; and
- in either case to 'lay a copy of the report before a meeting of the company's unsecured creditors summoned for the purpose on not less than 14 days' notice'.

This is the 'Section 48' meeting familiar to most practitioners (which the directors are not required to attend). The duties which an administrative receiver must fulfil following the establishment of a creditors' committee at a Section 48 meeting are considered in the Glossary at **3.21**.

The only occasion when an administrative receiver may avoid calling a meeting under s 48 is when the company has gone or goes into liquidation within three months of his appointment and when under the provision of s 48(4) the receiver has the option of instead reporting to the liquidator.

(vii) Duty of pay the preferential creditors

1.150 Section 40 imposes a duty upon administrative receivers to pay the preferential creditors out of assets caught by a charge which *as created* was a floating charge. The words 'as created' have been held to mean that where there is a liquidation during a receivership, the liquidation creditors *and the costs and expenses of the liquidation* rank ahead of the debenture holder. This decision (*Re Portbase Clothing Ltd* [1993] 3 All ER 829, BCC 96) could have serious repercussions for receivers holding funds under a floating charge unless subsequently overturned following referral to the Court of Appeal.

(viii) Duty to report on the conduct of unfit directors

1.151 The duty to submit a report to the Secretary of State where he suspects unfitness in a director, former director or shadow director is imposed by CDDA 1986 s7(3). This duty which applies to an 'office holder' (which under CDDA 1986 s7(3)(d) includes an administrative receiver) is dealt with in further detail at **1.96** in the section on administration orders.

(ix) Duty to file abstract of receipts and payments

1.152 Rule 3.32 requires that an administrative receiver sends to:
- the registrar of companies;
- the company;
- his appointor; and, if there is one,
- each member of the creditors' committee;

a summary of his receipts and payments account as receiver. The account is to be made up to a date 12 months from the date of his appointment and every subsequent period of 12 months and is to be sent within two months after the end of each accounting period. A final account is to be sent within two months after ceasing to act as receiver.

Failure to comply with this rule will make the receiver liable to a fine and, for continued contravention, to a daily default fine.

(x) Duty upon vacating office

1.153 An administrative receiver must give not less than seven days' notice of his intention to resign his office to:
1. the person by whom he was appointed;
2. the company or, if it is then in liquidation, its liquidator; and
3. in any case, to the members of the creditors' Committee (if any) (r 3.33).

Rule 3.35 requires him to give notice forthwith to 2 and 3 above upon vacating office and to file notice with the registrar of companies within 14 days (s45(4)).

Powers and responsibilities of directors following appointment of administrative receivers.

1.154 For all intents and purposes, the directors' powers cease upon the appointment of receivers, whereas their responsibilities remain. In reality, the management of the business is vested in the receivers and the directors may continue to exercise such management functions as may be required only with the express authority of the receivers.

This does not mean however that the directors are stripped of all powers outside of those powers to manage the business. Whereas it would be unreasonable to expect a receiver to continue or commence an action by the company against his appointor, the directors have the power to take such action on behalf of the company (*Newhart Developments Ltd v Co-Operative Commercial Bank Ltd* [1978] QB 814).

Directors may also commence an action against the receiver himself in respect of any improper exercise of his powers (*Watts v Midland Bank plc* (1986) 2 BCC 98,961).

The conduct of the receivership

(a) The involvement of the directors

1.155 The conduct of the receivership will be a matter for the receivers, but where possible an amicable and co-operative relationship with the directors will always be preferable to outright confrontation. The receiver will have many different situations arising upon appointment to deal with at the same time; claims for retention of title, securing the assets, dealing with day to day and statutory 'paperwork' and, where trading is to continue, persuading creditors to maintain continuity of supply and coming to terms with the work-force facing redundancy, to name but a few.

Although unlikely in the majority of cases to ensure any long-term involvement for the current directors, a 'united front' with the receivers will often help achieve better realisations or even a continuity of employment for at least some of the work-force following a sale of the business as a going concern.

(b) The decision to trade

1.156 In most instances the receivership strategy will have been determined before appointment and the receivers will know whether they intend to trade or not. The decision to trade is an aspect not always fully appreciated by directors or their advisers and merits further consideration. In theory there is no reason why, through trading, the receivers cannot generate sufficient profits to pay not only the debenture holder but also the preferential creditors and hand the company back to its directors with monies sufficient to discharge the unsecured creditors. Such a scenario, while rare, is not unknown.

The reality is likely to be quite different, the decision to trade being marginal and taken with the intention of realising a better price for the assets through the sale of the business as a going concern rather than on a break-up basis. This will often involve the receiver incurring trading losses which may be borne by the preferential creditors thereby risking possible criticism. A receiver who incurs trading losses through his own negligence is particularly vulnerable to attack by preferential creditors (*Westminster Corpn v Haste* [1950] Ch 442). If he trades and fails to achieve a sale he inherits the worst of all worlds for then he is left with a loss which will further reduce realisations below the break-up price he would have achieved upon an immediate shut-down.

The decision to trade is therefore not one which can be taken lightly and where any moral or social aspects concerning employment are secondary to the receiver's duty to his appointor and preferential creditors. The general practitioner can often help the directors to a better understanding of these problems thereby avoiding an unnecessary rift with the receivers which in the long term is unlikely to benefit anyone.

(c) The involvement of the general practitioner

1.157 Although perhaps not presenting the same opportunity for involvement as could be enjoyed in an administration there remain areas in which the general practitioner may continue to be involved in the receivership. Although neither the place nor the intention of this book is to invite general practitioners to attempt to frustrate receivers in the course of their duty it is nevertheless only right in the interests of the general practitioner to point out the important difference in protection that a general practitioner is afforded by virtue of s246 so far as his lien against an administrative receiver for unpaid fees is concerned and which is not available as against an administrator. (This is fully dealt with in Part 3.) He therefore has the opportunity under certain circumstances of holding the 'whip hand' at the outset of the receivership where he finds himself in possession of such of the company's books and records as the receiver requires for the fulfilment of his duties.

A general practitioner advising his client may well have been instrumental in assisting the receiver in his pre-appointment role of investigating accountant. A rapport established at this early stage could lead to a request for further professional involvement which could include updating accounting information, dealing with outstanding taxation matters and assisting in the preparation of the statutory Statement of Affairs. All of this not only helps the general practitioner by way of financial compensation but keeps him close to the company and in a better position to report to the directors in so far as he continues to act for them.

Life after receivership (case study)

1.158 Although often seen as the 'end of the road' there have been some spectacular 'revivals' out of receivership following the ability of the general practitioner and his client to create an innovative situation. The following story, drawn from an actual case, should illustrate the point.

CASE STUDY

> A Scottish whisky distillery was placed into receivership and shut-down by the receiver who then offered the assets of the company for sale. In today's terms, the bank would have been owed £1m with the receiver (in those pre-Insolvency Act days the 'receiver and manager') asking £600,000 for the building, plant and equipment. For legal reasons certain intellectual rights enjoyed by the company could not be passed on under a 'hive-down' of the assets to a subsidiary company and in any event, so far as the receiver was concerned, there was little point in such a manoeuvre as the tax losses (which often formed the real reason for selling in such manner) were lost with the cessation of trade.
>
> The general practitioner ascertained that whisky has by law to be allowed to mature for a minimum of three years before it may be sold as whisky. With this knowledge and, unknown to the receiver, he then successfully argued the principle with the local Inspector of Taxes that the maturation process formed an intrinsic and essential part of the company's trading activity, quite independent of distillation. The Inspector agreed that provided the distillation process re-commenced within three years from the shut-down, the tax losses, estimated to be worth in excess of £½ million in 'cash terms' against future profits, could be carried forward within the company.
>
> The general practitioner and his client then successfully negotiated with all the company's unsecured creditors to buy an assignment of their claims for 10% of their face value (but for this offer they would have received nothing following the receivership) and with the shareholders (all of whom were directors with loan accounts owing to them and therefore were to receive a 10% dividend thereon as creditors) to acquire their shares for £1.
>
> Although the bank refused to assign its debenture, it did agree to release the company from its charge and assign the entirety of its indebtedness for the receiver's asking price for the assets. In this manner the general practitioner's client purchased the company for £1, advancing £650,000 (subsequently repaid) against assigned debts of £1.5m with substantial tax losses available for set-off against future profits.
>
> The client gained a valuable business, the general practitioner a prestigious client.

VIII LIQUIDATION

The enforced alternative: the creditors' viewpoint

1.159 So far within the text, we have been looking at the preferred way forward through the eyes of the practitioner adivising a financially troubled company. Few practitioners would advise liquidation if they could help orchestrate some more palatable alternative, but we need to remember that while you are advising your insolvent client, others will be advising your client's creditors, and they may well be advocating compulsory liquidation as the most likely route to persuade your client to pay their debt (see **3.18** in the Glossary).

Creditors' Voluntary Liquidation as a 'last resort'

1.160 In the context of a practitioner advising an insolvent company, we have now reached the point where:
1   no monies are available to provide fresh working capital;
2   the bank cannot or will not appoint administrative receivers;
3   an <u>administration order</u> is unattainable;   *Konkursbeschluß*
4   an <u>informal moratorium</u> is out of the question; and
5   a CVA is unattainable;
leaving liquidation as the only answer if the directors are to avoid the possibility of a subsequent claim of wrongful trading by a future liquidator.

In such circumstances we would be talking about 'creditors' voluntary' liquidation as opposed to compulsory liquidation. (The only other type of liquidation is a MEMBERS' VOLUNTARY LIQUIDATION but this is not an insolvent liquidation and can only be carried out when the company will be in a position to pay all its creditors in full within 12 months).

The choice of liquidator: members v creditors

1.161 The first problem is the choice of insolvency practitioner to be liquidator. The company is put into liquidation by its members who appoint their own liquidator. At the subsequent meeting of creditors, a vote is taken to determine who will be liquidator and at which time the creditors might choose to ratify the members' choice of liquidator or prefer to elect some alternative insolvency practitioner.

Voting is by a straightforward majority by value only. Wherever possible, and to ensure continuity, it is always preferable to try to choose a liquidator who is likely to be acceptable to and whose appointment will be endorsed by the majority of the creditors.

Although this is sometimes easier said than done, it is often the case that the larger creditors let their personal preference be known well in advance of the meeting and 'joint appointments' between the creditors' candidate and the directors' nominee are frequently pre-arranged.

The continuing role of the general practitioner

1.162 It might be thought that if liquidation is inevitable, there is little more that the general practitioner can do, with the inclination simply to 'hand over' the client company to the chosen insolvency practitioner. Apart from being tantamount to a breach of faith, simply abandoning the client as it were, can be short sighted from the general practitioner's own point of view and positively harmful to the financial health of the client.

Consider firstly the purely mercenary aspect of the situation. Although the paying of commissions for the introduction of work is against all professional ethical guidelines, there is nothing whatsoever to stop the insolvency practitioner from retaining the instructing general practitioner with regard to certain specific aspects of the insolvency; for example agreeing the taxation and dealing with the initial statutory statement of affairs.

In fact it makes a great deal of sense for the general practitioner to be so involved. Firstly, who has a more intimate working knowledge of the company and is better placed to agree the taxation with the Inspector of Taxes in the most efficient and cost effective manner? Secondly, having already prepared the initial estimated Statement of Affairs which formed the basis of the decision to liquidate, again, who is better placed to assist the directors in 'fine tuning' that Statement of Affairs so as to comply with the statutory requirements?

The directors will be required by the liquidator to swear and lodge this Statement of Affairs within 21 days of liquidation; the liquidator has the power to authorise the reasonable costs thereof to be defrayed out of the assets within the liquidation. Thus you will be assisting your client in fulfilling his statutory obligations and at the same time earning fees for your own practice.

IX WHICH WAY FORWARD? – STRATEGIC PLANNING

Anticipating creditors' reactions

1.163 In the final analysis the choice of route forward is governed by a number of factors, most of which will be outside your direct control. With the whole picture now before you, begins what is tantamount to the thought process in a game of chess – 'if I make this particular move, what response is it likely to evoke'? For example:

> If I advise an informal moratorium, is any creditor likely to respond by immediately petitioning for the winding-up of the company? or,

> If we petition the court for the grant of an administration order, is the bank likely to appoint receivers?

Considering the position of the bank

(a) Nature of bank's security

1.164 Given that the bank's security holds the key to whether it can dictate the route forward irrespective of your advice or the client's wishes, the first concern must always be to address the position of the bank. It is from this point alternative avenues will open or close according to the facts of the particular case.

Thus, you need to ask the question: 'Does the bank hold a charge?'

If no charge has been taken by the bank it will be unable to appoint receivers and you will be free to consider all other available options.

If the bank holds a fixed charge only, although it could appoint a 'fixed-charge' receiver you could subsequently enforce his removal if the company were able to petition for and be granted an administration order.

Only if the bank holds a debenture which incorporates a floating charge (suitably drafted – see **1.71**) is it in a position to dictate the way forward through the appointment of administrative receivers.

That the bank will prefer to press ahead with its right to appoint must always be presumed; only if you are able to persuade the bank to some alternative course of action will you be able to follow another route.

(b) Persuading the bank to the administration route?

1.165 You must at all times be realistic and prepare for a disappointment. Take for example a hypothetical case where the bank holds fixed and floating charges over a company operating an hotel and where the preferential creditors for VAT and PAYE/NI are so great that they totally outweigh the value of the floating charge assets.

In such circumstances the bank could only ever expect to recover monies under its fixed charge so that its floating charge would seem to serve no purpose but to allow for the appointment of administrative receivers. On the other hand an administrator could run the company so that, on the face of it the bank has nothing to lose by simply 'sitting back' and allowing the directors to seek an administration order, with the administrator accounting to the bank in due course under its fixed charge out of the proceeds from the sale of the hotel.

We can take this scenario a stage further. An appointment of administrative receivers would not prevent a subsequent distraint by either the Customs and Excise or the Inland Revenue whereas the appointment of an administrator would stop *all* actions against the company, including distraint proceedings. Logic would therefore seem to have it that the bank would, if anything, be better off by doing nothing and allowing an administration order route to take its course.

Logic however is but one facet in our scenario where the choice of appointment is a highly emotive issue. Remember that an administrative receiver is the 'bank's man' whose primary duty is to the bank, the actual running of the business being of secondary importance. As we have seen in the earlier text, the role and duties of an administrator differ considerably and this is an aspect the bank will have very much in mind when considering any request by the directors not to pursue its powers of appointment.

(c) Dealing with a potential distraint

1.166 In practice there is even an answer to the problem of a potential distraint, for an administrative receiver could well persuade the Customs & Excise/Inland Revenue either not to distrain at all, or alternatively to take 'walking possession' (see **3.30** in the Glossary) over the furniture and equipment leaving everything in situ and receiving payment from the eventual sale proceeds of those assets.

(d) Leased assets: the balancing factor?

1.167 Where there are substantial assets leased by the company, the owners (or 'funders') of the goods would be free to recover their property (being 'goods in the company's possession') in an administrative receivership. This could in some instances have the effect of necessitating a close-down of the business. Within an administration however the position would follow the Court of Appeal decision in *Re Atlantic Computer Systems plc* [1990] BCC 859 which affords far more protection from repossession, subject to the principles therein established.

It is just possible that in extreme circumstances this one factor could influence a bank's decision as to whether or not to appoint administrative receivers.

In summary, although there will be instances when banks agree to allow the company to proceed along the administration route when they could have blocked the petition, realistically such instances will be few and far between.

(e) The bank as a 'partner'?

1.168 The late 1980s saw an 'invasion' of foreign banks keen to procure a share of the burgeoning UK property market. The early 1990s saw many of them facing unprecendented losses, but rather than simply 'cut and run' they often entered into imaginative schemes with the current management in an attempt to salvage the business. Invariably this involved the bank procuring the right to a share of the equity.

In certain instances this can make good sense. Just as a shareholder does not sustain a certain and definitive loss unless and until he sells his shares, so a lender locked into a depressed market might decide to take a long term view, giving up interest today for the chance of capital tomorrow.

In this country we are not accustomed to seeing risk or venture capital as an area in which the high street banks are prepared to experiment. Start-up capital is however one thing, a decision to consider equity participation and the provision of fresh working capital as an alternative to receivership, quite another.

Although we must continue to expect the banks to regard receivership as their most likely option given a degree of unacceptable exposure in an insolvent company, there are definite if cautious indications that in certain specific instances banks might be prepared to consider some alternative which gives them an equity stake.

It will be interesting to observe over the coming years how this widening of options develops. Should it gain momentum, it will add an entirely new spectrum to the reconstruction side of insolvency, with the 'Specialised Lending Services' departments (by whatever name) of banks' recovery units, assuming an increasingly important role.

The next consideration; the reaction of the creditors

1.169 Assuming, for whatever reason the bank is not going to appoint receivers, the next question to address is: 'What is the likelihood of the creditors agreeing to an informal moratorium?'

This possible if unlikely route forward has been fully considered at **1.26** and further analysed by virtue of the 'flow chart' in diagram 6. If not a viable proposition, then the remaining alternatives are CVA or an administration order.

In either instance there has to be an available cash flow to fund the company prior to any closedown, but for a CVA to be effected there needs to be a positive answer to the question:

'Can a CVA be achieved without any creditor successfully petitioning to wind up the company'?

If the answer to the question is 'no' then the only other available route as an alternative to liquidation is an administration order, from which a CVA could be put in place as a possible exit route.

We have already considered the requirements for an administration order. What we have not yet done is look at the position where liquidation is the *only* available route forward in the context of what could and should be done before any resolution to wind-up is passed.

Matters requiring attention *before* liquidation

1.170 Leaving all monetary considerations aside, there is often much that can and should be done for the client. If you are aware of any 'irregularity' within the company's accounts which, following a liquidator's scrutiny is likely to give rise to a claim by him requiring your client to make a financial contribution, then for a number of reasons it would probably be desirable that any monies due be paid to the company prior to passing the resolution to wind-up.

Such matters could be of considerable importance to the directors. The simple example below demonstrates the point.

EXAMPLE

> A director has a loan account of £110,000 standing to his credit in the company, which is reduced to £10,000 at the date of liquidation some eight months later in circumstances where the company was either insolvent at the time the directors withdrew the £100,000 or alternatively the withdrawal itself created the insolvency. A liquidator would be under a duty under s239 to seek repayment of those monies (preference within two years to a connected party).

Now at the same time, assume the director has guaranteed the bank account and that at the date of liquidation there is an estimated shortfall to the bank of £100,000. The company proceeds to liquidation and the liquidator, upon discovering the preference successfully brings an action to recover the £100,000. Those monies would not be paid into the bank account but would represent a recovery available for creditors generally. This could well result in the director then being left to face the majority if not the entirety of the (identical) shortfall to the bank, so that he will overall have to find up to £200,000.

Neither is the director able to escape repayment of the preference by paying-off the £100,000 shortfall under his guarantee *after* liquidation, at the same time claiming he was in effect repaying the preference. Following liquidation there is no mutuality of debit and credit; he would still be liable to repay the preference.

The only chance the director has of 'getting away' with paying £100,000 only, thereby discharging the preference and obviating the shortfall to the bank would be to repay the £100,000 *before* the resolution was passed placing the company into liquidation. Even then, there could be circumstances where the repayment itself created a preference to the bank which could be attacked by a liquidator, nevertheless, payment *before* liquidation represents the only chance of success available to the director.

Whatever the circumstances, should you ever find yourself in the position of having to give advice under similar circumstances, always ensure that the director receives legal advice before the company is placed into liquidation (see also TAXATION).

The personal position of the directors

1.171 It is impossible to leave the subject of corporate insolvency without contemplating the position of the directors in the context of an insolvent company. There are a number of pitfalls which face company directors and these are considered in Part 3. Certain of these pitfalls, in particular charges of either fraudulent or wrongful trading, could lead to a personal liability being incurred and most directors will be aware of these dangers and seek comfort before moving on to any formal insolvency route.

It is therefore important that the general practitioner should have sufficient knowledge of the relevant sections, ie s213 (fraudulent trading) and s214 (wrongful trading) to be able to advise the director. (Remember however the warning given at the beginning of this section, namely the possibility of a conflict of interest and the 'best advice' will often be that the directors seek urgent independent legal advice upon their personal positions.)

So far as wrongful trading is concerned, auditors should ensure that they give the appropriate timely advice to directors if they are not to expose themselves to the possibility of a claim against them in negligence. This could happen should the directors subsequently be found guilty to a charge of wrongful trading and to which possibility the auditors had failed to alert them (*Re Produce Marketing Consortium*).

These two important 'pitfalls' are considered in further detail below.

Fraudulent trading

(a) Definition

1.172   Section 213 defines fraudulent trading as when

> in the course of the winding-up of a company it appears that any business of the company has been carried on with intent to defraud creditors of the company or creditors of any other person, or for any fraudulent purpose.

and imposes the threat of a personal liability:

> The court, on the application of the liquidator may declare that any persons who were knowingly parties to the carrying on of the business in the manner above-mentioned are to be liable to make such contributions (if any) to the company's assets as the court thinks proper.

(b) Powers of the court

1.173   Note that it is (*only*) a liquidator who may make an application under this section. Until the introduction of this 'new' legislation first contained within the IA 1985 fraudulent trading was an offence against CA 1985 s 630 which could give rise to a personal liability being incurred by those concerned. Under that section a claim could also be brought (within the liquidation) by an individual creditor and the court had power to order the defendent to reimburse that creditor personally (*Re Cyona Distributors Ltd* [1967] Ch 889). Under s213 which replaces the earlier CA 1985 s630 legislation, any individual creditor wishing to bring a claim must make that claim through the liquidator and any sums ordered to be paid must be paid to the liquidator and held for the general body of creditors.

A further amendment gives the court power to direct that if a defendent to a charge of fraudulent trading is himself a creditor of the company, his own claim be postponed to rank *after* the claims of all other creditors (*Re Purpoint Ltd* [1991] BCC 121).

The court has power to impose a punitive element within any order. Such was the case in *Re a Company (No 001418 of 1988)* [1990] BCC 526 where a director was ordered to pay a penalty of £25,000 in addition to a compensatory award of £131,420. (Although this was a case decided under the 'old' Companies Act legislation it is generally held that the working of s213 is less restrictive than that of CA 1985 s630 so that there is no reason why the court would not order a punitive order under the new section – cf Wrongful trading where it has been held that the jurisdiction is primarily compensatory rather than penal, albeit in such terms as to 'leave the door open' for a punitive element to be included in any award.)

(c) Need for liquidator to prove dishonest intent

1.174 It has never been easy for liquidators to mount successful actions for fraudulent trading. To succeed it is necessary to establish not just that the individual was merely reckless or negligent but intentionally dishonest. The leading case is *Re William C Leitch Bros* [1932] 2 Ch 71, where the respondent had sold his business to a company the consideration for which was taken partly in shares and partly by way of a loan to the company, security for which was taken by way of a debenture over all assets, present and future. He was appointed managing director and ordered goods which were caught under his charge at a time when the company was sustaining losses. In finding him liable, the judge said:

> If a company continues to carry on business and to incur debts at a time when there is to the knowledge of the directors no reasonable prospect of the creditor *ever* receiving payment of those debts, it is in general a proper inference that the company is carrying on business with intent to defraud.

The word 'ever' was held to have an important meaning and gave rise to the 'Clouds and Sunshine' judgment of Buckley J in *Re White & Osmond (Parkstone) Ltd* (30 June 1960, unreported):

> Lastly it is said that the directors continued to incur credit in carrying on the business of the Company at a time when they know the company was insolvent. In my judgment, there is nothing wrong in the fact that directors incur credit at a time when, to their knowledge, the company is not able to meet all its liabilities as they fall due. What is manifestly wrong is if directors allow a company to incur credit at a time when the business is being carried on in such circumstances that it is clear the company will never be able to satisfy its creditors. However, there is nothing to say that directors who genuinely believe that the clouds will roll away and the sunshine of prosperity will shine upon them again and disperse the fog of their depression are not entitled to incur credit to help them to get over the bad time.

It is not difficult to imagine, given this judgment that liquidators could perceive a defence being put forward to any future action on the grounds that the director had a reasonably held genuine belief that the company would be in a position some time in the future to pay for credit taken at a time the company was knowingly insolvent.

Directors would however be unwise to rely on this case in view of the later Court of Appeal decision in *R v Grantham* [1984] BCLC 270, CA which dismissed an appeal against a conviction where the director had ordered a load of potatoes on one month's credit at a time when he knew the company would be unable to pay on the due date. Although generally held to be too harsh in the standard it lays down, this case nevertheless clearly places a limit on the time allowed for a change in the metaphorical weather-forecast so that the sunshine of prosperity must roll away the clouds and disperse the fog when the debt becomes due or *shortly afterwards*.

(d) Parties at risk

1.175 There are three further points worthy of note when discussing the subject of fraudulent trading. Firstly, s213 can only apply within a liquidation and within which section, despite its name, is not a criminal offence. It can however apply not only to a director but to any person who is knowingly a party to the carrying on of the business in the manner described within s213(1).

(e) Fraudulent trading as a criminal offence

1.176 Secondly, fraudulent trading *may* be a criminal offence carrying up to seven years' imprisonment under CA 1985 s458 and for which purpose insolvency of the company is not necessary for the purpose of an action being brought against those concerned.

(f) The position of a <u>financial adviser</u>, <u>company secretary</u> or <u>non-executive director</u>

1.177 Thirdly, and of particular interest to the general practitioner, in order to be liable, it is necessary to establish the person as being 'knowingly party' to the fraud. This would mean that a person would need to be in a position to know of the financial affairs of the company and have taken positive steps to defraud as a person concerned in the carrying on of the business. The company secretary or financial adviser is not so concerned merely because he fails to draw the attention of the directors to the insolvent state of the company (*Re Maidstone Building Provisions Ltd* [1971] 3 All ER 363). Neither does it seem that actions against 'non-executive' directors would be successful.

(g) Disqualification following an award

1.178 The general practitioner should point out in the context of any discussions upon the subject of fraudulent trading that any person having an award made against them could also face the possibility of a disqualification order being made under CDDA 1986.

(h) Fraudulent trading following the introduction of wrongful trading

1.179 In practice, there will inevitably be fewer cases brought by liquidators under s213 given the additional concept of wrongful trading introduced by s214, conviction under which section produces the same result so far as the creditors are concerned, but where an action is far easier for a liquidator to sustain given the less onerous standard of proof required.

Wrongful trading

(a) Need for the 'new law'

1.180 It was because of the perceived inadequacy of the law to deal with irresponsible, as opposed to blatantly dishonest trading that the Cork Committee recommended amendments which would allow liquidators to mount actions for 'unreasonable' conduct which would not require the same strict standards of proof which the courts insisted upon when considering charges of fraudulent trading.

Its recommendations included the continuing of fraudulent trading as a *criminal* offence, but that a new offence with a more relaxed standard of proof to be termed 'Wrongful Trading' be introduced to assume civil liability to pay compensation.

Instead, while introducing the concept of wrongful trading, the IA 1985 did so as an *addition* to the original concept of fraudulent trading. It also confined its scope to directors (including 'shadow directors') so that it does not extend to embrace others who might be party to the wrongful trading.

(b) Definition

1.181 There is no comprehensive statutory definition of wrongful trading, liability for which is established where:
1. the company has 'gone into insolvent liquidation'; and
2. the person concerned is (or was at the relevant time) a director (or shadow director); and
3. at a time when he knew or should have concluded there was no reasonable prospect that the company would avoid going into insolvent liquidation; he thereafter
4. failed to take 'every step' he ought to have taken with a view to minimising the potential loss to the company's creditors.

For the purpose of 1 above 'insolvent liquidation' is defined as if the company goes into liquidation at a time when its assets are insufficient for the payment of its debts and other liabilities and expenses of the winding-up.

(c) Defence to a charge of wrongful trading

1.182 As with the previous section s213 (fraudulent trading) a charge of wrongful trading may be brought only by a liquidator. The defence to wrongful trading is to be found within the wording of s214(3) from which 4 above is drawn, namely:

> The court shall not make a declaration under this section with respect to any person if it is satisfied that ... (he) took every step with a view to minimising the potential loss to the company's creditors.

What the legislation does not do, is to specify the 'every step' other than by the 'Interpretation of s214(2), (3)' given by s214(4) which reads:

> For the purpose of subsections (2) and (3), the facts which a director of a company ought to know or ascertain, the conclusions which he ought to reach and the steps which he ought to take are those which would be known or ascertained, or reached or taken, by a reasonably diligent person having both
> (a) the general knowledge, skill and experience that may reasonably be expected of a person carrying out the same functions as are carried out by that director in relation to the company, and
> (b) the general knowledge, skill and experience that that director has.

This section imposes an objective standard; a director can be liable even though unaware of facts, if it can be demonstrated that he ought to have known or ascertained them. In addition, (a) above calls for a minimum level of competence which every director will be presumed to possess, while (b) requires that if a director does in fact possess a higher level of knowledge, skill or experience he will be required to have demonstrated them in the discharge of his duties. Put in simple terms, although a director say in charge of transport operations cannot avoid liability for financial failure by pleading he knew nothing of the company's finances, it is likely that the qualified accountant financial director will be deemed to possess a higher degree of knowledge, skill and experience and be dealt with accordingly.

(d) Practical consequences for directors

1.183 The steps which a director ought to take to avoid the consequences of wrongful trading need to have a very firm foundation laid down throughout the life of the company. Those steps will include:
- Ensuring that accurate up to date accounting information is always available and that the financial affairs of the company are fully understood.
- Ensuring that the company is up to date with filing accounts at Companies House and complying with all statutory requirements.
- Where a director disagrees with board policy but elects to remain a director, ensuring that his dissent and views are accurately and fully minuted.
- Seeking immediate expert outside advice if the viability of the business is in any doubt and following any advice given. (Although this in itself may not protect the director from an action by a subsequent liquidator under s214, it should mean that the director would have a reciprocal right of action against the expert to the level of any award made against him as a direct result of following his advice.)

and/or thereafter:
- Avoiding taking further credit through the payment of cash for future supplies.
- Keeping a close eye on credit sales which might allow a creditor to receive goods and avoid payment by off-setting their value against monies owed.
- Avoiding any desperate attempts to rescue the situation other than through recognised insolvency procedures.
- Taking the appropriate steps to prevent any continuing losses, where necessary to include a cessation of trade or the commencement of formal insolvency proceedings. (But note below the observations on pessimism and timidity.)
- Cancelling all holidays or prolonged periods of absence from the business until viability is restored.

Directors of companies in financial difficulties undoubtedly face a dilemma. They must not be over-optimistic in assessing the chance of survival, nor unduly pessimistic without fairly weighing the options available. They should be neither unduly rash nor unduly timid, recognising that a premature cessation of trade or commencement of formal insolvency procedures could precipitate the very damage s214 requires them to avoid.

(e) Interpreting the new law

1.184 Traditionally, directors' duties have been owed to the company. Section 214 introduces a new concept in that once a company is in financial difficulties the directors' primary duty is to avoid further potential loss to the company's *creditors*.

Re Produce Marketing Consortium Ltd established that:
- any award is intended to be primarily compensatory rather than penal;
- a director could be liable if he was in ignorance not only of the facts which as a director he ought to know but also those which he ought to ascertain;
- directors of differing sizes of company owe differing standards of care. For example a director of a large public company would owe a greater duty then a director of a small private limited company.

(f) Assessing the award

1.185 There is no restriction on the court's discretion in determining the level of contribution awarded against a director although it would be reasonable to anticipate that this would normally be calculated by reference to the date when the director knew or ought to have realised there was no reasonable prospect of the company avoiding insolvent liquidation.

In *Re Produce Marketing Consortium Ltd* accounts for the year ended 30 September 1985 should have been filed with the Registrar of Companies no later than 31 July 1986 and the court held that those financial results should be assumed (for the purpose of s214) known to the directors by 31 July 1986 to the extent of the company's deficiency.

In *Re Purpoint Ltd* the company had 'commenced life' without any effective working capital in that, as a 'phoenix' company whose main asset was bought out of an earlier company which then went into liquidation, its assets were matched by loans. Nevertheless, the court held that to conclude the company was doomed to failure from inception was to impose too high a test. The company ceased trading in November 1987. Faced with the absence of proper accounting records, but in the knowledge that the director has been professionally advised on 28 May 1987 that liquidation was unavoidable the court held that all the evidence pointed to an insolvent period at a much earlier date but chose 1 January 1987 as the date upon which to base an order for compensation. Taking that date, Vinelott J quantified the amount by aggregating all debts, including crown debts incurred thereafter together with interest at the rate of 15% thereon from the date of liquidation and 16% from the date of judgment.

(g) Application of the award

1.186 Although the court has power to direct that the claim of any defaulting director as a creditor be postponed to rank after the claims of all other creditors (*Re Purpoint Ltd*) it had neither the jurisdiction to direct that any particular *class* of creditor be preferred nor that an award be paid to any individual creditor.

Any award will be paid to the liquidator.

The Cork Committee intended that the 'wrongful trading' proposals should provide a fund for a company's unsecured creditors. Nevertheless following the judgment in *Re Produce Marketing Consortium Ltd* it would seem clear that where the company has given a floating charge to its bank, that charge will attach to any sum received by the liquidator following an order under s214.

(h) Disqualification following an award

1.187 Although unlike fraudulent trading, wrongful trading can never be brought as a criminal offence, it shares in common with the earlier section the possibility that a judgment against a director could lead to a disqualification order being made against him under CDDA 1986

Wrongful trading compared with fraudulent trading

1.188 The following simple 'checklist' (diagram 8) highlights and compares the 'main features' of wrongful trading and fraudulent trading

Closing observations

1.189 There will inevitably be other matters which require consideration in planning a way forward; the aforegoing section should however be sufficient to guide the general practitioner through the 'initial period' and enable him to render constructive advice at the time when it is most urgently needed.

We end Part 1, as we began, with a note of caution. The requirement to identify the client – in this instance the company – and obtain separate representation for its director(s) thereby obviating any danger of the general practitioner finding himself in a conflict situation cannot be over stressed.

Consider the position of the insolvency practitioner who recommends the Centrebind procedure (see CENTREBINDING) to a company director/shareholder who is also guarantor to the company's lease. After liquidation the practitioner, in his capacity as liquidator, then successfully obstructs the landlord from distraining for arrears of rent. In attempting to act for all creditors to the detriment of the landlord he has unduly prejudiced the financial position of the director/guarantor who had followed his initial advice.

The way for the general practitioner to avoid finding himself in such a situation is always to remember that accountants prepare the figures and solicitors advise upon the law. By following that golden rule, the interests of all parties concerned with the financially troubled company should be fully protected at all times.

Diagram 8

	Fraudulent trading	*Wrongful trading*
Offences under section	213	214
Section applies to	Any person knowingly carrying on business in the manner described within the section	Directors and shadow directors only
Charge brought by	Liquidator only	Liquidator only
Criminal offence?	Not (under s213) in a liquidation but could be under CA 1985 s458	No
Liquidator must prove	Intent to defraud	Failure to exercise appropriate level of general knowledge, skill and experience (see s214(3))
Applicable to 'non-executive' directors?	Probably not	Yes
Potential liability on financial adviser for failure to warn directors of insolvency	No	Yes

PART 2

PERSONAL INSOLVENCY

Speak not of my debts unless you mean to pay them

Jacob Prudentun 1651

Introduction

2.1 There is nothing humorous about insolvency, but if corporate insolvency is bad enough, personal insolvency has to be especially traumatic for the individual concerned.

Nevertheless, as with any problem, if it is going to be faced up to and have any chance of being resolved then the general practitioner will need to develop the equivalent of the doctor's 'bedside manner' and be able to 'lift the patient' out of his understandable mood of despair and away from the edge of a potential nervous breakdown.

How this is achieved is very much down to the 'style' of the practitioner. 'It's only money' will not necessarily have the desired effect unless the client is able to relate to someone with even more serious worries, perhaps health problems, where all the money in the world will not help restore the position. You could point out to him that he should be thankful he is not living in the eighteenth century when, had he been convicted upon a complaint by a creditor for failure to surrender 'self or entire estate' to the Commission for Bankruptcy the only penalty was death by hanging, whereas today he would not even be given a suspended sentence!

One solicitor, well known for advising individuals with financial problems, could often break a client's near suicidal mood with the words: 'Come on, let's see you cheer up now. Remember, they haven't yet started to tax smiles and beer's still only 80p a pint.'

That was obviously some time ago and one would be careful not to speak in such terms to an individual whose expenditure on alcohol had helped bring about the very problems he now faced! The principle however remains intact; obtain the client's confidence and attention through any lawful means that will stop him feeling sorry for himself and start thinking positively.

The need to think positively

2.2 Having captured your client's attention so that he is in a 'receptive mood' the next step is to start him thinking positively. Bankruptcy should be regarded as the option of last resort and is often avoidable through an arrangement which benefits both debtor *and* creditor. This section of the book seeks to analyse the available alternatives, thereafter considering those aspects of bankruptcy upon which a general practitioner might anticipate being requested to advise.

Personal insolvency: 'individual' or 'collective'?

2.3 Insolvency is no respector of person, social standing or business reputation. It has caught many people unexpectedly and is not restricted to those who engage in business without the benefit of limited liability; thousands of individuals and couples found themselves insolvent following the spiral and then collapse in house prices in the late 1980s, being left with 'negative equity' having borrowed more money to buy the property than it proved to be worth following the collapse. Even more recently, hundreds of Lloyds' 'names' have seen their personal fortunes vanish overnight.

It is however likely that the general practitioner will find himself discussing the problem with someone who has either:
1   traded without the benefit of limited liability;
2   acted as guarantor to a company bank account;
3   acted as a director of a failed company and had an order made against him to contribute to the assets of the company (see FRAUDULENT TRADING and WRONGFUL TRADING); or
4   suffered from redundancy, illness or other incapacity which has led to debt problems. This route to insolvency became a hallmark of the early 1990s following the availability of easy credit in the 1980s, coupled, as mentioned above, with a fall in house prices.

When considering 1 above, the client could have been in business on his own as a sole trader and in which instance, as in the case of 2, 3 and 4 the general practitioner will be looking at an 'individual' situation where others are not involved. If however the individual has been in business with one or more partners and the partnership itself is insolvent the practitioner could be looking at 'collective' insolvency in the sense that although each individual partner may be insolvent in his personal capacity, it may be necessary to introduce a further aspect of insolvency law namely the 'Insolvent Partnerships Order' to deal with the collective position.

Within the text we will deal firstly with 'individual' insolvency, (Partnership insolvency is considered at **2.40**).

Initial involvement of the general practitioner

2.4   As with corporate insolvency, the first thing to ascertain is the individual's current financial position. This is done by preparing a statement of his assets and liabilities in 'Statement of Affairs' form.

(a)   Preparation of an up-to-date Statement of Affairs

2.5   A Statement of Affairs should be drawn up incorporating valuations based on a forced sale. Although the statement will be prepared on similar lines to the statement set out in diagram 2 in Part 1 (**1.19**) on corporate insolvency, this statement will differ in that it will include the client's personal and, where appropriate, business assets and liabilities.

Set out as diagram 9 is an example of a Statement of Affairs for a Mr J Smith who owns and runs a hotel business. The statement should be relatively self-explanatory and will certainly be easy to follow for any general practitioner who has studied the detailed notes covering the preparation of the corporate Statement of Affairs. This statement discloses that Mr Smith is insolvent to the extent that his liabilities exceed his assets by £172,000.

(b)   Reviewing the individual's current and future cash flow

2.6   If the client is to be saved from bankruptcy, the next step is to review his current and future anticipated income and expenditure to ascertain whether there might

Diagram 9

Mr J Smith
Estimated Statement of Affairs as at xx/xx/xx

		Estimated to Realise
	£	£
Assets specifically pledged		
Freehold of Sea View Hotel, Newtown		250,000
less: Amount due to Standard National Bank under first mortgage		(350,000)
Shortfall carried to unsecured creditors		(100,000)
Freehold of house at 23 Elm Road, Newtown		150,000
less: Amount due to Midwest Bank under first mortgage		(130,000)
Surplus carried down		20,000
Leyland Daf van D106XXX		7,500
less: due to Newtown Leasing Co under hire purchase agreement		(6,500)
Surplus carried down		1,000
Assets not specifically pledged		
Furniture and equipment in Sea View Hotel		5,000
Stock of food and drink at hotel		4,000
Personal household furniture and equipment		2,000
Vauxhall Cavalier F100XXX		7,000
Life policy with Midwest Bank		6,000
Surplus from Assets specifically pledged		
Freehold of 23 Elm Road		20,000
Leyland Daf van		1,000
Cash in hand		1,000
Assets available for preferential and unsecured creditors		46,000
Estimated Preferential Creditors		
Inland Revenue (re deduction of employees' PAYE)	5,000	
HM Customs and Excise (VAT)	18,000	
DSS (re deduction of national insurance)	3,000	
Total estimated preferential creditors		(26,000)
Amount available for unsecured creditors		(20,000)
Unsecured Creditors		
Shortfall to Standard National Bank re Sea View Hotel	100,000	
Bank overdraft at Midwest Bank Sea View Hotel Account		
Sea View Hotel Account	24,500	
Personal Account	2,500	
Estimated Trade Creditors of Sea View Hotel	65,000	
Total unsecured creditors		(192,000)
Estimated deficiency as regards trade creditors		(172,000)

Note: this statement takes no account of costs of realisation be surplus income which could be offered to creditors under some scheme more attractive to them than bankruptcy.

Where the individual is in paid employment, the exercise is relatively straightforward, with net income matched against expenditure. The position is more difficult where the client is engaged in a business and the preparation of a Business Plan incorporating a cash flow will probably be required. If the business is the client's only source of income it will need to generate sufficient income to support the client and his family before any surplus will be available for creditors.

If the cause of the client's financial problems is related to previous lack of profitability within his business this could clearly affect the creditors' decision as to whether to support a continuation of trade. A further problem could be funding ongoing trading. Any lender is likely to be reluctant to risk lending money to an insolvent individual and creditors will often prefer to see monies due to the debtor's business collected and held for dividend purposes rather than utilised within a continuing business.

(c) Selecting the appropriate option

2.7 With the client's financial review completed it will then be possible to consider the available options as an alternative to bankruptcy. There are three such possibilities, namely:
1 Informal moratorium;
2 Deed of Arrangement (DOA);
3 Individual Voluntary Arrangement (IVA).

Informal moratorium

2.8 Where possible, a simple informal moratorium with creditors is the most favoured and least expensive option. This will be on identical lines to its corporate counterpart fully considered at **1.26**.

For an informal moratorium to be effective, the agreement of all creditors is required and there is nothing to stop a dissenting creditor from petitioning for bankruptcy.

As an option, an informal moratorium is probably only achievable where there are but a handful of creditors who are supportive of and prepared to trust the debtor.

Deed of Arrangement

2.9 A Deed of Arrangement (DOA) is a formal alternative to bankruptcy which allows a debtor to enter into an arrangement with his creditors under the Deed of Arrangement Act 1914. Although available for over 75 years it has never achieved widespread use and seems destined to decline yet further as a realistic alternative, following the introduction of Individual Voluntary Arrangements in 1986.

The problem with DOAs has always been the time and difficulty in reaching the point where the deed becomes effective and binds any dissenting minority so giving any creditor determined upon bankrupting the debtor all the time in the world to achieve his objective. Until abolished with the new insolvency legislation in 1986, a creditor could petition for the bankruptcy of an individual if that person had committed an 'act of bankruptcy'. Ironically, attempting to enter into a DOA would itself have almost certainly constituted an 'act of bankruptcy' perhaps providing the one creditor favouring bankruptcy with the very weapon he needed to bring about the bankruptcy the DOA was intended to prevent!

Why DOAs are still with us is unclear. The CORK REPORT recommended its replacement with a new simplified procedure, the Individual Voluntary Arrangement. What we got instead was *additional* legislation, with the DOA remaining on the statute book. It is feasible in isolated instances that it might be possible to achieve a DOA where the newer more acceptable alternative, an Individual Voluntary Arrangement, is unattainable. This would be because in the latter, a majority in excess of 75% of creditors (by value only) must be achieved, whereas in the DOA the percentage is reduced to 50% (albeit in number *and* value).

To simply state the required majorities however is to disguise the difficulty in achieving those majorities, difficulties which had the cumulative effect of dissuading many insolvency practitioners from even considering attempting to effect a DOA. The required steps are as follows:

1. 'Sound out' the feelings of the principal creditors in order to gauge their likely reaction to the proposal.
2. Prepare the deed and convene a formal meeting of creditors. It will be necessary to involve an insolvency practitioner as only an insolvency licence holder may accept an appointment as trustee.
3. If the meeting accepts the proposals it will pass a resolution approving the DOA and appoint a trustee; assent forms will be circulated for signature. If the DOA is rejected the position of the debtor will effectively be held 'in limbo' unless he presents his own petition for bankruptcy or one of the creditors subsequently petitions.

    The first problem is persuading sufficient creditors to attend the meeting in order to achieve the majorities that are going to be required ultimately. The second problem is that it is not possible to bind any dissenting minority at this stage so that even with the required majorities committed to voting in favour, the debtor is still at risk from the minority sector.

4. The deed should then be executed by the debtor and the trustee and must be registered with the Registrar of Deeds of Arrangement within seven days of execution. (The Registrar is an official within the Department of Trade and Industry.)
5. The trustee must notify all creditors of the result of the meeting and request completion of assent forms from any creditors not attending.

For the deed to be effective, a majority in both number *and* value of *all* creditors (whether they attended the meeting or not) must have assented or the deed will otherwise fail. (Creditors owed £10 or under are, however, only counted in terms of value.)

Fortunately, we now have the newer alternative to bankruptcy, the Individual Voluntary Arrangement which has none of the logistical problems surrounding a DOA and has the additional advantage of offering immediate protection against any impending bankruptcy petition.

Individual Voluntary Arrangement

What is an Individual Voluntary Arrangment?

2.10 The Individual Voluntary Arrangement (IVA) is a simple system, introduced by IA 1986 which affords creditors the opportunity to decide for themselves what constitutes their best interests by enabling them to vote for a formal alternative to outright bankruptcy.

The general practitioner should *always* explore the possibility of achieving an IVA in advising any personal client facing insolvency. If the creditors can be persuaded that they will fare better (in terms of anticipated dividends) in an IVA than in a bankruptcy, they will invariably vote for the proposals.

The procedure in outline

2.11 The process is commenced by an application by the debtor to the court for an 'interim order' which, if granted, imposes an immediate moratorium on all creditors and creates a 'breathing space' in which the debtor's proposal can be formulated. However knowledgeable the general practitioner may be as regards the relevant procedures, it will still be necessary to involve an insolvency practitioner and seek his agreement to acting as 'nominee'. (The terminology can be confusing. The 'nominee' is the name given to the insolvency practitioner up to the point of the IVA being approved. Once the IVA is in place the insolvency practitioner becomes the 'supervisor', *but*, although the nominee and the supervisor will normally be one and the same person, they could be two entirely separate individuals.)

The proposal should give full details of all matters required by r 5.3 including an explanation as to why an IVA is considered desirable and the reasons as to why creditors should give it their support.

A meeting of creditors will be convened for the purpose of voting upon the proposal for which purpose a majority in excess of 75% in value only is required. Once approved, the IVA will bind every creditor who had notice of and was entitled to vote at the meeting (whether or not they attended or voted).

IVAs and the general practitioner

(a) Guiding the debtor

2.12 Given that an IVA requires the involvement of an insolvency practitioner, the general practitioner will, in most instances, have played his part long before the insolvency practitioner is consulted. With a general understanding of the principles involved and a thorough knowledge of his client's financial affairs, he is uniquely placed to formulate the proposal which is to form the basis of the IVA and thereafter work with the nominee towards achieving a successful outcome.

The general practitioner should also bear in mind that it is possible to attempt an IVA even after a petition for bankruptcy has been presented or as a route out of a formal bankruptcy.

(b) Guiding a creditor

2.13 The general practitioner could quite easily find himself 'acting for the other side' in advising a creditor who is being asked to vote in favour of a proposed IVA. Putting himself in the shoes of his client, the general practitioner should ask himself the following questions:
- What's in it for me?
- Why should I believe the proposal?

- What's the debtor trying to hide?
- Should I be suggesting modifications?

Q. 'WHAT'S IN IT FOR ME?'

2.14 The proposal itself should set out the financial implications of acceptance, and will seek to demonstrate the financial benefits to creditors over formal bankruptcy. Where the benefits are at best marginal, the general practitioner will need to balance carefully the 'safety' of bankruptcy against the relative freedom enjoyed by a debtor under an IVA and decide whether the risk in voting in favour can be justified on commercial grounds.

Q. 'WHY SHOULD I BELIEVE THE PROPOSAL?'

2.15 Although the figures as presented may look inviting, the general practitioner will need to try to 'look behind them' and assess their realism. While not suggesting over-cynicism, a healthly scepticism will never come amiss; the proposal is after all written to persuade creditors to accept the IVA and a degree of optimism inevitably will creep in from time to time.

General practitioners should also under the appropriate circumstances invite an application of the 'acid test' (see **3.1** in the Glossary).

Q. 'WHAT'S THE DEBTOR TRYING TO HIDE?'

2.16 It is possible that an unscrupulous debtor might seek to persuade his creditors to agree to an IVA knowing that he had neither the ability nor intention of adhering to its terms but with the sole intention of delaying the commencement of bankruptcy. There are certain transactions which, if entered into by an individual can be set aside *only* by a trustee in bankruptcy and then only if action for recovery is commenced within strict time limits. (PREFERENCES AND TRANSACTIONS AT AN UNDERVALUE are the most likely contenders: see **3.64** in the Glossary).

If the onset of bankruptcy can be delayed in order to render the relevant transactions 'time expired' the debtor could defeat any claim by an eventual trustee (although he would be laying himself open to criminal prosecution for misleading his creditors).

Q. 'SHOULD I BE SUGGESTING MODIFICATIONS?'

2.17 There will be occasions when the general practitioner could suggest modifications to the proposals as drafted. Where, for example, the debtor proposed an IVA of two year's duration with an estimated 30p in the £1 dividend, creditors might ask for the period to be extended to three years in order to increase the dividend prospects to 40p in the £1.

It should, however, be borne in mind that the debtor's consent is required to all modifications and if creditors insist on modifications to which he is not prepared to agree, the likely result will be bankruptcy.

One modification frequently called for by the Inland Revenue or Customs & Excise is the requirement for the supervisor to hold funds at all times for the purpose of petitioning for the debtor's bankruptcy in the event of a default under the IVA.

SETTING UP AN IVA – DETAILED PROCEDURES

2.18 For the general practitioner desiring to participate throughout the setting up of an IVA, a detailed review is contained within the Glossary (see INDIVIDUAL VOLUNTARY ARRANGEMENT at **3.39** in the Glossary.)

Bankruptcy

The 'avoidable option'?

2.19 In theory, with the IVA procedure available, the number of formal bankruptcies should be relatively low. In practice, this is clearly not the case. Where a debtor files his own petition for bankruptcy under s272 the court may appoint an insolvency practitioner to investigate the possible alternative of an IVA. There is no corresponding system in force where a creditor petitions for the bankruptcy and it is probable that many bankruptcies could be avoided were the debtor to realise the availability of the IVA route even after the presentation of a bankruptcy petition.

There are times however when creditors refuse to sanction an IVA, perhaps because they mistrust the debtor and are aware of assets which they fear may disappear within an IVA. Under such circumstances the general practitioner could point out that there is nothing to stop specific assets actually vesting in the supervisor thereby ensuring their protection.

From the viewpoint of a general practitioner guiding a creditor who is being asked to vote in favour of an IVA, bankruptcy should always be the favoured option when there is a suspicion that the debtor has entered into a preference or transaction at an undervalue or committed BANKRUPTCY OFFENCES (see **3.11** in the Glossary).

Bankruptcy and the general practitioner

2.20 It is unlikely that the general practitioner will require a full working knowledge of the bankruptcy procedures. Certain detailed aspects are however considered within the Glossary and are to be found as follows:

Subject	Para
Bankruptcy – Obtaining an Order	3.10
Bankruptcy Offences	3.11
Trustee in Bankruptcy *Konkursverwalter*	3.82
Preferences and Transactions at an Undervalue	3.64
Extortionate Credit Transactions	3.33

What the general practitioner does need is the ability to answer certain questions which debtors inevitably raise when the spectre of bankruptcy appears. Those questions are first set out below and then considered individually.

1. How could I be made bankrupt?
2. What will they take and will I be left with anything?
3. What about my home?
4. What about income I earn while the bankruptcy order in in force?
5. Will I face a public examination?
6. What restrictions will I face as an undischarged bankrupt?
7. How long will the bankruptcy last?
8. What is the effect of discharge?

Q. 'HOW COULD I BE MADE BANKRUPT?'

2.21 An individual is made bankrupt following the issue of a bankruptcy order by the court. The order itself follows a petition to the court filed either by the debtor himself or a creditor (or creditors) owed not less than £750. Once the order is made and the trustee appointed, the debtor's assets (with certain exceptions considered below) vest in his trustee.

Q. 'WHAT WILL THEY TAKE? AND, WILL I BE LEFT WITH ANYTHING?'

2.22 The short answer to these questions is that all the bankrupt's property vests in his trustee with the exception of certain personal belongings detailed in s283(2) and considered below.

Under s306, the bankrupt's estate vests in the trustee immediately his appointment takes effect. The 'estate' is defined in s283 as:
1. all property belonging to or vested in the bankrupt at the commencement of bankruptcy;
2. any property deemed by the Act to be comprised in the estate.

Property is defined in s436 as including money, goods, things in action, and every description of property wherever situated; which would seem to cover just about everything!

In addition the trustee may claim for the estate any property which has been acquired by or devolved upon the bankrupt after the date of the bankruptcy (s307 After Acquired Property). The bankrupt is under a legal obligation to inform the trustee of any such property.

The Act does, however, exclude certain items from the estate of the bankrupt in order that he be permitted a basic standard of living, together with the possibility of earning a living.

Section 283(2) excludes the following from the estate
1. such tools, books, vehicles and other items of equipment as are necessary for the bankrupt for use personally by him in his employment, business or vocation;
2. such clothing, bedding, furniture, household equipment and provisions as are necessary for satisfying the basic domestic needs of the bankrupt and his family.

Even these excluded items are not necessarily safe from the trustee. If it appears to the trustee that any excluded asset has a realisable value in excess of its replacement cost, he may claim the asset for the estate and replace it with a cheaper alternative (s308). This would apply, for example, to a piece of antique furniture which the bankrupt claimed as required to satisfy his basic domestic needs.

It will be noted that 'vehicles' are included within the assets which the debtor may retain under certain circumstances. Given that bankrupts are frequently able to demonstrate a need to keep their cars, tools and equipment and all their household furniture it is perhaps not too surprising after all that some debtors are content to accept bankruptcy without bothering to attempt to mount an IVA.

Q. 'WHAT ABOUT MY HOME?'

2.23 The house is very often the largest single asset available to the creditors, particularly where the individual has not been involved in a business or trade. The law is complex and it is essential that the general practitioner ensures his client seeks legal advice upon any matters concerning the effect of bankruptcy upon his residence.

The powers of the trustee in respect of the bankrupt's house depend upon two major factors:
1. right of the trustee to sell the house, particularly where there is co-ownership; and
2. rights of occupation of the bankrupt's:
    (a) spouse, and
    (b) children

The IA 1986 attempts to strike a balance between the interests of the bankrupt's creditors and the interests of his family.

(1) Right of trustee to sell the house (assume no rights of occupation)

2.24 Where there are no rights of occupation involved, the power of the trustee to sell the house depends upon its ownership.

(a) One registered owner

2.25 Where the bankrupt is sole registered owner, the trustee will be able to sell the property as he would any other asset, but he must have regard for any beneficial interest which might have been conferred upon another party. A beneficial interest may be acquired where direct or indirect monetary contributions have been made by the other party in respect of the house. Direct monetary contributions clearly refer to payments in respect of the purchase of the house. Indirect contributions would for example include payments to meet domestic expenses in so far as they enable the owner to make payments in respect of the purchase of the house. It should be noted that non-monetary contributions (housework etc) do not confer a beneficial interest. A trustee is not prevented from selling the property to which a beneficial interest relates, but he will hold part of the proceeds in trust for the beneficial interest holder.

(b) More than one registered owner

2.26 Where the house is registered to co-owners, the trustee cannot sell the property without the consent of the other co-owner, unless leave of court is obtained under LPA 1925 s30.

When considering an application from a trustee under LPA s30, the court will take account of IA 1986 s336, which sets out the factors for the court to consider in these circumstances.

The general requirement is that the court makes an order that is just and reasonable, having regard to:
1 the interests of the creditors;
2 the conduct of any spouse/former spouse in contributing to the bankruptcy (assuming the spouse is the co-owner);
3 the needs and financial resources of the spouse;
4 the needs of any children;
5 all other circumstances other than the needs of the bankrupt.

Section 336 also states that, one year after the vesting of the estate in the trustee, there is a presumption that the interests of the creditors are paramount and outweigh all other considerations, unless there are exceptional circumstances to the contrary.

(2) Rights of occupation

(a) Spouse (s336)

2.27 The Matrimonial Homes Act 1983 (MHA) gives a right of occupation to the spouse where not a registered owner/co-owner. The right takes the form of a charge on the house and is enforceable against the spouse (ie the owner) without the need for registration. However, the charge (in respect of occupation only, not ownership) is only effective against third parties if registered as a charge. (The MHA also provides that the right of occupation, even if registered, is ineffective against the owner spouse's trustee in bankruptcy, but this was reversed by IA 1986 s336.)

Section 336 states that where a right of occupation exists as a charge on the property of the owner spouse, the charge will continue in the bankruptcy and will be valid against the trustee. The right of occupation must, however, have occurred prior to the presentation of the petition. Nothing that happens between the presentation of the petition and the vesting of the estate in the trustee will give rise to rights of occupation. A bankrupt therefore getting married immediately after presentation of the petition in order to confer rights of occupation, will not succeed. The charge must be registered at some stage prior to the property vesting in the trustee.

Where a right of occupation exists for the spouse, the trustee may apply to the court to have the charge overturned to enable him to sell the property. (Clearly the trustee could sell the property regardless, but it is unlikely that a purchaser will be willing to buy a property to which rights of occupation attach.)

When considering the application of the trustee, the court will take account of the same factors as when considering an application for sale under LPA s30 (see above). Again, there is a presumption that the interests of creditors are paramount after one year unless there are exceptional circumstances to the contrary.

(b) Bankrupt and child (s337)

2.28 Section 337 confers a right of occupation on the bankrupt where he is entitled, prior to the bankruptcy, to occupy a house by virtue of some beneficial interest and has 'living with him' a child/children under 18 years of age, both at the date of presentation of the petition and at the date of the bankruptcy order.

Where the bankrupt and child are not in actual occupation at the commencement of bankruptcy, they may re-enter with the leave of the court. This would apply where the bankrupt has a number of homes. Where the bankrupt and child are in actual occupation, they may not be evicted except by leave of the court.

The right of occupation is deemed to be of the same nature as per MHA except that it is not registrable. It may be conferred notwithstanding any right of the spouse under s336 (ie there may be two rights of occupation).

The trustee must therefore apply to the court for leave to evict the bankrupt and child if he wants to sell the property. The court must make an order that is 'just and reasonable' having regard to:

1 the interests of the creditors;
2 the financial resources of the bankrupt;
3 the needs of the children;
4 all the circumstances of the case other than the needs of the bankrupt.

Again there is a presumption that after one year the interests of creditors outweigh all others unless there are exceptional circumstances to the contrary.

Charge taken by trustee on bankrupt's home

2.29 Where the trustee is unable to realise the property because of rights of ownership, rights of occupation or other reasons, he may apply to the court for an order imposing a charge on the property for the benefit of the bankrupt's estate (s313). Indeed, it is vital that the trustee seeks to obtain a charge since s332 prevents him from closing the bankruptcy where the bankrupt's estate comprises an interest in a property which has not been realised unless he has attempted to obtain a charge on the property.

Q. 'WHAT ABOUT INCOME I EARN WHILE THE BANKRUPTCY ORDER IS IN FORCE?'

2.30 The bankrupt is fully entitled to earn a living during the bankruptcy but is given a disincentive from earning too much by s310 (Income Payments Orders).

Under this section, the trustee may apply to the court for an order claiming for the bankrupt's estate part of the bankrupt's income for the period that the bankruptcy order is in force. The court cannot, however, make an order the effect of which would be to reduce the income of the bankrupt below what appears to the court to be necessary for meeting the basic domestic needs of the bankrupt and his family.

Q. 'WILL I FACE A PUBLIC EXAMINATION?'

2.31 Prior to 1976 every bankrupt faced a public examination in order both to assist with the identification of his estate and as an investigation into possible criminal offences. The law was changed however because it was not always considered necessary to incur the expense of an examination, or in every case to put the bankrupt through the ordeal of an examination.

Under s291, the bankrupt is under an obligation to deliver up his estate, together with all records concerned with the estate, to the Official Receiver (OR). In addition he must give the OR an inventory of his estate together with such other information as the OR requires, and must attend on the OR when reasonably required. If the bankrupt fails to co-operate, he is guilty of contempt of court.

In most cases, therefore, the provisions of s291 render a public examination irrelevant since the bankrupt will have provided all the required information. The OR may however still apply to the court for a public examination of the bankrupt under s290 when he considers that the bankrupt has not been fully co-operative.

Q. 'WHAT RESTRICTIONS DO I FACE AS AN UNDISCHARGED BANKRUPT?'

2.32
(a) By s360 he will be guilty of an offence if he obtains credit of £250 or more without declaring his status. This includes where goods are bailed to him under a hire purchase agreement and where he is paid in advance for the supply of goods and services. He is also guilty of an offence if he engages in any business under a name other than that in which he was adjudged bankrupt without disclosing his status to all persons with whom he enters into any business transactions.
(b) By s11 of CDDA 1986 it is an offence for an undischarged bankrupt to act as a director of a company or to be concerned in the formation or management of a company, except by leave of the court.
(c) By s427 he is disqualified from sitting in Parliament.

Q. 'HOW LONG WILL THE BANKRUPTCY LAST?'

2.33 Bankruptcy commences on the day the order is made and continues until discharge (s278).

In cases where there has been no previous bankruptcy within the last 15 years, and where there have been no Bankruptcy Offences, the bankrupt will obtain an automatic discharge. Section 279 states that:
1 Where a certificate of summary administration has been issued, discharge is after two years. Under s275, the court may issue such a certificate only on a debtor's petition where:
 (a) the total bankruptcy debts are below the bankruptcy level (currently £20,000;
 (b) there has been no previous bankruptcy nor composition or scheme of arrangement with creditors in the last five years.

(2) In other cases, discharge is after three years.

The OR may however apply to the court to extend the period in cases where the bankrupt has failed to comply with his obligations under the act.

Where there has been a previous bankruptcy within the last 15 years, or where there have been bankruptcy offences, there is no automatic discharge. The debtor must apply to the court for his discharge, but cannot do so until at least five years from the date of the bankruptcy order.

The court will request that the OR prepares a report on the circumstances of the present and previous bankruptcies, the levels of distributions to the creditors and whether the debtor has fulfilled his obligations under IA 1986. The court will base its decision upon this report.

Q. 'WHAT IS THE EFFECT OF DISCHARGE?'

2.34 Subject to certain exceptions listed below, the discharge will release the bankrupt from all bankruptcy debts. This includes all debts at the commencement of bankruptcy, all debts arising after the commencement of bankruptcy by reason of obligations incurred before, and all interest on bankruptcy debts.

The effect of this is to give the bankrupt a fresh start after discharge. Discharge will not, however, affect the trustee in carrying out his functions, and a creditor may still prove for a debt even after discharge. Nor will it affect the right of a secured creditor to enforce his security for the payment of a debt from which the bankrupt has been released (s281).

The IA 1986 makes certain exceptions to this general rule in order to prevent a debtor from petitioning for his own bankruptcy with the sole intention of avoiding certain liabilities. The exceptions are:

1   Any debt incurred as a result of fraud or breach of trust to which the bankrupt was party (s281(3)).
2   Any liability incurred in respect of a fine, except those relating to the public revenue, with the consent of the Treasury (s281(4)).
3   Any debt which arises out of a liability to pay damages for negligence, nuisance, breach of statutory/legal/other duty (s281(5)).
4   Any debt arising from an order made in family or domestic proceedings under the Matrimonial and Family Proceedings Act 1984 or the Magistrate Courts Act 1980 (s281(5)).
5   Any obligation relating to the Drugs Trafficking Offences Act 1986 (r 6.223).

The general practitioner as adviser to a bankrupt's creditor

2.35 General practitioners could also be called upon to advise a client owed money by a bankrupt and will need to know the answers to the following questions:
- How do I make a claim in the bankruptcy?
- What about interest on my debt?
- Do I have any say in the bankruptcy?
- Where do I stand in respect of dividends?

Q. 'HOW DO I MAKE A CLAIM IN THE BANKRUPTCY?'

2.36 Any creditor wishing to recover a debt must submit a written proof of debt on the prescribed form to the OR or trustee (r 6.96). The form will be sent to the creditor and must be completed in full, giving full details of the amount of the debt and how it was incurred. The OR/trustee may admit or reject the proof for dividend, either in whole or in part. Where a creditor is dissatisfied with this decision he may apply to the court for an order reversing or modifying the decision (see PROOF OF DEBT).

Q. 'WHAT ABOUT INTEREST ON MY DEBT?'

2.37 See interest on debts in a winding up at **3.47**.

Q. 'DO I HAVE ANY SAY IN THE BANKRUPTCY?'

2.38 The best way for a creditor to ensure that he has some say in the conduct of the bankruptcy is to stand for election to the creditors' committee (see **3.21**). The committee may require reports from the trustee on matters which concern them and may let their own views be known. (It should be noted that where the OR is the trustee, the powers of the committee are vested in the Secretary of State.) Where a creditor is dissatisfied with any act, omission or decision of the trustee, he may apply to the court for an order reversing or modifying that decision.

Q. 'WHERE DO I STAND IN RESPECT OF DIVIDENDS?'

2.39 It is inevitable that in the majority of bankruptcies there will be insufficient asset realisations to meet the claims of all creditors. A rigid set of rules has therefore been established by the IA as to the order in which realisations should be applied to creditors. There follows a summary of the regulations as per ss328, 329 and Sch 6.

1   Expenses of the bankruptcy

These have priority over all creditors' claims. Rule 6.224 contains a strict order for payment of expenses when there are insufficient funds to discharge them all in full.

2   Secured debts

Secured creditors will receive realisations from the sale of their security, less any expenses relating to that sale. Where this is insufficient to cover the whole of the debt, they may prove for the shortfall as an unsecured creditor.

3   Non secured debts

1   Preferential debts (see PREFERENTIAL DEBTS).
2   Ordinary debts – these include all debts which do not appear elsewhere on the list of priorities.
3   Statutory interest (see INTEREST ON DEBTS IN A WINDING-UP).
4   Transactions between spouses – where there is a debt due to a person who was the bankrupt's spouse at the commencement of bankruptcy, the debt will be payable after the preferential creditors, ordinary creditors and statutory interest (s329).

4   Surplus

Any surplus will be returned to the bankrupt. (Note under s282 the bankrupt may apply to court for an order to annul the bankruptcy order where all bankruptcy expenses, debts and interest have been paid in full.)

Partnership Insolvency

Introduction

2.40 When a general practitioner is faced with a partnership client experiencing financial difficulties, he should approach the problem broadly in the same way as he would for an individual client. A partnership is, after all, merely a group of individuals who are trading together without limited liability.

The rules surrounding partnership insolvency are, however, somewhat different from those for individuals. Whereas the business and personal assets of a sole trader may be lumped together for the purposes of a bankruptcy, the situation as regards a partnership is more complex. There has to be a separation of the business of the partnership (and its assets and liabilities) from the affairs of the individual partners (with their personal assets and liabilities). Yet the business and personal affairs are inextricably linked both by the unlimited liability of partners and by the joint and several liability of each partner in respect of partnership debts.

The insolvency of partnerships is governed by IA 1986 as modified by the Insolvent Partnerships Order 1986. This lays down rules both for the winding-up of the partnership, with or without the bankruptcy of the individual partners, and for the bankruptcy of the partners without the winding-up of the partnership. (Note that new legislation is intended to be introduced in 1994.)

(a) Involvement of the general practitioner

2.41 When advising on insolvent partnership, the general practitioner should:

(i) Avoid conflicts of interest

2.42 Where the partnership (as opposed to any individual partner) is the client the interests of the partnership may well conflict with those of the partners. For example, it might be possible for a partner to structure his own finances to limit any contribution he is able to make in respect of any shortfall in the partnership assets. This will clearly not be in the interests of the partnership or the partnership creditors, and all partners should be advised to obtain separate legal advice regarding their personal positions.

(ii) Ascertain the exact position of the partnership's financial affairs

2.43 The general practitioner should assist the partners in producing a statement of affairs for the partnership showing break-up values of the assets, together with all liabilities. This will be much the same as for a limited company (see diagram 1), and will show whether the partnership is likely to be able to meet its liabilities in the event of a break-up.

A break-up of the partnership may not, of course, be necessary since the partnership might actually be profitable. A thorough review of the business should therefore be carried out, and trading and cash flow forecasts produced. These will show whether there is any future for the business and whether a winding-up might be avoidable.

(iii) Consider the available options

2.44 The choice of option will clearly depend upon the outcome of the review into the partnership's financial position. The options are as follows:

1   Options outside the Insolvent Partnerships Order:
    (a) informal moratorium;
    (b) partners reach personal arrangement with creditors.
2   Insolvent Partnerships Order.

(b) Informal moratorium

2.45 This will usually be the simplest and least expensive of the methods, but is very much dependent upon a good relationship between the debtor and all his creditors. The absence of any mechanism for binding dissenting creditors means that one creditor may 'spoil the party' by attempting to wind-up the partnership and/or bankrupt the partners. It is unlikely therefore that an informal moratorium will be appropriate in any but a few exceptional cases.

(c) Formal arrangement with creditors

2.46 It needs to be understood at this point that there is currently no mechanism whereby the partnership (as opposed to each of the partners individually) can reach a formal arrangement with creditors either within or outside the Insolvent Partnerships Order. This has led to widespread criticism of the current partnership insolvency regulations. A draft revised insolvent partnerships order has, therefore, been produced and is expected to become law in early 1994. This draft contains provisions whereby partnerships can enter into voluntary arrangements or be subject to administration orders in much the same way as can a company (see also **2.48** below).

Until the law is changed the only way for a formal arrangement with creditors to be reached is for the individual partners to make separate but interlinking Individual Voluntary Arrangements. The implementation of each partner's arrangement will be dependent upon the approval of a similar arrangement for the remaining partners. The individual arrangements will make provision for partnership property and creditors together with the individual partners' personal property and creditors.

The logistics of obtaining the agreement of the creditors to all the individual arrangements can be difficult and usually requires the holding of simultaneous creditors' meetings. It is often more efficient for one insolvency practitioner to act as nominee in respect of all the arrangements.

(d) Insolvent Partnerships Order (IPO)

2.47 The IPO contains provisions for the three possible combinations of insolvency proceedings as regards the partnership and the individual partners.
1   Winding-up the partnership only, without the bankruptcy of the individual partners. This may occur for example when the firm is being wound up for reasons other than insolvency or when the firm is insolvent but the partners are able to make good the shortfall or to come to an arrangement in respect of the shortfall which avoids their own bankruptcy.
2   Winding-up the firm, with concurrent bankruptcy petitions in respect of two or more partners. This is perhaps the most common scenario whereby the creditors of the partnership petition for the bankruptcy of the wealthiest partners (or all the partners) in order to recoup their expected losses in the winding-up of the partnership. Each partner is, of course, jointly and severally liable for all

of the partnership liabilities, but has recourse to his fellow partners in the event that he has paid more than he should have under the partnership agreement.
3   Bankruptcy of individual partners without the winding-up of the firm. A creditor is fully entitled to take action against one or more individual partners without taking any action against the firm. This might be appropriate where, for example, the partnership has no assets.

Under the Partnerships Act 1890 s33, the bankruptcy of a partner will usually lead to the dissolution of the firm, although the firm might be able to survive if its articles displace s33.

When a partnership is wound up under the IPO the winding-up is the same as for an unregistered company under Part V of IA 1986. The main difference however is that there may be transfers of expenses or shortfalls to and from the estates of the partnership and any bankrupt partners. The rules relating to the conduct of a winding-up under the IPO are complex, and the general practitioner is unlikely to require a working knowledge. It should however be noted that the IPO contains provisions whereby partners are subject to the provisions of CDDA 1986 in the event that a partnership is wound up. A partner may therefore be disqualified from being a director of or being concerned in the management of a company for up to 15 years.

(e)   Revised Insolvent Partnerships Order

2.48   As noted above, it is likely that a revised IPO will become law in early 1994. The most important change proposed by the draft revised order is to make available the company voluntary arrangement and administration procedures to insolvent partnerships. The provisions of the draft order in respect of these procedures are almost identical to Part I and Part II of IA 1986 with changes in wording only where required to apply the law to partnerships instead of companies.

PART 3

GLOSSARY

CONTENTS TO GLOSSARY

'ACID TEST' 3.1
ADMINISTRATION ORDER 3.2
ADMINISTRATIVE RECEIVER 3.3
ADMINISTRATOR 3.4
AGRICULTURAL RECEIVER 3.5
    Fixed Charge
    Floating Charge
ANTON PILLER ORDER 3.6
ASSOCIATED AND CONNECTED PERSONS 3.7
AVOIDANCE OF CERTAIN FLOATING CHARGES 3.8
AVOIDANCE OF GENERAL ASSIGNMENT OF BOOK DEBTS 3.9

BANKRUPTCY 3.10
    Bankruptcy - obtaining an order
    Bankruptcy petition
    Grounds for petition
        (a) Creditor's petition
        (b) Debtor's petition
    Inability to pay debts (s268)
    Statutory demand
    Safeguarding the assets after presentation but before order
    Insolvency practitioner's report (debtor's petition only)
    Bankruptcy order
    Investigation by Official Receiver (OR)
    Duties of bankrupt to OR (s291)
BANKRUPTCY OFFENCES 3.11

CENTREBINDING 3.12
CLAYTON'S CASE 3.13
CHARGE 3.14
COMPANY DIRECTORS DISQUALIFICATION ACT 1986 3.15
    Grounds for making order
        (a) Conviction of indictable offence (CDDA 1986 s2)
        (b) Persistent breaches of companies' legislation (CDDA 1986 s3)
        (c) Fraud, etc in winding-up (CDDA 1986 s4)
        (d) Participation in wrongful or fraudulent trading (CDDA 1986 s10)
        (e) Undischarged bankrupt (CDDA 1986 s11)
        (f) Investigation of the company (CDDA 1986 s8)
        (g) Involvement in insolvent partnership
        (h) Unfit director of an insolvent company (CDDA 1986 s6)
    Matters for determining unfitness of directors (CDDA 1986 s9)
        Part I - matters applicable to all cases
        Part II - matters applicable where company has become insolvent
    Consequences of contravention of CDDA
        (a) Criminal penalties (CDDA 1986 s13)
        (b) Personal liability (CDDA 1986 s15)

112   *Glossary*

COMPANY VOLUNTARY ARRANGEMENT   3.16
COMPOSITION   3.17
COMPULSORY LIQUIDATION   3.18
   Definition
   When to petition?
   A general practitioner's guide to winding-up
   The winding-up petition
   Grounds for petition
   Inability to pay debts
   Who may petition (s124)
   Powers of court on hearing of petition (s125)
   Effects of the winding-up order
   Statement of affairs
   Investigation by official receiver
   Duty to report
CONNECTED PERSONS
CONTINUING PROFESSIONAL RELATIONSHIP   3.19
CORK REPORT   3.20
CREDITORS' COMMITTEE   3.21
   Committee within an administration
      (a)   Power to establish a committee
      (b)   Constitution
      (c)   Functions and meetings
      (d)   The chairman at meetings
      (e)   Quorum
      (f)   Procedure at meeting
      (g)   Resolutions by post
      (h)   Election to the committee
      (i)   Administrator's remuneration
      (j)   Expenses of members
   Committee within an administrative receivership
   Comparison with a creditors' committee in an administration
      (a)   Power to establish
      (b)   Constitution
      (c)   Functions and meetings
      (d)   The chairman at meetings
      (e)   Quorum
      (f)   Procedure at meetings
      (g)   Resolution by post
      (h)   Election to the committee
      (i)   Administrative receiver's remuneration
      (j)   Expenses of members
   Committee within a liquidation – 'Liquidation Committee'
      (a)   Power to establish
      (b)   Constitution
      (c)   Functions and meetings
      (d)   The chairman at meetings
   Committee within a bankruptcy
      (a)   Power to establish

  (b) Constitution
  (c) Obligation of trustee to committee
  (d) The chairman at meetings
  (e) Quorum
  (f) Voting rights and resolutions
  (g) Resolutions by post
  (h) Trustee's reports
  (i) Expenses of members
CREDITORS' VOLUNTARY LIQUIDATION – an overview 3.22
 Appointment of Liquidator
 Statement of affairs
 Section 98 meeting of creditors
 Voting for the liquidator
 Publicity
CROWN SET-OFF 3.23

DEBENTURE 3.24
DECLARATION OF SOLVENCY 3.25
DEED OF ARRANGEMENT 3.26
DISCLAIMER 3.27
 Companies
 Individuals
DISSOLUTION 3.28
 Revival of a dissolved company
DISTRAINT 3.29
DISTRESS 3.30
 Effect of insolvency – preferential creditors in a compulsory liquidation
 Effect of insolvency on right to distrain
  (a) Administrative receivership
  (b) Administration
  (c) Voluntary liquidation
  (d) Compulsory liquidation
  (e) Bankruptcy

EMPLOYEES IN INSOLVENCIES 3.31
 Employees' claims
  (a) Contractual claims
  (b) Claims arising under the Employment Protection (Consolidation) Act 1978 (EPA)
 Employees' preferential claims
 Guaranteed payments to employees
 Transfer of Undertakings (Protection of Employment) Regulations 1981 ('TUPER')
 TUPER and hiving-down
 Effect of insolvency on contracts of employment
  (a) Administrative receivership
  (b) Administration
  (c) Creditors' voluntary liquidation
  (d) Compulsory liquidation

ETHICS AND PROFESSIONAL CONDUCT OF INSOLVENCY
    PRACTITIONERS   3.32
    Obtaining insolvency work
    Professional independence
EXTORTIONATE CREDIT TRANSACTIONS   3.33

FIXED AND FLOATING CHARGES   3.34
    Fixed charges
    Floating charges
FRAUDULENT TRADING   3.35

GOING CONCERN   3.36
GUARANTOR – acting as   3.37

HIVE-DOWN   3.38
    In order to facilitate a continuation of trade
    Sale of business

INDIVIDUAL VOLUNTARY ARRANGEMENT (IVA)   3.39
    Application for interim order
    The proposal
    Nominee's report to the court (s256)
    Meeting of creditors
    Voting at the creditors' meeting
    Effect of approval (s260)
    Challenge of creditors' meeting decision (s269)
    Completion of voluntary arrangement (r 5.29)
    Default in connection with voluntary arrangement (ss264, 276)
INSOLVENCY ACT 1986   3.40
INSOLVENCY PRACTITIONER   3.41
    Security
INSOLVENCY RULES 1986   3.42
INSOLVENT LIQUIDATION   3.43
INSOLVENT PARTNERSHIPS ORDER 1986   3.44
INTERIM ORDER   3.45
INTERIM RECEIVER   3.46
INTEREST ON DEBTS IN A WINDING UP   3.47
    Advice of the general practitioner
        (a) Pre-liquidation interest
        (b) Post-liquidation interest (also called Statutory interest)
        (c) Bankruptcy

LAW OF PROPERTY ACT (1925)   3.48
LIENS – enforceability against insolvency office-holder   3.49
LIQUIDATION   3.50
LIQUIDATION COMMITTEE   3.51
LIQUIDATOR   3.52
    Appointment
    Functions
    Powers

Resignation and Removal
Remuneration
    (a)   Official Receiver (OR) as liquidator
    (b)   Liquidator not Official Receiver

MALPRACTICE (before and during liquidation)   3.53
'MAREVA' INJUNCTION   3.54
   Relevance to an office-holder
   Removal by a floating charge-holder
MEMBERS' VOLUNTARY LIQUIDATION   3.55
   Declaration of Solvency
   Appointment of the liquidator
   Insolvency in a Members' Voluntary Liquidation
   Meetings in a MVL
   Removal of the liquidator
MISFEASANCE   3.56

NOMINEE   3.57

OFFICIAL RECEIVER ('OR')   3.58
   Investigation
   Compulsory liquidation
   Bankruptcy
ONEROUS PROPERTY   3.59
ORIGINAL TENANT LIABILITY   3.60

PETITION   3.61
'PHOENIX' COMPANIES   3.62
    (a)   Sale of Business (r 4.228)
    (b)   Existing name (r 4.230)
PITFALLS FACING THE COMPANY DIRECTOR   3.63
PREFERENCES AND TRANSACTIONS AT AN UNDERVALUE   3.64
   Challengeable by an office-holder
   General Practitioner's need to identify
   Definition
    (a)   Preferences
    (b)   Transactions at an undervalue
   'Relevant time' and 'onset of insolvency'
    (a)   Company (s240)
    (b)   Individual (s341)
   Result of successful challenge by office-holder
PREFERENTIAL CREDITORS   3.65
PREFERENTIAL DEBTS   3.66
   Definition
   Order of priority
   Identifying preferential claims
   Preferential claims – the relevant date for calculating
    (a)   Creditors' voluntary liquidation
    (b)   Compulsory liquidation

Glossary

  (c) Administrative receivership
  (d) Company Voluntary Arrangement
  (e) Administration
  (f) Individual Voluntary Arrangement
  (g) Bankruptcy
 Payment of preferential claims
  (a) Administrative receiver's duty to pay
  (b) Assets available to meet preferential claims
 The effect of the decision in *Re GL Saunders Ltd* [1986] 1 WLR 215

PROOF OF DEBT   3.67
 Proofs of debt – liquidations
  (a) Provable debts
  (b) Treatment of various types of debt
  (c) Secured debts
 Proofs of debt – bankruptcy
  (a) Provable debts

PROVISIONAL LIQUIDATOR   3.68
PROXY   3.69

RECEIVER   3.70
RECEIVERSHIP UNDER THE LAW OF PROPERTY ACT (1925)   3.71
 Appointment of LPA receiver
 Powers of LPA receiver
 Application of monies by LPA receiver

RETENTION OF TITLE (ROT)   3.72
 Types of clause
 Incorporation
 Identification
 Tracing goods into work-in-progress or finished goods
 Tracing into proceeds of sale

RE-USE OF COMPANY NAME   3.73

SECURED CREDITOR   3.74
SET-OFF   3.75
SHADOW DIRECTOR   3.76
SPECIAL MANAGER   3.77
SOCIETY OF PRACTITIONERS OF INSOLVENCY   3.78
STATUTORY DEMAND   3.79
SUPERVISOR   3.80

TAXATION   3.81
 Taxation (direct) – corporate insolvency
  (a) Administration
  (b) Receivership
  (c) Liquidation
 Utilisation of trading losses
 Capital gains
 Solvent companies

Taxation (direct) – individual insolvency
    (a) Inland Revenue claim
    (b) Capital Gains Tax
TRUSTEE IN BANKRUPTCY   3.82
  Appointment
  Functions
  Powers
  Control over trustee
  Removal of the trustee
  Remuneration

UNSECURED CREDITOR   3.83

VALUE ADDED TAX   3.84
VAT BAD DEBT RELIEF   3.85
VOTING AT S98 CREDITORS' MEETING   3.86
  Proof of debt
  Proxy
  An individual attending and voting in his own name
  CA 1985 s375

WALKING POSSESSION   3.87
WINDING-UP ORDER   3.88
WINDING-UP PETITION   3.89
WINDING-UP RESOLUTION   3.90

3.1 'ACID TEST'

Insolvency practitioners are accustomed to being presented by directors, anxious to avoid a formal insolvency, with budget forecasts and business plans which bear no resemblance to current financial reality.

The enthusiasm of directors under such circumstances can be very persuasive. In order to prevent any element of 'getting carried away' insolvency practitioners will invariably apply, by whatever name, the 'acid test' which is usually sufficient to concentrate the mind upon realistic and relevant issues.

The general practitioner should invite an honest answer to the simple question: 'If things are so good, why are things so bad?' It is almost impossible for directors, however innocently, to deceive themselves or others, when the acid test is applied.

3.2 ADMINISTRATION ORDER

The expression 'Administration Order' may refer to the administration of insolvent estates of deceased debtors or to a county court order which allows an individual to pay off his debts by instalments.

Far more likely however for the general practitioner's purpose, it will apply to an order made by the court which places the company under the control of an INSOLVENCY PRACTITIONER who becomes the ADMINISTRATOR by virtue of the order.

See **1.62** for a detailed consideration of this subject.

3.3 ADMINISTRATIVE RECEIVER

When a bank or other lender who has advanced monies to a company and taken security which incorporates a FLOATING CHARGE the lender may appoint an administrative receiver to recover its monies. The appointee must be an INSOLVENCY PRACTITIONER.

Section 29 defines an administrative receiver as:

> a receiver or manager of the whole (or substantially the whole) of a company's property appointed by or on behalf of the holders of any debentures of the company secured by a charge which, as created, was a floating charge.

The first consideration for a general practitioner advising a client upon the possibility of the bank appointing a receiver is to establish (if necessary by means of a search at companies house) whether the bank has registered a DEBENTURE incorporating a floating charge. If the debenture is less than 12 months old, it *may* be invalid as against a liquidator or administrator but not against the company or a guarantor. (See AVOIDANCE OF CERTAIN FLOATING CHARGES).

The main point to remember is that if there is no floating charge registered then there can be no administrative receiver, sometimes abbreviated to RECEIVER.

See **1.105** for a detailed consideration of this subject.

3.4 ADMINISTRATOR

An INSOLVENCY PRACTITIONER appointed by the court pursuant to the grant of an ADMINISTRATION ORDER to achieve the purposes set out in the order.

See 'Administration Order' in **1.62**.

3.5 AGRICULTURAL RECEIVER

A receiver appointed under a fixed or floating charge pursuant to the Agricultural Credits Act 1928. Such a receiver is not an ADMINISTRATIVE RECEIVER and is not required to be an INSOLVENCY PRACTITIONER.

The charges can be granted by individuals who wish to raise finance for farming purposes. The Act describes the charges as follows:

Fixed Charge

A charge which is over 'such property forming part of the farming stock and agricultural assets belonging to the farmer at the date of the charge as may be specified in the charge.'

Floating Charge

A charge which is over 'the farming stock and other agricultural assets from time to time belonging to the farmer or such part thereof as is mentioned in the charge'.

The events which give the charge-holder the right to appoint a receiver will be specified in the charge. The powers of the receiver will depend upon the terms of the agricultural charge.

An agricultural receivership is generally conducted with a considerable degree of secrecy. The secured creditor is obliged only to notify the farmer concerned of the receiver's appointment. The receiver is neither obliged to advise third parties of his appointment nor of ceasing to act, his only duty in that regard being to apply to the charge-holder for his release from office.

3.6 ANTON PILLER ORDER

This is a court order which permits a person to enter the premises of another person in order to search for documents or assets. It takes its name from the case in which the order was first made, ie, *Anton Piller AG v Manufacturing Processes* [1976] RPC 719, CA.

Although most commonly used in respect of infringements of copyright, the Anton Piller order is also available to insolvency practitioners in order to assist them in their investigations into the whereabouts of assets or into the conduct of directors, etc. Although not a search warrant, it has the effect of placing any person who refuses to comply with the order in contempt of court.

It has, by way of example been used to allow administrative receivers to excavate a quarry where it was believed the directors had driven heavy plant and machinery to the bottom and then hidden it by filling in the quarry with rubble and then landscaping the surface to camouflage the site.

3.7 ASSOCIATED AND CONNECTED PERSONS

IA 1986 contains provisions which allow (in the case of a company) a LIQUIDATOR or ADMINISTRATOR or (in the case of an individual) a TRUSTEE IN BANKRUPTCY the opportunity of challenging certain transactions if they were carred out within a given period immediately prior to his appointment. Where the transactions in question were with an associated or connected person the period of time is carried further back.

The relevant sections are summarised as follows:

	Company	Individual
Transactions at an undervalue	s238	s339
Preferences	s239	s340
Avoidance of certain floating charges	s245	–

A person is deemed to be connected with a company if he is
1   a director or SHADOW DIRECTOR of the company or an associate of such a director or shadow director; or
2   he is an associate of the company (s249).

It is then necessary to look at s435 which describes the meaning of an 'associate' in the context of both an associate of a company or an individual.

If the section is difficult to read it is equally difficult to summarise without the danger of omission. It is therefore reproduced in full hereunder.

435 Meaning of 'associate'   (1) For the purposes of this Act any question whether a person is an associate of another person is to be determined in accordance with the following provisions of this section (any provision that a person is an associate of another person being taken to mean that they are associates of each other).

(2)   A person is an associate of an individual if that person is the individual's husband or wife, or is a relative, or the husband or wife of a relative, of the individual or of the individual's husband or wife.

(3)   A person is an associate of any person with whom he is in partnership, and of the husband or wife or a relative of any individual with whom he is in partnership; and a Scottish firm is an associate of any person who is a member of the firm.

(4)   A person is an associate of any person whom he employs or by whom he is employed.

(5)   A person in his capacity as trustee of a trust other than–
  (a) a trust arising under any of the second Group of Parts or the Bankruptcy (Scotland) Act 1985, or
  (b) a pension scheme or an employees' share scheme (within the meaning of the Companies Act),
is an associate of another person if the beneficiaries of the trust include, or the terms of the trust confer a power that may be exercised for the benefit of, that other person or an associate of that other person.

(6)   A company is an associate of another company –
  (a) if the same person has control of both, or a person has control of one and persons who are his associates, or he and persons who are his associates, have control of the other, or
  (b) if a group of two or more persons has control of each company, and the groups either consist of the same persons or could be regarded as consisting of the same persons by treating (in one or more cases) a member of either group as replaced by a person of whom he is an associate.

(7)   A company is an associate of another person if that person has control of it or if that person and persons who are his associates together have control of it.

(8) For the purposes of this section a person is a relative of an individual if he is that individual's brother, sister, uncle, aunt, nephew, niece, lineal ancestor or lineal descendant, treating –
   (a) any relationship of the half blood as a relationship of the whole blood and the stepchild or adopted child of any person as his child, and
   (b) an illegitimate child as the legitimate child of his mother and reputed father;
and references in this section to a husband or wife include a former husband or wife and reputed husband or wife.

(9) For the purposes of this section any director or other officer of a company is to be treated as employed by that company.

(10) For the purposes of this section a person is to be taken as having control of a company if –
   (a) the directors of the company or of another company which has control of it (or any of them) are accustomed to act in accordance with his directions or instructions, or
   (b) he is entitled to exercise, or control the exercise of, one third or more of the voting power at any general meeting of the company or of another company which has control of it;
and where two or more persons together satisfy either of the above conditions, they are to be taken as having control of the company.

(11) In this section 'company' includes any body corporate (whether incorporated in Great Britain or elsewhere); and references to directors and other officers of a company and to voting power at any general meeting of a company have effect with any necessary modifications.

3.8 AVOIDANCE OF CERTAIN FLOATING CHARGES

Section 245 provides that, where a company has had an ADMINISTRATION ORDER made against it or where it has been put into LIQUIDATION, certain FLOATING CHARGES taken out on its undertaking or property 'at a relevant time' prior to the administration/liquidation are invalid. This is designed to prevent one creditor obtaining an unfair advantage over others by securing his debt via a floating charge shortly before formal insolvency.

A 'relevant time' is defined as:
1. within two years of the onset of insolvency where the charge is created in favour of a CONNECTED PERSON;
2. within 12 months of the onset of insolvency where the charge is created in favour of a person not connected with the company;
3. in either case, at a time between the presentation of a petition for the making of an administration order and the making of an order on that petition.

The 'onset of insolvency' is defined as the commencement of the liquidation (which in the case of a COMPULSORY LIQUIDATION is the date of presentation of the petition, *not* the date of the winding-up order) or the date of presentation of the petition for the administration of the company on which the administration order is based.

General practitioners should take careful note that where the charge was created in favour of a person not connected with the company, the time is not a 'relevant time' unless the company was unable to pay its debts at the time of, or in consequence of making the charge, *but* this 'waiver' is not available to ASSOCIATED OR CONNECTED PARTIES. This means that when advising clients considering taking security by way of a floating charge to cover a past consideration, general practitioners should remember that the security will be open to challenge for a period of two years, should a liquidator or administrator be subsequently appointed.

A floating charge may however be valid, even if created at a relevant time:

1 where the consideration for the creation of the charge consists of money paid, or goods or services supplied, *at the same time or after*, the creation of the charge;
2 where the consideration consists of the discharge or reduction of a debt to the company *at the same time or after* the creation of the charge.

In addition a bank may be able effectively to create a valid floating charge in relation to 'new advances' to the company even if taken at a relevant time and for past consideration (see CLAYTON'S CASE).

The points to remember are that either an administrator or a liquidator can seek to set aside a floating charge granted to an unconnected party within the previous 12 months unless:

1 it was granted for fresh consideration and taken at the same time (or before) the new advance was made; or
2 the company was solvent at the time the charge was created; and that
3 the period of 12 months is extended to two years if granted to a connected party, whether or not the company was solvent at the time.

The general practitioner advising any client intending to grant or take a floating charge as security would do well to study the Court of Appeal decision given on 20 May 1993 in the case of *Power v Sharp Investments Ltd & Chandru Mahtani* [1993] BCC 609. This was a case brought by the liquidator of Shoe Lace Ltd, a company which went into compulsory liquidation after having granted a debenture to a company for past consideration at a time it was undoubtedly insolvent. That it was *intended* a debenture be granted at the time the advance was made or that the advance was made in consideration of the debenture being granted was not in dispute. The delay between execution of the debenture and earlier payment of the monies forming the consideration varied from 17 weeks down (in the case of the final tranche of monies advanced) to eight days.

Hoffman J in the court of first instance had found in favour of the liquidator who had claimed £180,710 subsequently paid by Shoe Lace to the order of the debenture holder prior to liquidation on the grounds that the debenture was invalid by virtue of s245. In upholding that judgment, the Court of Appeal held that, inter alia,

1 for the purpose of s245(5) the date of winding-up in a compulsory liquidation is the date of presentation of the petition and not the date of the order; and
2 the wording of s245(2) which renders the charge invalid unless the consideration is given to the company 'at the same time as, or after, the creation of the charge' is to be literally construed.

It is therefore not sufficient that monies be advanced on the understanding, strict or otherwise and in consideration of a (future) debenture being granted, unless in the words of Sir Christopher Slade 'the interval is so short that it can be regarded as de minimis – for example a "coffee-break" '.

3.9 AVOIDANCE OF GENERAL ASSIGNMENT OF BOOK DEBTS

Where a person engaged in business makes a general assignment to another person of his existing or future book debts, and is subsequently adjudged bankrupt, the transaction is subject to the provisions of s344.

Any such assignment is void against the trustee of the bankrupt's estate as regards book debts which were not paid before the presentation of the bankruptcy petition, unless the assignment has been registered under the Bills of Sale Act 1878.

A general assignment of book debts does not however include the following:
1. an assignment of debts from specified debtors or of debts becoming due under specified contracts;
2. an assignment of book debts included either in the transfer of a business made in good faith and for value or an assignment made for the benefit of creditors generally.

Note that there is no corresponding provision relating to insolvent companies.

3.10 BANKRUPTCY

Bankruptcy - obtaining an order

A consideration of the alternatives to bankruptcy is included in Part 2 (see **2.7**).

Set out below is a brief outline of the various steps leading to a bankruptcy order.

Bankruptcy petition

A bankruptcy order can only be made following the presentation of a petition (s264). The following persons may petition:
1. a creditor or creditors;
2. the debtor himself;
3. the supervisor of a voluntary arrangement.

The grounds for the petition must be stated.

Grounds for petition

(a) Creditor's petition

Inability to pay debt exceeding £750 or no reasonable prospect of being able to pay (s267).

(b) Debtor's petition

Unable to pay debts (s272).

Inability to pay debts (s268)

1. non compliance with a statutory demand within 21 days of service; or
2. execution in respect of a judgment debt returned unsatisfied.

Statutory demand

Must be on prescribed form (see r 6.1 – r 6.5).

Safeguarding the assets after presentation but before order

- restrictions on disposal of property (s284);
- restrictions on proceedings (s285);
- Interim receiver (s286).

Insolvency practitioner's report (debtor's petition only)

In certain circumstances the court will appoint an insolvency practitioner to investigate the affairs of the debtor and to report whether or not a meeting of creditors should be summoned to consider a voluntary arrangement (s273).

Bankruptcy order

OFFICIAL RECEIVER becomes receiver and manager of bankrupt's estate until appointment of TRUSTEE IN BANKRUPTCY (s287)

Official receiver decides whether to summon a meeting of creditors in order to appoint a trustee. If not, the official receiver is the trustee (s293)

The bankrupt must provide the official receiver with a statement of affairs within 21 days of the bankruptcy order (creditor's petition only) (s288).

Investigation by Official Receiver (OR)

It is the duty of the OR to investigate the affairs and conduct of every bankrupt and make such a report (if any) to the court as he thinks fit (s289).

Any report will be taken into account when considering the discharge of the bankrupt (see **2.33**).

Duties of bankrupt to OR (s291)

- to deliver possession of his estate;
- to deliver up all relevant books, records etc;
- to give the OR any such information as requested.

3.11 BANKRUPTCY OFFENCES

The IA 1986 creates a series of criminal offences designed both to punish fraud/dishonesty by bankrupts and to establish minimum standards in the control of businessmen and the conduct of businesses.

These offences are contained in ss350–362 and the general practitioner should refer to those sections where detailed information is required. The broad categories of offences are as follows:
1. improper dealings in property both before and after the making of the bankruptcy order;
2. failure to disclose and to deliver up all assets to the trustee;
3. actions which defraud creditors; and
4. culpability of the bankrupt leading to the bankruptcy.

3.12 CENTREBINDING

Centrebinding is a name given to the practice of placing a company into immediate liquidation, following the decision in *Re Centrebind Ltd* [1967] 1 WLR 377. Up to the implementation of the Insolvency Act 1986, the old rules (Companies Act 1948 s293, Companies Act 1981 s106 and Companies Act 1985 s588) required that a statutory meeting of creditors had to be held on the same day or that following the members' meeting and at least seven day's notice of the members' meeting had to be given (the company being placed into liquidation by the members at the members' meeting).

The practice of avoiding the seven day notice requirement (which notice had the effect of alerting creditors to the impending insolvency) was usually done to defeat a threatened execution of a judgment or a distraint by HM Customs & Excise or a landlord (but note that a 'Centrebind' does *not* in fact prevent a landlord from distraining) in order to maintain such assets as were available for the benefit of all creditors.

The Insolvency Act 1986 effectively recognises the apparent inconsistency between the requirements of the various Companies Acts and the 'Centrebind' judgment and 'legalises' the practice of 'Centrebinding' being content instead to restrict the powers of the liquidator until such time as the creditors either ratify his appointment or replace him at the creditors' meeting.

Under the new rules the company is firstly (as before) placed into liquidation by the passing of a resolution to wind up the company by not less than 95% of the members who consent to short notice of an extraordinary general meeting placing the company into immediate voluntary liquidation. Thereafter, a meeting of the company's creditors should be held within 14 days and during which time, the liquidator's powers are (without the leave of the court) restricted to allow him to:

1   take into his custody or under his control all the property to which the company appears to be entitled;
2   dispose of perishable goods and other goods the value of which is likely to diminish if they are not immediately disposed of; and
3   do all other things as may be necessary for the protection of the company's assets (s166(3)).

On an historic note it is interesting to consider the effect that *Re Centrebind* has had upon shaping current insolvency law. In the original Centrebind case, the acts of the company and liquidator were carried out in good faith but it did not take the unscrupulous or 'cowboy' element among insolvency practitioners at the time long to realise that by centrebinding a company they could take immediate control of its assets and thereafter deliberately delay the convening of the creditors meeting, often idefinitely, notwithstanding this constituted a technical breach of the Companies Act. From this was born the practice of unscrupulous liquidators, nominated by the directors, under-selling the assets to connected purchasers, with the creditors powerless to take any action.

It was this abuse which led to the call not only to license insolvency practitioners but also to bring about a thorough overhaul of insolvency law.

3.13   CLAYTON'S CASE

Clayton's Case (1816) 1 Mer 572 is of importance to banks when considering their position as preferential creditors for wages paid or their floating charge security in the context of the provisions of s245, AVOIDANCE OF CERTAIN FLOATING CHARGES.

In the former, where a bank has paid wages and is therefore deemed to 'stand in the shoes' of the employees for purpose of a preferential claim, its claim could be eroded by virtue of monies paid into the credit of the bank account. It is for this reason that banks often insist upon a 'Wages Account' being opened to prevent any erosion of their preferential claims should formal insolvency occur.

In the latter, the rule in *Clayton's Case* operates to the banks' advantage in that debits to a bank account subsequent to the creation of a floating charge are deemed to constitute a fresh advance. It is because of this that where a bank has been granted a floating charge at a time the company was insolvent and the charge was for a past consideration (in other words no concurrent increase in facility was made) the bank will not necessarily have to wait the full 12 months before that charge is valid as against a subsequent liquidator or administrator.

By way of example, a bank is owed £100,000 by an insolvent company against which it holds no security. The company requests an increase in facility which the bank refuses, offering instead to continue the existing facility provided the company agrees to execute a debenture in the bank's favour granting fixed and floating charges.

Over the next three months, the company pays £140,000 into the bank account during the ordinary course of business and the bank allows cheques to be paid out, which, with charges etc total £136,000. The following month, the bank appoints administrative receivers.

But for the rule in *Clayton's Case*, the floating charge would by virtue of s245 be void as against a liquidator and it would have been in the interests of the unsecured creditors to petition immediately for the compulsory winding up of the company. However, following the rule in *Clayton's Case*, the bank will be deemed to have advanced the entirety of the overdraft, ie £96,000 (£100,000 + £136,000 - £140,000) subsequent to the taking of the charge; in other words for fresh consideration and the charge is thereby now safe from attack by a liquidator.

Had the bank subsequently advanced less than the original overdraft balance following creation of the charge, the difference would still be open to challenge by a liquidator. (It is unlikely that an administrator could challenge the charge as the court cannot grant an administration order without the agreement of the administrative receiver to vacate office – which would be highly unlikely under the circumstances.)

3.14 CHARGE

See FIXED AND FLOATING CHARGES

3.15 COMPANY DIRECTORS DISQUALIFICATION ACT 1986

One area of constant concern to all company directors is the extent to which they may be exposed to a personal liability in fulfilling their function as a director – the PITFALLS FACING THE COMPANY DIRECTOR.

The general practitioner can advise his director clients by reference to the various matters which are contained within Sch 1 to the Company Directors Disqualification Act 1986 (CDDA) which consolidated previous legislation regarding the disqualification of directors. It enables the court to make a disqualification order which prohibits a person from:
1   being a director of a company;
2   being a liquidator, administrator, receiver or manager of a company;
3   being connected or taking part in the promotion, formation or management of a company.

The Act provides for a minimum disqualification of two years up to a maximum of 15 years for the most serious cases. An application to the court for a disqualification order will usually be made by The Secretary of State, the liquidator of the company concerned or the official receiver, although s16 CDDA also permits an application by any member or creditor of the company.

Grounds for making order

A disqualification order may be made on the following grounds:

(a) Conviction of indictable offence (CDDA 1986 s2)

The court may make a disqualification order against a person where he is convicted of an indictable offence in connection with the promotion, formation, management or liquidation of a company or with the receivership or management of the company's property.

(b) Persistent breaches of companies' legislation (CDDA 1986 s3)

The court may made a disqualification order against a person who has been persistently in default in relation to provisions under the CA in respect of making returns or delivering documents to the Registrar of Companies.

(c) Fraud, etc in winding-up (CDDA 1986 s4)

The court may make a disqualification order against a person where it appears in the course of the winding-up of a company that he is guilty of FRAUDULENT TRADING (regardless of whether convicted) or has otherwise been guilty, while an officer or liquidator of a company or receiver or manager of its property, of any fraud or breach of duty in relation to the company.

(d) Participation in WRONGFUL or FRAUDULENT TRADING (CDDA 1986 s10)

Where the court has made an order requiring a person to contribute to a company's assets under s213 or s214 (IA 1986), the court may, it if thinks fit, also make a disqualification order against that person.

(e) Undischarged bankrupt (CDDA 1986 s11)

This section provides that it is an offence for an undischarged bankrupt to be a director of or be concerned with the promotion, formation or management of a company, except by leave of the court.

(f) Investigation of the company (CDDA 1986 s8)

Where the Secretary of State has ordered an investigation into the company under CA 1985 ss431–441, he may apply to the court where he believes it to be in the public interest that a disqualification order be made against any director or SHADOW DIRECTOR of the company.

The court may make such an order if it is satisfied that the conduct of the person in question makes him unfit to be concerned in the management of a company.

(g) Involvement in insolvent partnership

Under the Insolvent Partnership Order 1986 the court may use a person's conduct in respect of an insolvent partnership in determining whether that person is unfit to be concerned in the management of a company.

(h) Unfit director of an insolvent company (CDDA 1986 s6)

The court is obliged to make a disqualification order under this section where it is satisfied that a person's conduct as a director or shadow director of an insolvent company makes him unfit to be concerned with the management of a company.

For the purpose of this section a company becomes insolvent if it goes into liquidation where its assets are insufficient to meet its liabilities and the expenses of winding-up, if an administration order is made against it or if an administrative receiver is appointed to the company.

The application for an order under this section will usually be made by the Secretary of State (or by the official receiver under direction of the Secretary of State). Under CDDA 1986 s7, the liquidator or other office-holder must report cases of unfitness to the Secretary of State. This reporting requirement is reinforced by the Insolvent Companies (Reports on Conduct of Directors) Rules 1986, which obliges office holders to return reports on the prescribed forms ('D Forms') in the following cases:

- a creditors' voluntary liquidation;
- a voluntary liquidation which began as a members' voluntary liquidation but now found to be insolvent;
- an administrative receivership.

The report should cover all directors and shadow directors for the three years prior to the commencement of the relevant insolvency procedure.

Matters for determining unfitness of directors (CDDA 1986 s9)

Section 9 provides that the court should have regard for CDDA 1986 Sch 1 in determining whether a person is unfit to be concerned in the management of a company. (The liquidator and administrative receiver should have regard for the same factors when preparing their reports on directors.)

Schedule 1 is divided into two parts. Part I applies in all cases, whereas Part II provides additional factors for consideration where the company is insolvent.

Part I - matters applicable to all cases

1 Any misfeasance or breach of any fiduciary or other duty owed by the director to the company.
2 Any misappropriation of assets by the director or any conduct giving rise to an obligation to account for assets.
3 The extent of a director's responsibility for the company entering into any transaction liable to be set aside under IA 1986 s423 (transactions defrauding creditors).
4 The extent of the director's responsibility for the failure of the company to keep proper accountancy records and registers and to file annual returns at Companies House under CA 1985.
5 The extent of the director's responsibility in the failure of the company to prepare annual accounts.

Part II - matters applicable where company has become insolvent

6 The extent of the director's responsibility for the cause of the company becoming insolvent.
7 The extent of the director's responsibility for the failure of the company to provide goods and services when they have been paid for in whole or in part.
8 The extent of the director's responsibility for the company entering into any transaction which is voidable as a preference or is at undervalue (IA 1986 s238-240).
9 The extent of the director's responsibility for any failure to summon a creditors' meeting in a creditors' voluntary liquidation under IA 1986 s98.
10 The failure of the director to comply with the various procedural requirements imposed upon the directors under the IA (eg statement of affairs, duty to co-operate etc).

Consequences of contravention of CDDA

(a) Criminal penalties (CDDA 1986 s13)

If a person acts in contravention of a disqualification order he is liable, on conviction or indictment, to imprisonment for not more than two years or a fine or both.

(b) Personal liability (CDDA 1986 s15)

A person is personally liable for all the 'relevant debts' of a company if at any time he is involved in the management of a company in contravention of a disqualification order. In addition any person involved in the management of a company who is willing to act on the instructions given by a person whom he knew to be subject to a disqualification order, will be similarly personally liable.

By 'relevant debt' is meant all debts incurred at the time the person was involved in the management of the company.

3.16 COMPANY VOLUNTARY ARRANGEMENT

A Company Voluntary Arrangement is a procedure introduced by the IA 1986 whereby a plan of reorganisation is effected which may involve deferring or compounding creditors' claims, capital restructuring or an orderly disposal of assets. The arrangement will be proposed to creditors and shareholders at separate meetings (in practice often held concurrently) and, if accepted, will be under the control of an insolvency practitioner acting as SUPERVISOR.

For more detail, refer to Part 1, **1.47**.

3.17 COMPOSITION

A composition is an agreement between a debtor and his creditors whereby the compounding creditors agree with the debtor and between themselves to accept less than would have been required to settle their claims in full. Such an arrangement often forms the central feature of the proposals in a COMPANY VOLUNTARY ARRANGEMENT.

3.18 COMPULSORY LIQUIDATION

Definition

A compulsory liquidation is the winding-up of a company by order of the court. This usually follows a PETITION to the court by a creditor.

When to petition?

In advising a client creditor of a company whether or not to go to the expense of petitioning to wind up the debtor company, care needs to be taken in balancing the costs involved with the likely benefit to be achieved. It is always worth considering when there is a well-founded suspicion that the directors have spirited away assets or preferred other creditors at a time the company was insolvent (see PREFERENCES and TRANSACTIONS AT AN UNDERVALUE). General practitioners should however remember that although it is their client who is going to be asked to pay for the cost of the petition, any benefit will be for *all* creditors.

Care should also be taken not to fall foul of s127 which states:

In a winding-up by the court, any disposition of the company's property, and any transfer of shares, or alteration in the status of the company's members, made after the commencement of the winding-up is, unless the court otherwise orders, void.

The date of the winding-up following a winding-up order will be deemed to have been the date of presentation of the petition and this, coupled with s127 has led to more than one petition 'back-firing' against the original petitioner. This follows the use of the threat of a petition as a weapon to persuade the debtor company to pay its outstanding account. Given that the company will almost certainly be insolvent, it could be argued that by *not* petitioning the client creditor is in effect giving fresh consideration and therefore creating a shield against any future potential claim by a liquidator for repayment of the monies as constituting a preference under s239.

The problem could arise if the client is forced to proceed with his threat to petition, with the debtor company then paying off the debt before the hearing to wind up. Once presented, a petition cannot be withdrawn without the consent of the court and although your client may have received payment in full, another creditor may well 'adopt' the petition with the result that at the hearing, a winding-up order is granted anyway. This would leave your client having received 'a disposition of the company's property ... after the commencement of the winding-up' under such circumstances as would be void against the liquidator (and therefore repayable to him) unless the court was prepared to order otherwise.

When considering the use of a petition as a threat to obtain payment of a debt, legal advice is essential. The general practitioner could however consider advising his client where a petition has actually been issued, to attempt to persuade the directors of the debtor company to effect payment of the debt *personally*, leaving them to worry about any other creditor thereafter adopting the petition.

A general practitioner's guide to winding-up

It is unlikely that the general practitioner will need anything more than a general outline of the procedures involved. For those requiring detailed information, reference should be made to the relevant sections of the IA 1986 and the IR 1986.

A brief outline of the procedures by reference to the various 'steps' in a compulsory winding-up is set out below:

The winding-up petition

- must be in prescribed form;
- must give full details of company against which petition is made;
- must state grounds for petition (s122).

Grounds for petition

Usually either:
- company is unable to pay its debts; or
- just and equitable that the company should be wound up.

Inability to pay debts

Defined in s123. General practitioners should note that it is not necessary for a judgment to be obtained against a company in order to be able to petition for its winding-up provided one of the sub-sections in s123 is satisfied.

Who may petition (s124)

Powers of court on hearing of petition (s125)

Note power to make an interim order providing for the appointment of a PROVISIONAL LIQUIDATOR and SPECIAL MANAGER.

Effects of the winding-up order

- company in compulsory liquidation;
- liquidation deemed to have commenced at date petition presented;
- official receiver becomes liquidator unless and until 'outside' liquidator appointed;
- all legal action against the company halted;
- s127 (see above) applies;
- any attachment, sequestration, distress or execution against the estate of the company is void (s128);
- right to inspect company's statutory registers ceases (s155);
- floating charges crystallise at the date of the winding-up order.

Statement of affairs

The official receiver may require that a statement of affairs be submitted to him (s131).

Investigation by official receiver

It is the duty of the official receiver to carry out an investigation into the cause of the company's failure (s132).

Duty to report

It is the duty of the official receiver to report at least once to creditors and contributories (r 4.43) and, if he decides to hold a meeting of creditors for the purpose of appointing someone else as liquidator must hold that meeting within four months of the winding-up order (s136(5)).

CONNECTED PERSONS

See ASSOCIATED AND CONNECTED PERSONS

3.19   CONTINUING PROFESSIONAL RELATIONSHIP

See ETHICS AND PROFESSIONAL CONDUCT OF INSOLVENCY PRACTITIONERS

3.20   CORK REPORT

The Cork Report is the name given to the report of the Insolvency Law Review Committee which formed the basis for the IA 1986. The committee was chaired by Sir Kenneth Cork.

3.21 CREDITORS' COMMITTEE

There are provisions for the formation of a committee chosen from the general body of creditors to represent creditors in an administration, administrative receivership, liquidation and bankruptcy

Confusingly the committee is referred to as a 'creditors' committee' in the case of administration and administrative receivership, whereas in a liquidation it is referred to as a 'liquidation committee'.

Committee within an administration

(a) Power to establish a committee

The power to establish a creditors' committee within an administration is contained within s26 which section also empowers the committee, on giving not less than seven day's notice, to require the administrator to attend before it at any reasonable time and furnish it with such information relating to the carrying out of his functions as it may reasonably require.

The constitution of the committee and its functions are governed by the Insolvency Rules. Rule 2.32 deals with the constitution as follows:

(b) Constitution

(1) Where it is resolved by a creditors' meeting to establish a creditors' committee for the purpose of the administration, the committee shall consist of at least 3 and not more than 5 creditors of the company elected at the meeting.

(2) Any creditor of the company is eligible to be a member of the committee so long as his claim has not been rejected for the purpose of his entitlement to vote.

(3) A body corporate may be a member of the committee, but it cannot act as such otherwise than by a representative appointed under Rule 2.37.

(c) Functions and meetings

Once again it is to the Insolvency Rules (r 2.34) that we have to turn to discover the statutory authorities which are set out thus:

(1) The creditors' committee shall assist the administrator in discharging his functions, and act in relation to him in such a manner as may be agreed from time to time.

(2) Subject as follows, meetings of the committee shall be held when and where determined by the administrator.

(3) The administrator shall call a first meeting of the committee not later than 3 months after its first establishment; and thereafter he shall call a meeting –
    (a) if so requested by a member of the committee or his representative (the meeting to be held within 21 days of the request being received by the administrator), and
    (b) for a specified date, if the committee has previously resolved that a meeting be held on that date.

(4) The administrator shall give 7 days written notice of the venue of any meeting to every member of the committee (or his representative designated for that purpose), unless in any case the requirement of notice has been waived by or on behalf of any member.

Waiver may be signified either at or before the meeting.

(d) The chairman at meetings

Rule 2.35(1) provides that administrators should be chairman, subject to r 2.44(3). (This deals with the chairing of meetings covered under s26 where the committee has summoned the administrator to give information and at which meeting the committee may elect one of their own members to be chairman of the meeting in place of the administrator or his nominee.)

> The chairman at any meeting of the creditors' committee shall be the administrator or a person nominated by him in writing to act.

Rule 2.35(2) states that:

> a person so nominated must be either –
> (a) one who is qualified to act as an insolvency practitioner in relation to the company, or
> (b) an employee of the administrator or his firm who is experienced in insolvency matters.

(e) Quorum

Rule 2.36 states:

> A meeting of the committee is duly constituted if due notice of it has been given to all the members and at least 2 members are present or registered.

(f) Procedure at meeting

At any meeting of the committee, the procedures are governed by r 2.42 which states:

> (1) At any meeting of the creditors' committee each member (whether present himself or by representative) has one vote; and a resolution is passed when a majority of the members present or represented have voted in favour of it.
>
> (2) Every resolution passed shall be recorded in writing, either separately or as part of the minutes of the meeting.
>
> (3) A record of each resolution shall be signed by the chairman and placed in the company's minute book.

(g) Resolutions by post

Rule 2.43 allows the administrator to dispose of holding a formal meeting requesting instead that the committee members signify their agreement or otherwise to a resolution by post. Any member who feels that a meeting is called for, may, within seven business days from the date the administrator sends out the resolution, require him to summon a meeting of the committee to consider the matters passed by the resolution. As with a full meeting, a resolution by post is deemed to have been passed following written notification by a majority of the committee members and a copy of any resolution passed must be placed in the company's minute book.

(h) Election to the committee

The creditors' committee in an administration order is simply an extension of the older 'Committee of Inspection', since the Insolvency Act, re-titled a 'Liquidation Committee' in a liquidation. As such we have over many years seen how insolvency practitioners have attempted to deal with the often vociferous demands by creditors to be elected to a committee when the Act restricts the numbers to not more than five. Common practice saw the 'co-option' of additional 'members' onto a committee who in effect had the right to be 'seen and not heard'. In reality they often made more noise than the rest of the committee put together, which was perhaps their personal revenge for being denied a formal vote, seeking instead to influence the elected members by virtue of their rhetoric!

A further problem was the 'spread' of creditor representation of the committee, with many an argument that the 'widow's mite' was just as important as the largest claim and that the committee should not be 'swamped' by the largest creditors at the expense of the smaller creditor. This issue now seems to be resolved following *Re Polly Peck International plc* [1991] BCC 503 with r 2.32 being read as if the committee will be elected following a single ballot, with the five creditors who attract the greatest number of votes being chosen to form the committee.

(i) Administrator's remuneration

Although r 2.34(1) sums up the committee's function in a single sentence, ie:

> (to) assist the administrator in discharging his functions and acting in relation to him in such manner as shall be agreed from time to time.

one of the committee's main functions, so far as the administrator himself is concerned, is to fix his remuneration!

Rule 2.47(3) states '… it is for the creditors' committee (if there is one) to determine …' the method of fixing the administrator's remuneration.

(j) Expenses of members

Rule 2.45 allows for the reasonable travelling expenses directly incurred by members of the creditors' committee to be defrayed by the administrator out of the assets of the company as an expense of the administration. It should be noted however that no expenses are allowed in attending a meeting within three months of a previous meeting unless the meeting in question was summoned at the request of the administrator.

Note also that this section applies only to *expenses* incurred; time costs are not allowable as an expense.

Committee within an administrative receivership

Unless the company is placed also into liquidation within three months of an administrative receiver being appointed, the receiver is obliged by s48 to convene a meeting of the company's creditors and report to them in due form (see IA 1986 s48 for relevant data).

At that meeting, the creditors may if they wish establish a creditors' committee.

Comparison with a creditors' committee in an administration

For all intents and purposes the purpose and function of the committee are identical within an administrative receivership and an administration.

(a) Power to establish

So far as the *sections* are concerned, s49 in an administrative receivership compares with s26 in an administration; in other words it confers power to establish a committee and for the committee to summon the administrative receiver to attend a committee meeting for the purpose of furnishing information.

Everything else is covered by the IR 1986 which follows the text of the corresponding rules within an administration. Using the same order as used above for a creditors' committee within an administration, the Rules themselves are to be found as follows:

		Rule
(b)	Constitution	3.16
(c)	Functions and meetings	3.18
(d)	The chairman at meetings	3.19
(e)	Quorum	3.20
(f)	Procedure at meetings	3.26

Note that whereas in an administration order it is a requirement (r 2.42(3)) that a record of each resolution be signed by the chairman and placed in the company's minute book, r 3.26(3) requires that in the case of administrative receivership, the signed resolution be kept as part of the records of the receivership.

(g)	Resolution by post	3.27
(h)	Election to the committee	3.16

Election will be by a single ballot with the five creditors who attract the greatest number of votes being elected.

(i) Administrative receiver's remuneration

Unlike the powers conferred by r 2.47(3) to the creditors' committee in an administration, there are no provisions for the creditors' committee in an administrative receivership to become involved in the question of the receiver's fee.

(j)	Expenses of members	3.29

Committee within a liquidation – 'Liquidation Committee'

(a) Power to establish

'Liquidation Committee' is the name given to a committee of creditors appointed under the provisions of s101, at a meeting of creditors held pursuant to s98 (being the meeting held to appoint a liquidator).

Unlike the power to establish in the case of an administration order or an administrative receivership, the Act (as opposed to the Insolvency Rules) actually specifies a committee 'of not more than 5 persons ...' making no reference to a minimum number (but see *(b)* below).

A liquidation committee may also be established under s141 where a winding-up order has been made by the court. Thereafter the constitutional differences between the two committees are contained within the relevant Rules. In this text, reference will be restricted to a liquidation committee formed pursuant to s101 in a creditors' voluntary liquidation.

(b) Constitution

Rule 4.152(2) states that 'The committee must have at least three members before it can be established.' Thus by combing s101 (which restricts the maximum number to five but calls for no minimum) and r 4.152(2) (which calls for a minimum number of three but mentions no maximum) we are back to the requirements of the Rules in the instance of both an administration order and an administrative receivership, where there must be at least three and no more than five members constituting a committee!

(c) Functions and meetings

Under r 4.153, the liquidation committee does not come into being and accordingly cannot act, until the liquidator has issued a certificate of its due constitution.

In order to consider the full extent of the liquidation committee's functions, it is once again necessary to have regard to both the Act and the Rules. Section 103 gives the committee power to sanction the continuance of the powers of directors after liquidation.

The Rules deal with the committee's functions almost as if from a negative angle. The Rule in question is r 4.155 'Obligations of liquidator to committee' which throws the onus on the liquidator to bring to the attention of the members of the committee, 'all such matters as appear to him to be, or as they have indicated to him as being, of concern to them with respect to the winding up.'

Rule 4.156 deals with the question of meetings, thus:

(1)   Subject as follows, meetings of the liquidation committee shall be held when and where determined by the liquidator.

(2)   The liquidator shall call a first meeting of the committee to take place within 3 months of his appointment or of the committee's establishment (whichever is the later), and thereafter he shall call a meeting-
  (a) if so requested by a creditor member of the committee or his representative (the meeting to be held within 21 days of the request being received by the liquidator), and
  (b) for a specified date, if the committee has previously resolved that a meeting be held on that date.

(3)   The liquidator shall give 7 days' written notice of the venue of a meeting to every member of the commitee (or his representative, if designated for that purpose), unless in any case the requirement of the notice has been waived by or on behalf of any member.

Waiver may be signified either at or before the meeting.

Although the committee cannot act until the liquidator has issued a certificate of its due constitution, by virtue of r 4.153(3) and (3A) it is possible for the first meeting of liquidation committee to be held immediately following the meeting at which the liquidator is appointed.

(d) The chairman at meetings

Under r 4.157 the chairman at any meeting of the liquidation committee will be the liquidator or an employee of the liquidator or his firm who is experienced in insolvency matters or some other independent insolvency practitioner.

Committee within a bankruptcy

(a) Power to establish

The power to establish a committee is contained in s301 which bears the overriding heading 'Control of Trustee'. This section enables the creditors at a general meeting to establish a committee to supervise the trustee. Section 301(2) states that no committee shall be formed where the Official Receiver acts as trustee, his role being supervised by the Secretary of State.

Again, as in corporate insolvency, the constitution of the committee and its functions are governed by the Insolvency Rules, which are summarised as follows (note that the headings do not compare exactly with those in corporate insolvencies).

		Rule
(b)	Constitution	6.150
(c)	Obligation of trustee to committee	6.152

Unless he is without funds, the request is frivolous or unreasonable or the cost of complying excessive in relation to the importance of the information, a trustee has a duty to report to members of the committee all such matters as appear to him to be, or as they have been indicated to him as being, of concern to them with respect to the bankruptcy.

(d)	The chairman at meetings	6.154
(e)	Quorum	6.155
(f)	Voting rights and resolutions	6.161
(g)	Resolutions by post	6.162
(h)	Trustee's reports	6.163

The trustee can be required to submit two-monthly reports to the committee or at such less frequent periods as they direct. In the absence of specific directions he must report not less often than in every period of six months.

(i)	Expenses of members	6.164

In addition to the above there are numerous other rules, with which the trustee must comply, which are unlikely to be of interest to a general practitioner guiding an insolvent individual or monitoring a trustee in bankruptcy on behalf of a creditor client.

3.22 CREDITORS' VOLUNTARY LIQUIDATION – an overview

The voluntary winding-up of a company commences with the passing of a resolution to wind up the company at a general meeting of members (see WINDING-UP RESOLUTION). Where a DECLARATION OF SOLVENCY has been sworn by the directors prior to the resolution, the company will be wound up in a MEMBERS' VOLUNTARY

LIQUIDATION. Where no such declaration has been made, the winding-up will be continued as a creditors' voluntary liquidation (CVL).

The following overview of the more important procedures pertinent to a CVL are intended to give the general practitioner a broad understanding of the subject. It is not intended to be fully comprehensive and general practitioners should consult the IA 1986 and IR 1986 for detailed legislation.

Appointment of Liquidator

Under s100 a liquidator may be nominated by the company for the purposes of winding-up the company's affairs. This will usually take place at the meeting convened to pass the resolution to wind up.

At the meeting of creditors convened under s98 the creditors may also nominate a person to act as liquidator. Where creditors nominate a different liquidator it is the creditors' nomination that takes precedence.

If a resolution to wind up the company has been passed by the members in general meeting but no liquidator has been appointed, (and there is to be a delay before the meeting of creditors), the directors are able only to exercise limited powers (s114). Unless the directors obtain sanction of the court, the directors powers are restricted to:
1   disposing of perishable goods and goods the value of which is likely to diminish;
2   doing all such things necessary for the protection of the company's assets.
See also CENTREBINDING.

Statement of affairs

The directors of the company are required under s99 to prepare a Statement of Affairs of the company (on Form 4.19). This statement must be verified by some or all of the directors and must show the prescribed information including:
1   particulars of the company's assets, debts and liabilities;
2   the names and addresses of the company's creditors;
3   the security held by the creditors and dates created.
The statement must be made up to a date no earlier than 14 days before the winding-up resolution, and must be laid before the meeting of creditors by the director nominated as chariman of the meeting.

Section 98 meeting of creditors

The company is obliged under s98 to hold a meeting of creditors within 14 days of passing the resolution to wind up the company although in practice it will usually be held on the same day and immediately following the members' meeting.

The main purposes of the meeting are to:
- inform the creditors of the financial position of the company;
- lay a statement of affairs before the creditors;
- enable the creditors to nominate and elect a liquidator;
- appoint a liquidation committee.

All creditors must be given at least seven days' notice of the meeting, and the notice should also be advertised in the *Gazette* and in two newspapers circulating in the locality of the company's principal place of business. Although it is the responsibility of the directors to organise the meeting and appoint one of their number as chairman the insolvency practitioner who has been nominated as liquidator by the members will usually ensure that the provisions of the IA 1986 have been followed.

A quorum at the meeting is one creditor present in person or by proxy. Proxies must be lodged prior to midday on the business day immediately before the meeting in order to be valid.

Voting at the s98 meeting: (see VOTING AT S98 CREDITORS' MEETING).

Voting for the liquidator

Where two persons have been nominated, the one with the most support in terms of value is appointed. There is no requirement for a majority of all those present and entitled to vote as in a compulsory liquidation.

After the liquidator has been appointed the chairman must ratify the appointment on the prescribed form but only after having received a written statement from the liquidator that he is an insolvency practitioner and qualified to act in respect of the company.

Publicity

The publicity required for a voluntary liquidation (whether creditors' or members') is as follows:
1. the resolution to wind up the company must be gazetted within 14 days (s85) and filed at Companies House within 15 days by the company (s84);
2. the appointment of the liquidator must be gazetted and filed at Companies House within 14 days by the liquidator (s109);
3. within 28 days of the s98 meeting of creditors, the liquidator must send to all creditors and contributories:
   (a) a copy or summary of the statement of affairs;
   (b) a report on the proceedings at the meeting;
4. Under s188, every invoice, order for goods or business letter issued by or on behalf of the company, together with every document issued by the liquidator where the company's name appears, should contain a statement that the company is being wound up.

3.23 CROWN SET-OFF

Where one government department owes an insolvent company money – for example a VAT repayment, that department will first of all enquire within other government departments as to whether they are owed monies by the insolvent company. If so, the repayment will normally be offered to the creditor department by way of crown set-off. This is permissible because the crown is treated as a single entity.

The one exception to the rule is where the company has granted its bankers a fixed charge on book debts. Under such circumstances it is customary for the debtor government department to recognise the charge and effect repayment direct to the company.

See also SET-OFF.

3.24 DEBENTURE

There is no statutory definition of the word 'debenture'. The word itself derives from the Latin (*debere* 'to owe') *debentur mihi* 'there are owed to me'. It is, in effect a written acknowledgement of debt, defined in *Levy v Abercorris Slate and Slab Co*

(1887) 37 Ch D 260 as 'a document which either creates a debt or acknowledges it'.

It is by virtue of a debenture granting a FLOATING CHARGE over a company's assets that the lender is empowered to appoint an ADMINISTRATIVE RECEIVER.

3.25 DECLARATION OF SOLVENCY

See MEMBERS' VOLUNTARY LIQUIDATION

3.26 DEED OF ARRANGEMENT

A deed of arrangement is a means by which an individual (as opposed to a company) may come to an arrangement with his creditors under the Deeds of Arrangement Act 1914, and so avoid bankruptcy. This method is now little used, having been replaced almost completely by INDIVIDUAL VOLUNTARY ARRANGEMENTS. (For further details refer to **2.10**).

3.27 DISCLAIMER

The IA 1986 contains provisions whereby the liquidator of a company or the trustee in bankruptcy of an individual may disclaim any property within the estate which they consider to be 'onerous'. This disclaimer may be carried out without need to seek leave of the court, and serves to release the company or individual from further obligations in order that liability may be quantified.

Companies

A liquidator may, by giving notice, disclaim any onerous property, notwithstanding that he has taken possession of it, endeavoured to sell it or otherwise exercised rights of ownership in relation to it (s178).

Onerous property includes the following-
1. any unprofitable contract; and
2. any other property of the company which is unsaleable or not readily saleable or is such that it might give rise to a liability to pay money or perform any other onerous act.

Onerous property might include, for example, a lease which contains unfavourable repairing convenants, or a plot of land which is highly contaminated.

The effect of a disclaimer is to determine, as from the date of the disclaimer, the rights, interests and liabilities of the company in or in respect of the property disclaimed. It does not however affect the rights and liabilities of any other person, except so far as is necessary for the purpose of releasing the company from any liability.

In order for a disclaimer to be effective, the liquidator must complete a notice of disclaimer containing full particulars of the property disclaimed. The notice must be signed by the liquidator and filed in court, together with a copy. The court then seals and endorses the document with the date of filing and returns the copy to the liquidator (r 4.187).

The liquidator must within seven days of the date on which the copy notice is returned to him, send copies of the notice to every person who, to his knowledge, claims an interest in the property or is under any liability in respect of the property (r 4.188).

Where the notice is in respect of an unprofitable contract, he must give copies to all persons whom he knows to have an interest therein. Where the property disclaimed is of a leasehold nature, he must send a copy to every person who, to his knowledge, claims under the company as an underlessee or mortgagee (s179). If it comes to the liquidator's knowledge subsequently that any other person is entitled to receive notice, he should send a copy forthwith.

Any person sustaining loss or damage in consequence of the operation of a disclaimer is deemed to be a creditor of the company and may prove for the loss or damage in the winding up. An interested party may however apply to the court within three months of becoming aware of the disclaimer for an order vesting the disclaimed property in the applicant (s181). The court will make such order as it thinks fit.

The general practitioner advising a landlord whose tenant is a company in liquidation should bear in mind that his client can force the liquidator into making a decision whether to disclaim or not. Understandably, liquidators often 'hedge their bets' continuing to occupy a property, perhaps in the hope of obtaining a premium on a sale of the lease (although less likely since the late 1980s collapse in the property market). The landlord may write to the liquidator requiring a decision and if within 28 days no disclaimer has been made, the liquidator is thereafter unable to issue any notice of disclaimer (s178(5)).

For general practitioners advising clients who have given personal guarantees in support of leases, see also GUARANTOR - ACTING AS.

Individuals

The provisions for disclaimer in a personal insolvency under ss315–321 are virtually identical to those set out above for companies, the only significant difference being the provision regarding dwelling houses (s318). Disclaimer will not take place in the case of a dwelling house unless notice has been served on every person in occupation at or claiming a right to occupy.

3.28   DISSOLUTION

Dissolution is the process by which the existence of a company is terminated. There are two main ways in which this may occur.
1 dissolution as the final stage of a liquidation. General practitioners requiring details of the procedures involved should refer to the IA 1986 as follows:
   (a) dissolution in a members' or creditors' voluntary liquidation – ss94, 106 and 201;
   (b) dissolution in a compulsory winding-up – ss 202–205;
2 dissolution as a result of the company's name being struck off by the Registrar of Companies under CA 1985 s652. The registrar may invoke this procedure in two circumstances:
   (a) if he has reasonable cause to believe that a company is not carrying on business;
   (b) if, where a company is being wound up, he has reasonable cause to believe either that no liquidator is acting, or that the affairs of the company are fully wound up, and the returns required to be made by the liquidator have not been made for a period of six consecutive months.

Revival of a dissolved company

CA 1985 contains two methods by which a dissolved company may be revived:

(i) *Declaration that dissolution is void (CA 1985 s651).* Within two years of the dissolution an application may be made to court by the liquidator or any person interested to have the dissolution declared as having been void. The object of this section is to cater for assets or liabilities which might have been overlooked.

(ii) *Restoration of a company struck off by the Registrar (CA 1985 s653).* Where the registrar has struck off a company under CA 1985 s652, an application may be made under CA 1985 s653 by the company or by any person who, at the date of dissolution, was a member or creditor. The application for restoration of the company may be made within 20 years of the gazetting of the dissolution. The court must be satisfied that the company was carrying on business at the time of the striking off, or that it is otherwise just for the company to be restored.

3.29 DISTRAINT   *Beschlagnahme*

See DISTRESS

3.30 DISTRESS

Distress is the action of distraining, being the legal seizure and detention of chattels in order to satisfy a debt or claim out of the proceeds of sale. The right to distrain is a common law remedy reinforced by statute. Insolvency practitioners have to deal frequently with distraint or attempted distraint by the HM Customs and Excise for VAT or the Commissioners for other taxes, and landlords, for arrears of rent.

In order to levy distress it is necessary for a bailiff to gain peaceful entry to the premises during daylight hours on any day but Sunday (where the landlord is an individual, he may distrain in person (Law of Distress Amendment Act 1888)). Notwithstanding a right to distrain involves a right to enter for the purpose of effecting the distraint, there is no right of forceable entry. Once peaceful entry has been gained the goods are 'seized' and then 'impounded' by being placed in the custody of the law in preparation for sale. In practice it is common for goods to be impounded on the premises by agreement with the debtor, which practice is known as 'taking walking possession'.

While the Inland Revenue and HM Customs and Excise may distrain upon any goods not belonging to third parties, there are some interesting restrictions upon distress by a landlord. The general practitioner should be aware that a landlord may not under any circumstances distrain against the following:
- wild animals;
- money not in a closed container;
- perishable articles;
- wearing and bedding apparel up to the value of £100;
- tools up to a value of £150.

Effect of insolvency – preferential creditors in a compulsory liquidation

In a compulsory liquidation, s176 preserves the preferential status of the preferential creditors over goods and their proceeds of sale which have been the subject of a distraint within the three months period prior to the winding-up, to the extent that the other property of the company is insufficient to meet them. Where a person who has so distrained is required to surrender goods or make a payment to the company, the preferential status of those creditors who receive the benefit of his distraint is subrogated to him to the extent of the payment.

There are no similar provisions which so preserve the property of the preferential creditor within a creditors' voluntary winding-up. Note however that under s112 the liquidator (or any contributory or creditor) may apply to the court to determine any matter arising in the winding-up.

Effect of insolvency on right to distrain

(a) Administrative receivership

The appointment of an administrative receiver has no effect upon a landlord's right of distraint.

(b) Administration

Administration does prevent any distraint except with the leave of the court.

(c) Voluntary liquidation

Placing a company into creditors' voluntary liquidation will not in itself defeat, for example, a landlord's right to distrain. Distraint can however be frustrated where peaceful entry is unobtainable. Application may also be made to the court under s112.

(d) Compulsory liquidation

Again, subject to s112, distraint prior to a presentation of the petition could proceed but would not be available as a remedy after presentation of a petition.

(e) Bankruptcy

It is possible for a landlord to distrain against a bankrupt's trustee, but only to a limit of rent outstanding for up to six months accrued due to the commencement of the bankruptcy.

3.31 EMPLOYEES IN INSOLVENCIES

The insolvency of a business invariably affects its employees, and the general practitioner advising individuals caught up in this situation needs to be aware of their statutory rights.

The subject is comprehensive and is covered below under the following headings:
- employees' claims;
- employees' preferential claims;
- guaranteed payments to employees;
- Transfer of Undertakings (Protection of Employment) Regulations 1981;
- effects of insolvency on contracts of employment.

Employees' claims

Where the employee is made redundant he will have certain monetary claims upon his employer.

(a)   Contractual claims

These claims arise out of the employee's employment contract and may include the following:
- arrears of pay at the date of redundancy;
- arrears of holiday pay in respect of holiday accrued but not taken;
- expenses incurred by the employee not reimbursed;
- pay in lieu of notice (ie damages for breach of contract by the employer in terminating the contract without giving notice. The damages will take account of lost pay, pension rights, etc).

The employee will be able to claim in full all amounts to which he is entitled by virtue of his employment contract (whether he will receive payment in full is a different matter). As will be seen below part of this claim may be preferential.

(b)   Claims arising under the Employment Protection (Consolidation) Act 1978 (EPA)

The EPA legislation was designed to consolidate the provisions of previous employment legislation and to provide a framework for protecting the rights of employees. It does not restrict itself to insolvent situations, although it does contain specific provisions in this respect.

Where a claim is admitted under the EPA, the government will place the liquidator (or other office holder) in funds (to certain maximum limits – see below) to discharge employees' claims, thereafter 'standing in the shoes' of the employees and claiming within the insolvency. It should be noted that to be eligible for consideration under the EPA scheme, employees must be 'on the books'. Sub-contractors (with or without valid certificates) or 'consultants' are not protected by the EPA scheme (see 'guaranteed payments to employees' below).

The EPA provides for the following claims against an insolvent employer.

(i)   Statutory pay in lieu of notice. This is designed to impose statutory minimum periods of notice on employment contracts. Where the contracts include a longer notice period, the employee may make a claim based on the contract. When however the employment contract contains no provision for notice or contains a notice period below the statutory minimum, the following statutory periods should be used.

Period of employment	Notice period
4 weeks – 2 years	one week
2 – 12 years	one week for each completed year of employment
over 12 years	12 weeks

Since however pay in lieu of notice represents damages in respect of loss of earnings, the employee will be required to mitigate his claim by deducting:
- any earnings received during the notice period;
- unemployment benefit entitlement (whether received or not) during the notice period;
- any protective award relating to the notice period (see below);
- any award for unfair dismissal in excess of the basic award (see below).

Notional tax will be deducted from any payment made to the employee in the insolvent administration.

As discussed below, the claim may be wholly or partly guaranteed under the EPA.

(ii) *Statutory redundancy pay.* The EPA provides that where an employee has been continually employed for over two years since his eighteenth birthday and is made redundant, he is entitled to receive a redundancy payment from the employer. The rules relating to what constitutes continuous employment are complex and are set out in Sch 13 to the EPA. Employment would be deemed to be continuous if, for example, there was a change of ownership of the business or where the employee had been reinstated after wrongful dismissal. In order to qualify for redundancy payment, an employee will have had to work for more than 16 hours per week.

The level of redundancy pay is determined by the employee's age and length of service, thus:

Age	Weeks' pay for each complete year of employment
18-21	½
22-40	1
41-65 (men) } 41-60 (women) }	1½

(iii) *Protective awards.* The EPA contains provision that, where an employee's job is recognised by an independent trade union, the employer must consult the trade union prior to the dismissal of the employee. This applies equally to solvent and insolvent companies.

Consultation must commence at the earliest opportunity and in any case:

1. where a hundred or more employees at one establishment are to be dismissed, at least 90 days before the dismissal takes effect;
2. where 10 employees at one establishment are to be dismissed, at least 30 days before dismissal takes effect.

Where the employer fails to consult, the union may take the case before an industrial tribunal. The employer may be able to avoid liability where he can show that there were special circumstances which made the appropriate consultation impossible. It has been held, however, in *Clarks of Hove v Bakers Union* [1979] 1 All ER 152, that insolvency per se is not a special circumstance.

Where the tribunal finds that the employer has contravened the consultation regulations, it may order that the employer pays a protective award to compensate the employees. This will represent one week's pay for each week of the award. The award should be 'just and equitable' and should not exceed 90 days (where one hundred employees have been dismissed) or 30 days (where 10 or more dismissals have occurred).

(iv) *Unfair dismissal.* The EPA provides that where an employee has been continually employed for two years, he has the right not to be unfairly dismissed. Since (straightforward) redundancy would not normally constitute unfair dismissal, it would be unusual for claims for unfair dismissal to arise simply by virtue of the insolvency of the employer. In order for a redundant employee to have been dismissed unfairly, he must show that he was unfairly selected for dismissal or that the manner of his dismissal was unfair.

Any award in respect of unfair dismissal is made in two parts:

1. Basic award – this is a statutory award based on length of service, age and pay, and is calculated as per a redundancy payment. The award will be reduced by any actual redundancy payment made, thus normally cancelling the basic award completely.

2   Compensatory award – this should be commensurate with any loss suffered. The employee is under a duty to mitigate the loss.

Employees' preferential claims

Under IA 1986 Sch 6, employees may rank as PREFERENTIAL CREDITORS for certain amounts owed to them by an insolvent employer. Preferential debts must be assessed to the 'relevant date' (see PREFERENTIAL CREDITORS). These debts include the following:
1   Amounts owed in respect of accrued holiday entitlement which had not been taken or paid at the 'relevant date'. This claim has no monetary or time restrictions.
2   Amounts owed relating to remuneration in respect of the four months prior to the 'relevant date', up to a monetary limit (currently £800). This includes employees' contributions which have not been paid into an occupational pension scheme.

All other employees' claims are treated as unsecured.

Only employees of a company are entitled to make the preferential claims outlined above and problems frequently arise as to whether certain persons are employees (and thus preferential) or independent contractors (and non-preferential).

It should be noted that preferential debts include subrogated claims from the Department of Employment in respect of guaranteed payments (see below).

Guaranteed payments to employees

The EPA provides for certain payments out of government funds ('the Redundancy Fund') in cases where an employee loses his job following his employer's insolvency. Payment is administered by the Department of Employment which will then take over any claim which the employee had against the employer in respect of payments made. Any subrogated claim will follow the employee's original right to claim preferentially or rank unsecured.

The state guaranteed payments are as follows:
1   Arrears of pay up to a maximum of eight weeks and subject to the monetary limit (currently £205 per week).
2   Accrued holiday pay up to a maximum of six weeks and subject to the monetary limit (currently £205 per week).
3   Payments in lieu of notice, based upon the statutory notice periods contained within the EPA, up to the monetary limit (currently £205 per week).
4   Payments in respect of an unpaid basic award by an industrial tribunal for unfair dismissal.

It should be noted that the scheme covers payments until the later of the commencement of winding-up and the termination of employment. In practice the office holder will liaise between the employees and the Department of Employment, with payments made to the office holder who will then pass them over to the employees. Many insolvency practitioners have a specialist department to deal with EPA claims.

Transfer of Undertakings (Protection of Employment) Regulations 1981 ('TUPER')

The Transfer of Undertakings (Protection of Employment) Regulations were introduced in 1981 in consequence of an EC directive designed to protect the rights of employees in transfers of undertakings. The regulations apply to all companies but have particular relevance as regards insolvency where a receiver or administrator sells a business as a going concern.

Prior to TUPER the sale of a business would have resulted in the termination of all employment contracts. The employees would have received new contracts but would have broken their continuity of service, thus restricting their rights if they were made redundant subsequently. In certain instances this gave rise to the paradox of employees effectively being made redundant, receiving their full statutory entitlement and then continuing uninterrupted doing the same job but for a different employer.

In order to prevent this, TUPER provides that, for a relevant transfer, all rights and obligations of the employment contract are automatically transferred. There is no effective termination of employment contracts, with employees able to treat their employment as having been continuous. (A relevant transfer is defined as a transfer of an undertaking situated within the UK.) TUPER states that the regulation applies only to persons employed by the transferor immediately before the transfer.

The regulations also provide that where an employee who is dismissed either before or after the transfer and the principal reason for the dismissal is the transfer, the dismissal is to be treated as an unfair dismissal for the purpose of the EPA. The dismissal will not be unfair however if made for 'an economic, technical or organisational reason'.

TUPER has introduced a great deal of uncertainty into the sale by insolvency practitioners of businesses as going concerns. Purchasers are clearly reluctant to accept liability for the claims of employees who are not required as part of the sale of the business. One method of attempting to avoid liability was to persuade the receiver to make redundancies a few hours before the transfer of the business so that the employees were not employed 'immediately before' the transfer. This route has, however, been blocked by the decision of the House of Lords in *Litster v Forth Dry Dock & Engineering Co Ltd* [1989] IRLR 161.

The case involved 12 former employees of Forth Dry Dock who were dismissed by the receiver one hour prior to the sale of the business as a going concern. The purchaser then employed new workers at lower wages. It was held that the employees had been unfairly dismissed under TUPER because the transfer was the reason for their dismissal. Furthermore, it was held that 'immediately before' should include those who would have been so employed had they not been unfairly dismissed. The purchaser was therefore liable for the employees' claims.

Had it been shown, however, that the dismissal had been for an 'economic, technical or organisational reason' the dismissal would not have been unfair and the purchaser not liable. The length of time between the dismissal and the transfer is not relevant. In *Secretary of State for Employment v Spence* [1986] IRLR 248, the Court of Appeal held that employees who were dismissed by the receiver for economic reasons just three hours prior to the sale of the business were not employed 'immediately before' the transfer. It has been successfully argued subsequently that where dismissal by a receiver was at the request of a purchaser who would not have bought the business had the dismissal not been made, then the dismissals were for 'economic, technical or organisational' reasons. However this decision, by an industrial tribunal in the case, *Re DMG (Realisations) Ltd* (1990) – unreported, is contrary to the Litster judgment and until tested in the courts cannot be safely relied upon as a precedent.

TUPER and hiving-down

The regulations also contain specific provisions relating to the use of hiving-down by receivers and administrators (see HIVE DOWN). Where a business and assets have been hived down to a subsidiary, the transfer of employees' contracts to the subsidiary is deemed not to have occurred until the sale of the subsidiary to the ultimate purchaser.

Effect of insolvency on contracts of employment

The effect of the insolvency of an employer upon the contract of employment of the employees is governed by case law for most types of insolvency. The current situation regarding each type is as follows:

(a) Administrative receivership *Zwangsverwaltung*

The appointment of an administrative receiver does not, of itself, automatically terminate the contract of employment *Griffiths v Secretary of State* [1974] QB 468. Certain actions of the administrative receiver may however have the effect of so doing. These might include closing the business or changing the nature of employment so that it is incompatible with the old contract. Alternatively a contract might be deemed terminated where the employment of a particular employee is clearly inconsistent with the role of the administrative receiver – this might include a managing director who operated independently of board control.

Section 44 is a source of potential trouble for administrative receivers who could be deemed to have personally adopted employees contracts after a period of 14 days. It is therefore usual to find administrative receivers dismissing all unrequired staff within the first 14 days following appointment and writing to all remaining staff within the same time-scale advising that they will not be adopting their contracts personally but will attempt to procure that the company is placed in funds to continue their employment for as long as may be required.

(b) Administration

The grant of an administration order will have no automatic effect on the contract of employment. An administrator is given the power to employ and dismiss employees in IA 1986 Sch 1 and, since he is deemed (IA 1986 s14) to be acting as agent of the company, it follows that there is no automatic termination. The administrator's actions after appointment, like those of an administrative receiver, may subsequently terminate employees' contracts – cf see *(a)* above.

(c) Creditors' voluntary liquidation

Case law has produced the general rule that voluntary winding-up does not in itself terminate contracts of employment. In practice liquidators seldom continue the employment of the directors or employees with the effect that all contracts of employment will be terminated on liquidation.

(d) Compulsory liquidation

It has been held that a winding-up order serves to terminate employees' contracts of employment. (*Re Oriental Bank Corpn* (1884) 28 ChD 634). Employees are therefore effectively dismissed as of the date of the order. This clearly has implications for an administrative receiver appointed prior to the winding-up order. If the administrative receiver requires that the employees continue to work for the company after winding-up, he will have to draw up new contracts of employment upon which he may be personally liable.

3.32 ETHICS AND PROFESSIONAL CONDUCT OF INSOLVENCY PRACTITIONERS

Despite isolated instances of bad publicity, insolvency practitioners are subject to stringent ethical guidelines with respect to their professional conduct and business dealings. Not only must they adhere as members to guidelines issued by their authorising body (eg ICAEW, Law Society, etc) but they must also comply with specific provisions concerning their conduct as insolvency practitioners.

Obtaining insolvency work

Insolvency practitioners are not allowed to offer valuable consideration or commission for the introduction of appointments.

It is also an offence under s164 for an insolvency practitioner to offer a member or creditor of a company any valuable consideration with a view to securing nomination as liquidator.

The guidelines also prohibit harassment of creditors soliciting when for proxies.

Professional independence

The insolvency practitioner must consider carefully the implications of accepting an appointment in respect of any company or individual, and should satisfy himself that his objectivity will not be compromised by, for example, a conflict of interest.

In order to ensure his independence, the guidelines state that an insolvency practitioner should not accept an appointment where he has had a material professional relationship with the company/individual. This applies to all appointments except a liquidator in a solvent liquidation.

A material professional relationship arises where a principal or an employee of a practice has carried out during the previous three years, material professional work for the company or individual. Material professional work would include:

1. where a practice or person has carried out or had been appointed to carry out, audit work for the company/individual;
2. where a practice or person has carried out one or more assignments, whether of a continuing nature or not, of such overall significance that a member's objectivity could be impaired.

It should be noted that prior to 1 July 1993, the guidelines spoke of a 'continuing professional relationship' rather than a 'material professional relationship'. The change was made because it was felt that significant 'one-off' work could still impair objectivity but would not constitute a continuing relationship.

There is one area which from time to time raises criticism both within and outside of the insolvency profession. The guidelines state that a material professional relationship will not normally arise where the relationship is one which springs from the appointment of a practice by a creditor of the company/individual to investigate, monitor or advise on the affairs of the company/individual. This enables, for example, a bank to request a firm of accountants to investigate the affairs of a company and to appoint subsequently that firm as administrative receiver of the company. Notwithstanding, there are from time to time suggestions that accountants instructed by banks to report on a company's viability should not subsequently be allowed to accept an appointment as administrative receiver upon the basis of their own recommendation.

3.33 EXTORTIONATE CREDIT TRANSACTIONS

IA 1986 contains provisions whereby a liquidator or administrator of a company, or the trustee in bankruptcy of an individual, may apply to court to have set aside any extortionate credit transaction entered into prior to insolvency.

Extortionate credit transactions are applicable both to companies (s244) and individuals (s343). The office holder (ie the administrator, liquidator or trustee) may apply to the court where he believes that an extortionate credit transaction was entered into within the three years ending with the onset of insolvency.

A credit transaction is deemed to be extortionate if, having regard for the risk accepted by the person providing the credit, the terms either require extortionate payments to be made in respect of the provision of the credit or otherwise grossly contravene the ordinary principles of fair trading. Where the office holder applies to court under this section, there is a refutable presumption that the transaction is extortionate.

The court may make any order it thinks fit, including setting aside any security and setting aside or varying the rate of interest charged.

3.34 FIXED AND FLOATING CHARGES

Fixed and floating charges play important roles within the framework of insolvency legislation.

For example, most lenders will rely upon a fixed charge as their principal security, whereas a floating charge, while of secondary importance in security terms, can be of great importance in its own right in that it allows the lender to appoint an ADMINISTRATIVE RECEIVER (whereas under a fixed charge, a LAW OF PROPERTY ACT RECEIVER only may be appointed).

Fixed charges

A fixed charge prevents the borrower from dealing with the assets over which the security is granted and will usually be taken over assets which are of a permanent nature and not frequently traded. It is common to find lenders taking fixed charges over:

- freehold and leasehold property;
- fixed plant and machinery (in practice probably restricted to a central heating system or similar equipment which effectively becomes a part of the building);
- intellectual property rights;
- book debts (but see below);
- goodwill; and
- uncalled share capital.

The position with regard to fixed charges on book debts merits further consideration, for in essence we are talking about *future* book debts where common sense might suggest that a floating charge would be more appropriate. It was principally the efforts by banks to create additional security to cover lendings which led in the 1970s to fixed charges being taken over future book debts. Although the decision in *Siebe Gorman & Co Ltd v Barclays Bank Ltd* [1979] 2 Lloyd's Rep 142 confirmed the ability of banks to take fixed charges on book debts, subsequent cases, eg the *Re New Bullas Trading Ltd* [1993] BCC 251 make it clear that the chargee must take and actually exercise control over the proceeds of those debts (eg by ensuring that they are collected through an account held by the bank) if the charge is to be treated as fixed as opposed to floating.

General practitioners advising non-banking clients upon the taking of charges over book debts in order effectively to create a fixed charge should always ensure that specialist legal advice is sought to minimise the risk of a future liquidator or administrator successfully proving the charge to be in substance a floating security.

Floating charges

Under a floating charge the company may continue to use the assets caught by the charge in the normal course of business until such time as the charge crystallises.

The crystallisation of floating charges constitutes an area of technical debate in its own right. For the general practitioner's understanding there would appear to be a consensus that a floating charge crystallises upon one of the following events taking place:
- when a receiver is appointed under a floating charge;
- when the company ceases carrying on business;
- on the company going into liquidation;
- by agreement between the parties on the occurence of a specified event (eg the application for an administration order).

Floating charges will normally be taken over:
- stocks;
- work in progress;
- fixtures and fittings;
- motor vehicles (not on lease or hire-purchase); and
- (non-fixed) plant and machinery.

See also AVOIDANCE OF CERTAIN FLOATING CHARGES.

3.35   FRAUDULENT TRADING

For a detailed consideration of this subject see Part I, **1.172**.

3.36   GOING CONCERN

An expression used by insolvency practitioners to define a basis of valuing a business or its assets on the premise that the business continues to trade (see also Part I, **1.18**).

3.37   GUARANTOR – acting as

Every general practitioner will understand both the definition of a guarantee and the implications of acting as a guarantor.

There are however two aspects not always fully understood which merit special consideration. First, where a client acts as a 'joint and several' guarantor, in the event of a default the lender may pursue any one or more of the guarantors for the entirety of the debt. There is nothing which says they must seek payment equally or at all from any of the other guarantors and neither can the chosen 'victim' seek to bring in his fellow guarantors at that stage in an attempt to avoid payment of the full amount. Once he has paid in full under the guarantee he may well have a right of contribution against his fellow guarantors; the point being he will first of all have to pay off the entirety of the amount outstanding.

A second problem can be the possible taxation implications where an asset held personally is offered as security to a lender and both the amount advanced and value of the security have increased substantially over the years. Where this occurs in such manner that a disposal of the asset creates a chargeable gain (assessed upon the guarantor as beneficial owner) but the entirety of the proceeds of sale are required to discharge the guarantee liability, the guarantor will be left to find the tax payable, whether or not he has the funds available.

In advising clients contemplating giving joint and several guarantees the general practitioner should seek, wherever possible, to limit their guarantee to a fixed amount, while recognising that banks will normally insist on a joint and several liability. Where the guarantee is to be supported by collateral which could give rise to a future assessable gain as contemplated above, the general practitioner should seek to ensure that the guarantee is restricted to any *net* realisation from a sale of the asset, after providing for any capital gains tax arising upon the disposal.

3.38 HIVE-DOWN

A hive-down is a technique whereby the valuable assets, profitable contracts and key employees of a company in receivership or administration ('the transferor company') are transferred to a newly formed subsidiary ('Newco'). The consideration for the transfer will usually be in the form of an unsecured loan, the amount of which will be determined at a later date.

There are a number of reasons for a receiver or administrator to contemplate hiving-down

In order to facilitate a continuation of trade

Where it is intended that trade should continue, hiving-down may be beneficial in that Newco will not be in administration or receivership and will therefore be able to operate without many of the problems which surround an insolvent company.

Hiving-down can be particularly useful where the company is also in liquidation as the receiver will not be deemed to act as agent of Newco thereby enabling trade to continue without the receiver assuming a personal liability.

Sale of business

There could be advantages where a receiver or administrator intends to sell the business as a going concern. *arbeitendes Unternehmen*
1   it might be possible to transfer tax losses from the transferor company to Newco, although rule changes in the TA 1988 made this much more difficult to accomplish.
2   since unprofitable contracts will remain with the transferor company, it should be possible for the prospective purchaser to determine precisely the profitability of Newco. Additionally the purchaser will be able to buy a going concern company without the liabilities of the old company.

Despite these reasons for hiving-down, receivers and administrators tend to make less use of the device than in the past due mainly to the difficulties involved in transferring tax losses. In addition the Transfer of Undertakings regulations mean that a purchaser is likely to assume the employment liabilities in respect of employees taken on and could even assume liabilities for those not transferred (see EMPLOYEES IN INSOLVENCY: TRANSFER OF UNDERTAKINGS (PROTECTION OF EMPLOYMENT) REGULATIONS 1981).

Under TA 1988 s343, Newco is able to use the unrelieved tax losses of the transferor company to offset against its own future profits of the same trade. Newco may also assume any benefits of unrelieved capital allowances subject to the requirements of the section which include a provision that the trade has not been discontinued. Where the transferor company has ceased to trade but Newco has continued the business it is deemed that trade has not been discontinued where at least three-quarters of the shares of the two companies have been in common ownership at some time within one year before the hive-down and at any time within two years after. In addition the transfer must have been made at a time where a group relationship existed between the two companies. It is the beneficial ownership of the shares which is important and the losses may not be transferred to Newco when the transferor is in liquidation since beneficial ownership will have been lost: *IRC v Olive Mill Ltd* [1963] 1 WLR 712. Beneficial ownership is also deemed to have been lost when there is already a binding contract for the sale of Newco *before* hive-down: *Wood Preservation v Prior* [1969] 1 WLR 1077.

As already indicated, the ability of a purchaser of a hived-down business to make use of the unrelieved losses had been curtailed by TA 1988. Section 768 limits the use of the losses where, within a period of three years, there has been both a change in the ownership of the company and a major change in the nature or conduct of its trade or where after a change in ownership the activities of the company have become small or negligible prior to any revival of trade.

It is s343(4) however which 'bites' even when all other criteria are satisfied. In simple terms the legislation is based on the principle that the available losses in the transferor company are reduced to the extent that those losses have been borne, not by the company, but by its creditors.

3.39 INDIVIDUAL VOLUNTARY ARRANGEMENT (IVA)

An overview of the IVA procedure and the role of the general practitioner is contained in Part 2, **2.10**.

For the general practitioner requiring a more detailed analysis of procedures involved in setting up an IVA, the various stages referenced to IA 1986 and IR 1986, are summarised below.

Application for interim order

The first stage is for the debtor to obtain an INTERIM ORDER under s253. Prior to the application the consent of an INSOLVENCY PRACTITIONER to act as nominee must be obtained.

An interim order will initially be granted for 14 days where the court is satisfied that the debtor intends to make a proposal to his creditors for a voluntary arrangement. The purpose of the order is to provide a breathing space during which to prepare a proposal to put to creditors. While the interim order is in force:

1   no bankruptcy petition may be presented or proceeded with against the debtor; and
2   no other proceedings, executions etc. may be commenced or continued with against the debtor except with the leave of the court (s252).

The application must be accompanied by an affidavit (r 5.5)

The proposal

The proposal should give a brief explanation as to why a voluntary arrangement is desirable and give reasons why the creditors may be expected to accept the arrangement. It should also give full details of the financial position of the debtor together with other matters as required by r 5.3. The proposal will also give details of how much the creditors are expected to receive and the timing of the arrangement.

Nominee's report to the court (s256)

The nominee must submit a report to the court stating whether, in his opinion, a meeting of creditors should be convened to consider the debtor's proposal. He should also provide a statement of affairs for the debtor as per r 5.8. This report should be presented before the end of the interim order, although the nominee may apply to court for an extension.

Meeting of creditors

A meeting must be summoned by the nominee to be held not less than 14 days and no more than 28 days from the date his report is filed in court, giving 14 days' notice of the meeting to all known creditors (r 5.13). There should be sent with the notice:
1   a copy of the debtor's proposal;
2   a copy of the statement of affairs;
3   the nominee's comments on the proposal.
    The nominee will normally act as chairman at the meeting

Voting at the creditors' meeting

Every creditor who was given notice of the meeting may vote, either in person or by proxy (r 5.17). The requisite majority for any resolution to accept a proposal or modification thereof is one in excess of 75% in *value* of the creditors *present* (in person or by proxy) at the meeting.

If any other resolution is proposed at the meeting the percentage is reduced from 75% to 50%. Where the majority includes votes cast by associates of the debtor, the resolution will not be passed if more than 50% of those voting against are unconnected with the debtor.

Effect of approval (s260)

Where approval has been given to the debtor's proposal (with or without modifications), the scheme will bind every creditor who had notice of and was entitled to vote at the meeting, regardless of whether he was actually present or represented. No modification may be approved until agreed by the debtor. Note that the scheme does *not* bind creditors who were not given notice of the meeting

Challenge of creditors' meeting decision (s269)

An application may be made to court by the debtor or a creditor to challenge an IVA on one or both of the following grounds:
1   that the IVA unfairly prejudices the interests of a creditor or the debtor; or
2   that there was some material irregularity at or in relation to the meeting

Completion of voluntary arrangement (r 5.29)

When the voluntary arrangement is complete, the supervisor must prepare a report summarising all receipts and payments made by him in respect of the arrangement and explaining any difference between the expected and actual outcome. This report should be sent to the debtor, the Secretary of State and the creditors.

Default in connection with voluntary arrangement (ss264, 276)

The supervisor of the arrangement or any creditor bound by it may present a bankruptcy petition to the court where:
1. the debtor has failed to comply with his obligations under the IVA; or
2. the debtor had supplied false or misleading information in obtaining the approval of the creditors; or
3. the debtor failed to do all such things as reasonably required by the supervisor.

The court may appoint the supervisor as trustee in bankruptcy.

3.40 INSOLVENCY ACT 1986

Insolvency law and practice encompasses many statutes and statutory instruments. Central however to insolvency legislation is the IA 1986 which emerged as the primary legislation following the CORK REPORT.

3.41 INSOLVENCY PRACTITIONER

One of the most important changes introduced by the IA 1986 was the requirement that all practitioners of insolvency must be properly qualified. This was designed both to protect society from the rogue liquidator and to ensure that insolvency procedures were carried out with a high level of skill and competence.

Section 388 defines an insolvency practitioner as someone who acts:
1. as liquidator, administrator, administrative receiver or supervisor of a voluntary arrangement in respect of a company;
2. a trustee in bankruptcy, interim receiver, trustee under a deed of arrangement or supervisor of a voluntary arrangement in respect of an individual.

Anyone who acts as an insolvency practitioner who is not qualified to do so commits a criminal offence and is liable to imprisonment, a fine or both (s389).

The following persons are disqualified from acting as insolvency practitioners (s390):
1. a body corporate;
2. an undischarged bankrupt;
3. a person subject to a disqualification under CDDA 1986;
4. a mental patient within the meaning of the Mental Health Act 1983.

There are two routes via which an individual may obtain authorisation to act as an insolvency practitioner:
1. by membership of a recognised professional body and by achieving the requirements in respect of experience and insolvency qualifications set down by the body. At present, the following bodies are recognised:
   - Institute of Chartered Accountants in England and Wales,
   - Chartered Association of Certified Accountants,
   - Institute of Chartered Accountants in Ireland,
   - Institute of Chartered Accountants in Scotland,
   - Insolvency Practitioners Association,
   - The Law Society,
   - The Law Society of Scotland;
2. by authorisation from the Secretary of State. The Secretary of State must be satisfied that the person is a fit and proper person to act as an insolvency practitioner and that he possesses the required qualifications and practical experience.

Note that since March 1991, the requirements as regards qualifications in either case may be demonstrated only by passing an examination set by the Joint Insolvency Examination Board (JIEB).

Security

Before an insolvency practitioner is qualified to act in relation to a particular office, he is required to give security for his appointment. This is designed to protect creditors from losses incurred through a default by the practitioner.

1. prior to accepting an appointment the insolvency practitioner must possess security for the proper performance of his functions under which a surety undertakes to be jointly and severally liable for the proper performance by the practitioner of his duties in a general penalty sum of £250,000;
2. the insolvency practitioner must submit a monthly declaration of the appointments accepted by him to be covered under his bond. The value of this bond will depend upon the value of the company's assets, subject to certain restrictions in an administrative receivership for sums payable to secured creditors.

3.42 INSOLVENCY RULES 1986

The Rules (as amended) which set out the detailed procedures to the statutes within the INSOLVENCY ACT 1986.

3.43 INSOLVENT LIQUIDATION

Section 214 describes an insolvent liquidation (for the purposes of determining wrongful trading) as one in which the company's assets are insufficient for the payment of its debts and other liabilities and the expenses of winding up.

For a company to be wound up as a MEMBERS' VOLUNTARY LIQUIDATION the directors have to swear a declaration that in their opinion the company will be able to pay its debts in full, together with interest 'at the official rate' (see INTEREST ON DEBTS IN A WINDING-UP) 'within such period, not exceeding 12 months from the commencement of the winding up' (s89). Thus, by virtue of this section, although a company may be insolvent at the time of passing the resolution to wind up, on the basis that it is unable to meet its debts as and when they fall due, it is deemed to be solvent for the purpose of the winding-up provided it can meet the required criteria.

So far as the general practitioner is concerned any other liquidation must be regarded as an insolvent liquidation if, not being a members' voluntary liquidation, its assets are insufficient to pay its debts and other liabilities (where appropriate to include statutory interest) including the costs of winding-up.

3.44 INSOLVENT PARTNERSHIPS ORDER 1986

This is the statutory instrument by which the provisions of the IA 1986 are modified in order to be applicable to insolvent partnerships. (To be replaced by new legislation to be introduced in 1994. Please refer to **2.48**.)

3.45 INTERIM ORDER

An interim order may be granted by the court to an individual who intends to propose an individual voluntary arrangement to his creditors. The interim order provides a 'breathing space' during which the debtor can work on his proposal, since bankruptcy and other proceedings are precluded while the order is in force (see **2.11** for further details).

3.46 INTERIM RECEIVER

The expression 'interim receiver' is to be found within s286 as follows:

> The court may, if it is shown to be necessary for the protection of the debtor's property, at any time after the presentation of a bankruptcy petition and before making a bankruptcy order, appoint the official receiver to be interim receiver of the debtor's property.

The interim receiver fulfils the same role in a personal insolvency as a PROVISIONAL LIQUIDATOR in a corporate insolvency, and may be appointed following an application by the debtor, a creditor or by the insolvency practitioner appointed under s273 in respect of a debtor presenting his own petition.

The powers of the interim receiver are determined by the court but will usually extend only to taking possession of the debtor's property. The debtor must co-operate fully in providing an inventory of his property and assisting the interim receiver in carrying out his functions.

During the period of interim receivership, the debtor's assets enjoy the same protection as if a bankruptcy order had been made.

3,47 INTEREST ON DEBTS IN A WINDING-UP

Advice of the general practitioner

This is an area which, so far as most practitioners and their clients are concerned, is shrouded in mystery and yet, properly advised there are few areas where (with apologies to Josh Billings) the adage 'Twice blest is he whose cause is just; thrice blest he who gets his blow in – fust' can place an unsecured creditor in a position of advantage when dividends become available on unsecured claims.

General practitioners should consider advising all their clients to follow a set procedure when debts become overdue so that they might be in a position to add interest to the principal debt in the event of an ensuing insolvency. In simple terms, interest is not allowed to accrue *after* the date of liquidation, unless and until all debts have been paid in full, when statutory interest will apply to all debts in respect of the period after liquidation before any surplus is available for shareholders. On the other hand, interest *can* accrue on debts overdue as at the date of liquidation, providing the necessary criteria are satisfied.

The position may be summarised as follows:

(a) Pre-liquidation interest

Where a debt proved in the liquidation bears interest at a previously agreed specified rate, that interest is provable as part of the debt up to the date on which the winding-up order is made (the date of liquidation). It should be borne in mind however that if the interest rate is extortionate, the liquidator may be able to obtain a court order setting it aside under IA 1986 s244 (Extortionate Credit Transactions).

In cases where interest had not been reserved or agreed, pre-liquidation interest may be claimed in two circumstances:

1 if the debt is due by virtue of a written instrument and payable at a certain time, interest may be claimed for the period from that time to the date when the company went into liquidation (r 4.93(3));
2 if the debt is due otherwise, interest may only be claimed if, before that date a demand for payment of the debt was made in writing by or on behalf of the creditor, and notice given that interest would be payable from the date of the demand to the date of payment (r 4.93(4)). Again, interest may only be proved in respect of the period up to the date of liquidation.

The rate of interest to be claimed under r 4.93(3)(4) is the 'official rate' as at the date of the liquidation, except where under r 4.93(4) a lower rate has been specified in the notice. The official rate is as specified in s17 of the Judgments Act 1838 — currently 8%. The Lord Chancellors Department has the power by statutory instrument to alter this rate in line, broadly, with prevailing market conditions.

The general practitioner should note that a sales invoice does *not* constitute a written instrument under r 4.93(3). Interest will therefore be payable on such a debt only if the creditor has made a formal demand for payment, stating that interest will be charged. The creditor may then prove for interest from the date of the formal demand to the date of liquidation.

(b) Post-liquidation interest (also called Statutory interest)

Under IA 1986 s189 interest may be paid on all debts in respect of the period after the date of liquidation, but only when all creditors' claims have been paid in full. Any surplus of funds after the payment of all liquidation expenses and creditors' claims will be applied to the payment of post liquidation interest, with all debts ranking equally for interest purposes, irrespective of whether the debt was preferential or unsecured.

The interest rate payable is the greater of:
1 the defined rate specified in Judgments Act 1838 s17; and
2 the rate applicable to the debt apart from the winding-up (ie as per pre-liquidation interest).

Post liquidation interest is not provable – it is paid statutorily.

(c) Bankruptcy

The same provisions apply to interest on a bankruptcy debt under IA 1986 s328 and r 6.113. The only significant difference is that in a bankruptcy post bankruptcy interest is paid after all debts except debts to the bankrupt's spouse, which are paid after statutory interest has been paid.

3.48 LAW OF PROPERTY ACT (1925)

See RECEIVERSHIP UNDER THE LAW OF PROPERTY ACT 1925

3.49 LIENS – enforceability against insolvency office-holder

The general practitioner can be forgiven for any confusion experienced in trying to decide whether or not he holds a lien for unpaid fees over a company's books and records following formal insolvency.

The section with which he needs to concern himself is s246 which is entitled 'Unenforceability of liens on books, etc.' and which states:

(1) This section applies in the case of a company where –
  (a) an administration order is made in relation to the company, or
  (b) the company goes into liquidation, or
  (c) a provisional liquidator is appointed;

and the 'office-holder' means the administrator, the liquidator or the provisional liquidator, as the case may be.

(2) Subject as follows, a lien or other right to retain possession of any of the books, papers or other records of the company is unenforceable to the extent that its enforcement would deny possession of any books, papers or other records to the office-holder.

(3) This does not apply to a lien on documents which give a title to property and are held as such, ie by way of lien *Re SEIL Trade Finance Ltd* [1992] BCC 538.

Thus, at this stage we can establish that whereas a solicitor could for example claim a lien over the title deeds to a company's freehold property where he was acting in the purchase or sale, general practitioners and solicitors may not withhold a company's books etc from a liquidator or administrator by virtue of claiming to have a lien over them for unpaid fees. Note that this section applies only to 'books, papers and other records'. Other categories of goods are not caught by this section, although in the case of an administration it will be necessary to seek the leave of the court to enforce the lien (*Re Paramount Airways Ltd* [1990] BCC 130).

The above section deals effectively with the position so far as an administrator or liquidator is concerned, but what about the position of an administrative receiver or supervisor under a company voluntary arrangement? The good news from the general practitioner's point of view is that there are no provisions which would assist in setting aside a claim to a lien in either an administrative receivership or a Company Voluntary Arrangement. General practitioners should however 'watch out' for insolvency practitioners requesting books and other records of the company to be surrendered to them on the grounds that any lien is unenforceable against them. If challenged – and they seldom are – they would doubtless refer the general practitioner to s234, which, whilst making no direct reference to liens, states:

(1) This section applies in the case of a company where –
  (a) an administration order is made in relation to the company, or
  (b) an administrative receiver is appointed, or
  (c) the company goes into liquidation, or
  (d) a provisional liquidator is appointed;

and 'the office-holder' means the administrator, the administrative receiver, the liquidator or the provisional liquidator, as the case may be.

(2) Where any person has in his possession or control any property, books, papers or records to which the company appears to be entitled, the court may require that person forthwith (or within such period as the court may direct) to pay, deliver, convey, surrender or transfer the property, books, paper or records to the office holder.

If the general practitioner was aware of the existence and relevance of s246 and compared it with the above section he would realise that he was being (perhaps unintentionally) misled for it seems clear that s234 was never intended as a 'lien defeater' and that any order to hand over the records would be accompanied by an order that the general practitioner's account be paid.

In practice, the majority of general practitioners seem to accept the inevitability of having lost their lien over a company's 'books, papers and records' following an insolvency appointment. The simple truth is that this only applies in either a liquidation or administration. Under any other circumstances the general practitioner remains in a strong position to negotiate his fees with an office holder against company documents held.

3.50 LIQUIDATION

When a company has reached the end of its useful life then unless it has neither assets nor liabilities (and in which event the directors may apply to the registrar of companies for the company to be struck off) its legal existence must be ended by liquidation or winding-up, whereby its assets are disposed of and the proceeds distributed to its members and creditors. DISSOLUTION will follow liquidation and will finally terminate its existence.

Liquidation may take the form of a
- MEMBERS' VOLUNTARY LIQUIDATION;
- CREDITORS' VOLUNTARY LIQUIDATION;
- COMPULSORY LIQUIDATION.

For a company to proceed to members' voluntary liquidation it is necessary for the members to swear a STATUTORY DECLARATION OF SOLVENCY prior to passing the resolution to wind up (see MEMBERS' VOLUNTARY LIQUIDATION).

3.51 LIQUIDATION COMMITTEE

See CREDITORS' COMMITTEE at **3.21**.

3.52 LIQUIDATOR

A liquidator is an INSOLVENCY PRACTITIONER appointed to wind up a company (see WINDING-UP ORDER and WINDING-UP RESOLUTION).

Appointment

The detailed provisions relating to the appointment of liquidators are covered under the headings COMPULSORY LIQUIDATION, CREDITORS' VOLUNTARY LIQUIDATION and MEMBERS' VOLUNTARY LIQUIDATION.

It should be noted that it is an offence for any person to give or offer to give any member or creditor of a company any valuable consideration with a view to securing his own appointment or nomination as liquidator of the company (IA 1986 s164). If he does so he is not only liable to a fine but the court may disallow his remuneration as liquidator.

Functions

The liquidator performs two distinct functions:
1. to get in, realise and distribute the assets of the company in accordance with IA 1986; and
2. to perform such investigations as may be necessary into the promotion, formation and management of the company. These investigations may lead to criminal proceedings in respect of offences against IA 1986 or Companies Acts and also to actions to recover funds in respect of (inter alia) PREFERENCES AND TRANSFERS AT AN UNDERVALUE.

Under IA 1986 s218 the liquidator is obliged to make a report to the official receiver (in a compulsory liquidation) or the Director of Public Prosecutions (in a voluntary liquidation) where it appears to him that any past or present officer of the company, or any member has been guilty of an offence in relation to the company.

(See also a liquidator's duty to report under CDDA 1986).

Powers

The liquidator is given wide ranging powers under the IA 1986 in order that he may be able to effectively perform his duties. These powers are contained in IA 1986 ss166–69 and Sch 4.

It should be noted that some powers require the sanction of the creditors' committee or the court before they may be exercised.

Resignation and Removal

In certain circumstances, a liquidator may resign his office by giving notice of his resignation to the Registrar of Companies (in a voluntary liquidation) or to the court (in a compulsory liquidation).

The permitted circumstances are as follows:
1. ill health;
2. intention to cease in practice as an insolvency practitioner;
3. there is some conflict of interest or change of personal circumstances which precludes or makes impracticable the further discharge by him of the duties of liquidator; or
4. where two or more persons are acting as liquidator jointly, any one of them may resign where, in the opinion of the other(s), it is no longer expedient that there should continue to be the present number of liquidators.

A liquidator may be removed by an order of the court or by a general meeting of the company's creditors summoned specifically for that purpose in accordance with the rules (ie IR 1986 rr 4.113–4.122).

The relevant legislation is contained in s 172 (COMPULSORY LIQUIDATION) and ss108 and 171 (MEMBERS' or CREDITORS' VOLUNTARY LIQUIDATION).

Remuneration

The method of determining the remuneration of the liquidator depends upon the nature of the winding-up.

(a) Official Receiver (OR) as liquidator

When the OR is acting as liquidator, his remuneration is calculated as a percentage on realisations (excluding sums paid to secured creditors out of their securities) together with a percentage of distributions.

Under the Insolvency Regulations 1986, the OR's scale is as follows:

	Realisation Scale (%)	Distribution Scale (%)
First £5,000 or part thereof	20	10
Next £5,000 or part thereof	15	7.5
Next £90,000 or part thereof	10	5
All further sums	5	2.5

(b) Liquidator not Official Receiver

(i) Compulsory and creditors' voluntary winding-up. Under r 4.127, a liquidator is entitled to receive remuneration for his services which shall be fixed either:
1. as a percentage of the value of assets realised or distributed; or
2. by reference to the time properly given by the insolvency practitioner (as liquidator) and his staff in attending to matters arising in the winding-up.

It is for the LIQUIDATION COMMITTEE (if there is one) to determine which method is to be used although there are provisions in the IR 1986 giving the court a residual discretion to fix a liquidator's fees where there is no committee, the committee fails to fix the remuneration or the liquidator is unhappy with the fees awarded to him.

(ii) Members' voluntary winding-up. The remuneration of the liquidator is determined by the company in a general meeting. As with a compulsory or creditors' voluntary winding-up, the remuneration will be based either on a percentage or a time basis.

3.53 MALPRACTICE (BEFORE AND DURING LIQUIDATION)

Chapter X Pt IV of IA 1986 (ss206–219) contains provisions for the penalisation of company directors and officers in respect of actions before or during the liquidation.
1. Sections 210–11 provide for penalties or fines and/or imprisonment for those guilty of offences of fraud, deception etc.
2. Section 212 provides for compensation to be paid to a company in the event of an officer, liquidator, administrator or administrative receiver having retained or misapplied property of the company or been guilty of any misfeasance or breach of any fiduciary or other duty in relation to the company.
3. Sections 213–15 deal with FRAUDULENT and WRONGFUL TRADING.
4. Sections 216 and 217 contain provisions in respect of the re-use of company names where the company has gone into insolvent liquidation, together with personal liability of directors, managers, etc for debts where the provisions have been contravened.

3.54 'MAREVA' INJUNCTION

So called following the decision in *Mareva Cia Neviera SA v International Bulk Carriers Ltd* [1975] 2 Lloyd's Rep 509.

Relevance to an office-holder

Liquidators, trustees in bankruptcy and other office holders may seek a 'Mareva' Injunction, which is a court order, where they believe assets in which they claim an interest on behalf of creditors are at risk of disappearing – particularly abroad and from the court's jurisdiction.

Removal by a floating charge-holder

A holder of a crystallised FLOATING CHARGE is entitled to have a 'Mareva' Injunction discharged *(Cretanor Maritime Co Limited v Irish Marine Management Ltd* [1978] 1 WLR 966).

3.55 MEMBERS' VOLUNTARY LIQUIDATION

The voluntary winding-up of a company commences when a resolution to wind up the company is passed by its members at a general meeting (see WINDING-UP RESOLUTION). For a company to be wound up as a Members'Voluntary Liquidation (MVL) a declaration of solvency must be sworn by the majority of the directors prior to the passing of the resolution to wind up. Where such a declaration has not been made, the liquidation will proceed as a CREDITORS' VOLUNTARY LIQUIDATION (CVL). This section highlights the major areas where an MVL differs from a CVL.

Declaration of Solvency

Under s89 the majority of the directors may make a statutory declaration (on Form 4.70) to the effect that, having conducted a full enquiry into the affairs of the company, they are of the opinion that it will be able to pay its debts in full, including interest at the official rate, within a period not exceeding 12 months from the declaration.

In order to take effect the declaration must be made within five weeks *before* the date of the winding-up resolution. In addition it must include a statement of the company's assets and liabilities at the latest practicable date. The declaration must be delivered to the Registrar within 15 days of the date of the winding-up resolution.

It is a criminal office, punishable by imprisonment and/or fine for any director to make a declaration of solvency without having reasonable grounds for believing that the company will be able to pay its debts in full within the specified period. In the event that the debts are not paid within the period there is a refutable presumption in law that the directors did not have reasonable grounds.

Appointment of the liquidator

In an MVL, the company must, in general meeting, appoint one or more liquidators for the purposes of winding-up the company's affairs and distributing the assets (s91). This will normally be done in the same meeting in which the resolution to wind up the company is passed.

Unlike a CVL there is no provision for the creditors of the company to be able to appoint a liquidator of their choice. Similarly, a members' voluntary liquidator (cf **3.32**) may have had a material professional relationship with the company. Note however that the liquidator must be an insolvency practitioner. It is common therefore for companies to appoint as liquidator either an insolvency practitioner on the recommendation of their auditors or in cases where there is no doubt that the company's assets will meet all its liabilities and expenses of the liquidation, one of their auditors' insolvency partners.

Insolvency in a Members'Voluntary Liquidation

Where a company is being wound up as an MVL and the liquidator discovers that it will be unable to pay its debts in full (together with interest at the official rate) within

the period stated in the directors' declaration of solvency, the liquidator must take the necessary steps to convert the liquidation into a creditors' voluntary winding-up (s95). These steps are:
1   summon a meeting of creditors for a day not later than the twenty-eighth day after the day on which he formed that opinion;
2   send notices of the creditors' meeting to the creditors by post not less than 7 days before the day on which that meeting is to be held;
3   cause notice of the creditors' meeting to be advertised once in the *Gazette* and once at least in two newspapers circulating in the locality in which the company's principal place of business in Great Britain was situated during the relevant period; and
4   during the period before the day on which the creditor's meeting is to be held, furnish creditors free of charge with such information concerning the affairs of the company as they may reasonably require.

The liquidator must also make out a statement of affairs for the company in the prescribed form, giving full details of the company's assets and liabilities. The liquidator should lay the statement before the creditors' meeting and should attend and preside at that meeting.

Under s96 from the day on which the creditors' meeting is held under s95, the liquidation will proceed as if the directors had never made a declaration of solvency. The creditors' meeting (and the company meeting at which the winding-up resolution was passed) will be treated as if they were the meetings under s98 in a CREDITORS' VOLUNTARY LIQUIDATION.

From this date, the liquidator should also consider his own position where he has had a continuing professional relationship with the client. In cases where it appears that the company will eventually be able to pay its debts in full, although not within the period per the declaration of solvency, he may accept nomination by the creditors and, if approved, continue as liquidator. In other cases he should not accept nomination.

Meetings in a MVL

Under s93, the liquidator must summon a general meeting of the company at the end of the first year prior to the commencement of the winding-up and at each anniversary thereof. He should lay before the meeting an account of the winding-up.

When the company's affairs are fully wound up, the liquidator must call a general meeting and lay before it an account of the liquidation. This account should be filed with the Registrar of Companies.

Removal of the liquidator

The liquidator may be removed in two ways:
1   By a general meeting of the company (s171). However the members cannot compel the company to hold a general meeting unless:
    (a) the power to do so is contained within the articles,
    (b) where members representing one tenth of the paid up equity capital request the directors to hold a meeting (CA 1985 s368),
    (c) under CA 1985 s371 the members may apply to court for a general meeting to be held;
2   The liquidator may be removed by the court under s108 'on cause shown'.

3.56 MISFEASANCE

A misfeasance is a breach of duty by a director or manager of a company in respect of company money or property. It may also apply to an office holder (eg liquidator, receiver etc) who is in breach of duty in relation to an insolvency procedure.

3.57 NOMINEE

A nominee is an INSOLVENCY PRACTITIONER appointed to consider proposals of a debtor in respect of an INDIVIDUAL VOLUNTARY ARRANGEMENT or COMPANY VOLUNTARY ARRANGEMENT. The nominee reports to the court on whether, in his opinion, a meeting of creditors members should be held to consider the proposals. (For further details see **1.55** (company) and **2.11** (individual).)

The nominee will usually (but not necessarily) be appointed the SUPERVISOR of the approved scheme.

3.58 OFFICIAL RECEIVER ('OR') *Konkursverwalter*

An OR is a salaried civil servant who works for the Government Insolvency Service, and is appointed by the Secretary of State. Each OR's office will be headed by an OR with jurisdiction for specified insolvency districts. Every High Court and County Court in the land is assigned to an insolvency district.

The OR is involved in a range of matters concerning the insolvency of individuals and companies. His primary functions are as follows:

Investigation

In a compulsory liquidation the OR is required to investigate both the affairs of the company and the conduct of its directors. In a bankruptcy he investigates the affairs and conduct of the bankrupt.

The OR will use the resulting information to decide whether a criminal offence has been committed, and will, where necessary, make a report to the Secretary of State via the prosecution unit.

Compulsory liquidation

- Liquidator: unless the court appoints a liquidator the OR will become the liquidator until another liquidator is appointed. (ie by a meeting of creditors). The OR will also act as liquidator where any vacancy occurs in the office due to resignation, death or removal of the liquidator.
- Provisional liquidator: the court may appoint either the OR or an insolvency practitioner to act as provisional liquidator prior to the making of a winding-up order. The primary function of the provisional liquidator is to safeguard the assets of the company in respect of which he is appointed pending the hearing of the winding-up petition (s135).

Bankruptcy

- Interim receiver: the court may appoint the OR as interim receiver in order to protect a bankrupt's assets prior to issuing a bankruptcy order (s286)

- Trustee : the OR will become trustee in bankruptcy in a number of circumstances including:
  (a) where the OR notifies the court that he does not intend to call a first meeting of creditors to appoint a private sector trustee;
  (b) where a certificate of summary administration is issued by the court;
  (c) where a vacancy occurs in the office of trustee.

The OR has no direct role in voluntary liquidations, administrative receiverships or administrations although he may petition for a winding-up by the court.

3.59 ONEROUS PROPERTY

See DISCLAIMER.

3.60 ORIGINAL TENANT LIABILITY

Although not an area of direct relevance to IA 1986, the concept of original tenant liability has created severe problems for many companies in recent years and a number of otherwise solvent businesses have been rendered insolvent by virtue of its application. If the general practitioner has a client with a potential liability in this area he should ensure that his client obtains legal advice as soon as possible since the liability will not disappear and is likely to increase by the day.

Original tenant liability arises from property leases. In English Law a lease not only creates a legal estate between the landlord and the tenant but also a contractual relationship for the term of the lease under the principle of privity of contract. In layman's terms this means that where an original tenant assigns a lease, he is liable to the landlord in the event that the assignee (and subsequent assignees) default on the lease. His liability is a direct and primary liability and not the liability of a surety: *Warnford Investments Ltd v Duckworth* [1979] Ch 127. The landlord is able therefore to seek immediate recourse against the original tenant without pursuing an action against the current tenant.

The problems caused by original tenant liability have been exacerbated in recent times by the high level of company insolvencies combined with the collapse in the property market. Landlords have frequently been unable to re-let their properties following the insolvency of a current tenant and have looked instead to the original lessee. This has led to companies who had assigned leases many years ago being pursued. Since many of them have not kept a record of the assigned leases these claims have come as an unwelcome and often very expensive surprise.

The problems of original tenant liability were recognised by the Law Commission in their review of 1988. The Law Commission recommended substantial change in the law, but none is planned at present. Until the law is changed, it will continue to have devastating effects for many original tenants.

3.61 PETITION

A petition is a request by way of a written application to court for the grant of an order (eg WINDING-UP PETITION, BANKRUPTCY petition, petition for the grant of ADMINISTRATION ORDER, etc).

3.62 'PHOENIX' COMPANIES

The name itself derives from the practice (prevalent prior to IA 1986) of new companies 'rising out of the ashes' of insolvency, with the same directors trading with similar or even identically named new companies to the extent that quite often long established customers were unaware of any change.

IA 1986 contains provisions in respect of the re-use of company names where a company has gone into INSOLVENT LIQUIDATION. Under s216 a person who was a director or SHADOW DIRECTOR of the insolvent company within 12 months of the date of liquidation may not (except by leave of the court) be a director of a company with a 'prohibited name' for a period of five years following the date of liquidation.

A prohibited name is defined as either:
1. a name by which the company in liquidation was known at any time in the 12 months prior to the liquidation; or
2. a name which is so similar as to suggest an association with that company.

IR 1986 however contain provisions permitting the re-use of company names in the following circumstances:

(a) Sale of Business (r 4.228)

Where a company acquires the whole or substantially the whole of the business of an insolvent company which is in liquidation, administration, administrative receivership or subject to a voluntary arrangement, the successor company may use a 'prohibited name', subject to notice being given to the creditors of the insolvent company.

Notice must be given within 28 days of the completion of the sale of business, and must state the names used and proposed to be used by the two companies. The notice must also state the names of any directors or shadow directors which the companies have in common.

(b) Existing name (r 4.230)

A director or shadow director may be involved with a company with a 'prohibited name' so long as the company had been known by that name for a period of 12 months prior to the date of liquidation, and had not been dormant during that time.

3.63 PITFALLS FACING THE COMPANY DIRECTOR

The modern company director faces a vast array of rules, directives and regulations with which he is expected to comply. These include:
- health and safety laws;
- environmental regulations;
- Companies Act provisions;
- taxation requirements.

most of which are outside the scope of this book. For guidance thereon the practitioner should refer to a specialist publication.

Here however, we are addressing those particular pitfalls which face the director of an insolvent company. Those pitfalls are to be found identified under COMPANY DIRECTORS' DISQUALIFICATION ACT 1986, MALPRACTICE (BEFORE AND DURING LIQUIDATION); AND GUARANTOR – acting as.

3.64 PREFERENCES AND TRANSACTIONS AT AN UNDERVALUE

Challengeable by an office-holder

IA 1986 contains provisions which enable:
- a liquidator; or
- an administrator; or
- a trustee in bankruptcy.

(and no one else) to attack what are known as 'preferences' and/or 'transactions at an undervalue' which have taken place within specified periods of time (the 'relevant time') immediately prior to the 'onset of insolvency'.

Although preferences and transactions at an undervalue are dealt with under separate sections of IA 1986, they are inter-linked and may conveniently be considered 'side by side'. Both companies and individuals are subject to the relevant provisions.

General Practitioner's need to identify

Any general practitioner guiding his client during a period of financial difficulty will need to have particular regard to the possibility of a preference or transaction at an undervalue having taken place. No insolvency practitioner is allowed to accept an appointment as supervisor in a scheme of INDIVIDUAL VOLUNTARY ARRANGEMENT or COMPANY VOLUNTARY ARRANGEMENT unless he has investigated and satisfied himself that none has occurred or that arrangements have been made to restore the position for the benefit of creditors generally.

Definition

(a) Preferences

Under s239, a company is deemed to have given a preference to a person if:
1. that person is one of the company's creditors or a surety or guarantor for any of the company's debts or liabilities; and
2. the company does anything or suffers anything to be done which has the effect of putting that person into a position which, in the event of the company going into INSOLVENT LIQUIDATION, will be better than the position he would have been in had the thing not been done.

The identical wording, suitably adapted, applying to an individual is contained in s340.

(b) Transactions at an undervalue

Under s238 a company is deemed to have entered into a transaction at an undervalue with a person if:
1. the company makes a gift to that person or otherwise enters into a transaction with that person on terms that provide for the company to receive no consideration; or
2. the company enters into a transaction with that person for a consideration the value of which, in money or money's worth, is significantly less than the value, in money or money's worth, of the consideration provided by the company.

The identical wording, suitably adapted applying to an individual is contained in s339 extended to include any transaction entered into with a person in consideration of marriage.

'Relevant time' and 'onset of insolvency'

For the office-holder to bring an action under either of these sections the transaction must have taken place within a 'relevant time' ending with the 'onset of insolvency'.

The 'onset of insolvency' is described as being:

(a) *Company (s240)*

- Administration or liquidation following administration. The date of presentation of the petition on which the administration order was made.
- Liquidation (other than following administration)
  (a) *Voluntary.* The date of passing the resolution to wind-up.
  (b) *Compulsory.* The date of presentation of the petition on which the winding-up order was made.

(b) *Individual (s341)*

The day of the presentation of the bankruptcy petition on which the individual is adjudged bankrupt.

The 'relevant time' is described in detail within the sections, summarised as follows:

	Company	*Individual*
Transaction at an undervalue	2 years	5 years
Preference to an ASSOCIATED or CONNECTED PERSON not involving a transaction at undervalue	2 years	2 years
Any other preference not involving a transaction at an undervalue	6 months	6 months

Result of successful challenge by office-holder

The court has wide powers under s241(company) and s342(individual) to make any order it sees fit to set aside the preference or transaction at undervalue. General practitioners requiring more detailed information should consult the appropriate section. Note also however that the sections give relief where an innocent third party has acquired an interest or received a benefit in good faith.

3.65 PREFERENTIAL CREDITORS

The definition of a preferential creditor is contained in s258(7) as follows:

> In this section "preferential debt" has the meaning given by section 386 in Part XII; and 'preferential creditor' is to be construed accordingly.

Put another way round, a preferential creditor is someone to whom a preferential debt is owed.

3.66 PREFERENTIAL DEBTS

Definition

A preferential debt is one, which but for the 'special treatment' offered by law, would otherwise be unsecured (in strict technical terms it is unsecured!). It is therefore hardly surprising that this special or preferential treatment favours Crown debts.

In simple terms a debt is preferential in that it is to be satisfied out of a company's assets subject to a floating charge in priority to the claims of the holder of that charge.

Order of priority

Preferential claims rank before those of the holder of a floating charge and unsecured creditors, but after the claims of a debenture holder secured by and under a fixed charge (*Re Lewis Merthyr Consolidated Collieries Ltd* [1929] 1Ch 498. They rank equally among themselves after the expenses of winding-up and abate in equal proportions if the available assets are insufficient to meet all preferential claims in full (s175(2)(a)).

Identifying preferential claims

In most instances, preferential claims will comprise up to:
- 12 months' arrears of PAYE
- 12 months' arrears of NI
- 6 months' arrears of VAT; and
- employees' arrears of Holiday Pay and, to a maximum per employee – currently £800 – up to 4 months' arrears of wages.

The definitive list of preferential claims is to be found within IA 1986. Section 386 sets the scene:

> (1) A reference in this Act to the preferential debts of a company or an individual is to the debts listed in Schedule 6 to this Act (money owed to the Inland Revenue for income tax deductions at source; VAT, car tax, betting and gaming duties; social security and pension scheme contributions; remuneration etc. of employees; levies on coal and steel production); and references to preferential creditors are to be read accordingly.

It will therefore be necessary for the general practitioner requiring a definitive list to refer to Sch 6 for a complete list of preferential debts.

Preferential claims – the relevant date for calculating

The relevant date from which to 'work back' in order to calculate the preferential period is determined by reference to the nature of the insolvency. Thus:

(a) Creditors' voluntary liquidation

The date of the passing of the resolution to wind-up.

(b) Compulsory liquidation

The date of presentation of the petition to wind up (and not the date of the winding-up order) (s387(3)(c)); unless compulsory liquidation follows immediately upon the discharge of an administration order (see below).

(c) Administrative receivership

The date of appointment of the administrative receiver (s387(4)).

(d) Company Voluntary Arrangement

The date of the creditors' approval of the scheme (s387(2)(b)) unless an administration order is already in force, in which case the date of the making of the order (s387(2)(a)).

(e) Administration

There are no preferential creditors within an administration. When however the company is subsequently placed into compulsory liquidation, the relevant date is deemed to be the date of the making of the administration order (s387(3)(a)).

If a Company Voluntary Arrangement follows an administration order which is in force at the time of the approval of the voluntary arrangement then the relevant date is the date of the making of the administration order (s387(2)(a)).

Note that there are no provisions for protecting the position of creditors enjoying preferential status where a company in administration proceeds to Creditors' Voluntary Liquidation and where the relevant date would be the date of the passing of the resolution to wind up. As it is likely that at least six months and perhaps 12 months will have elapsed since the granting of the administration order, the entirety of the 'preferential period' could now be within the period of the administration itself, leaving claims as at the date of administration unsecured.

It is because of this that it is customary to include a proposal preserving the status of preferential claims within an administration in order that creditors who could otherwise lose their status be encouraged to vote in favour. (In *Re Scotlane Ltd* (1986) unreported Harman J held that the administration order should not be discharged unless the unsecured creditors waived their claims to put the preferential creditors in the same position in the voluntary winding-up as they would have been in a compulsory winding-up.)

(f) Individual Voluntary Arrangement

Where the debtor is not an undischarged bankrupt, the date of the interim order (made under s252) with respect to his proposal (s387(5)).

(g) Bankruptcy

Where at the time the bankruptcy order was made there was an interim receiver appointed (under s286), the relevant date is the date on which the interim receiver was first appointed after the presentation of the bankruptcy petition (s387(6)(a)).

Where no interim receiver has been appointed, the relevant date is the date of the making of the bankruptcy order (s387(6)(b)).

Payment of preferential claims

(a) Administrative receiver's duty to pay

Section 40 imposes a positive duty upon administrative receivers to discharge the preferential claims (*IRC v Goldblatt* [1972] Ch 498).

Note however that this duty is effectively removed by virtue of s11(5) where an administrative receiver vacates office under s11(1)(b) subsequent to the making of an administration order.

An administrative receiver therefore has a duty not only to recover monies outstanding and due to the debenture holder, but also to pay the preferential creditors, before vacating office and handing 'control' to a liquidator or, in the absence of a liquidator, back to the directors.

(b) Assets available to meet preferential claims

Section 40 provides that payment shall be made out of assets caught by a charge which *as created* was a floating charge. Section 251 reinforces the wording by repeating:

> "floating charge" means a charge which, as created, was a floating charge.

Put in other words, even if it is proved possible for a floating charge to crystallise prior to the appointment of administrative receivers, so as to become a fixed charge upon appointment, the assets caught thereby would still be available for the benefit of the preferential creditors in priority to the debenture holder.

(See also **1.115** and **1.149** concerning the decision in *Re Portbase Clothing Ltd*.)

The effect of the decision in *Re GL Saunders Ltd* [1986] 1 WLR 215

The decision in this case follows an application by receivers to the court for directions and deals with the position where a debenture holder is repaid out of assets caught by a fixed charge, leaving an available surplus. In this specific case, floating charge realisations were insufficient to pay preferential creditors in full. Nourse J took the view that payment in full of the debenture holder's debt out of fixed-charge monies not only redeemed the fixed charge but simultaneously redeemed the floating charge and that under such circumstances any equity remaining following discharge of the fixed charge could never be caught by the floating charge.

The practical effect of this decision is that under such circumstances any available surplus fixed charge realisations must be paid to the company or – as will be the case in most instances – to the liquidator.

3.67 PROOF OF DEBT

When a creditor of a company in liquidation or an individual in bankruptcy submits a claim to the liquidator or trustee, he is said to be 'proving his debt'. The document by which he seeks to establish the claim is called a 'proof of debt'.

Proofs of debt – liquidations

In a compulsory winding-up, all creditors wishing to claim in the liquidation must submit proofs to the liquidator on Form 4.25. This form will usually be sent to the creditors with the first notice calling a meeting of creditors and must be completed by the creditor showing full details of the debt. No proof is required in a voluntary liquidation for dividend purposes unless the liquidator so requires, although no creditor may vote at the s98 creditors' meeting unless he has detailed his debt to the chairman before the vote is taken. The chairman will decide whether claims should be admitted or rejected, in full or in part. Creditors who disagree with the chairman's decision may apply to the court to have the decision varied or modified. The application must be made within 21 days of receiving notice of the chairman's decision.

(a) Provable debts

The general rule is that a liquidator may only pay debts which are legally enforceable against the company. A 'debt' is defined as a liability at the date of liquidation, a liability arising after the date of liquidation by reason of an obligation incurred before that date, or pre-liquidation interest on that debt.

(b) Treatment of various types of debt

(i) Assigned debts. The assignee may prove for the full amount of the debt even though he may have bought it for less.

(ii) Debts arising from improper use of company's powers. These are voidable at the instance of the liquidator where the creditor had notice of the impropriety.

(iii) Debts arising from illegal transactions. Illegal transactions are void and the debts unenforceable.

(iv) Statute-barred debts. The statutory limitation period is six years for most debts, although there are exceptions (eg 12 years for contracts under deed). The liquidator should not pay debts which are statute barred at the date of commencement of the liquidation.

(v) Discounts. Rule 4.89 requires that creditors should deduct from the claim all discounts which would have been available to the company but for its liquidation. Clearly this would not include discounts for early payment.

(vi) Payments of a periodic nature (eg rent). A creditor may prove for any amounts due and unpaid until the date of liquidation, accruing on a day-by-day basis. (r 4.92).

(vii) Debts payable at a future date. The debt is provable as if it was a present debt (r 4.94). When a dividend is paid before the debt is due, the liquidator must reduce the amount of the proof by a percentage, calculated as follows:

$$\% = \frac{I \times M}{12}$$

where $I = 5\%$
M = number of months between date of dividend and date debt is due (r 11.13).

(viii) Contingent debts. A contingent debt is one which will only arise on the occurrence of an uncertain event. For example, where a company has consented to pay a pension, the claim depends upon how long the person will live.

The liquidator must estimate the value of the contingent claim, taking into account the likelihood of the contingency. (r 4.86)

(ix) Unascertained debts. These debts are admissible for proof, but the liquidator must estimate the value. An example of an unascertained debt would be a claim for unliquidated damages in tort (r 4.86).

(x) Foreign debts. These are normally admissible and should be converted into sterling at the spot rate at the date of liquidation (r 4.91). Foreign taxes are however not admissible.

(xi) Post liquidation interest. Interest on debts from the date of liquidation is not provable but will be paid under s189 after all creditors' claim have been paid in full (see INTEREST ON DEBTS IN A WINDING-UP).

(c) Secured debts

The general rule is that a secured creditor may only prove for any unsecured part of his debt. The general practitioner should refer to rr 4.95–4.99 for the regulations concerning the valuation of his security by a secured creditor, the liquidator's right to redeem the security, the realisation of the security and other related matters.

Proofs of debt – bankruptcy

Creditors wishing to claim in a bankruptcy must submit a proof on Form 6.37, giving full details of the debt. The form will usually accompany the first correspondence received from the trustee/official receiver.

The trustee will decide whether the claim should be admitted or rejected although a creditor may apply to the court to have the decision varied or reversed.

(a) Provable debts

The rules concerning provable debts are largely the same as for liquidation. The major exception is the deferred status for debts to the bankrupt's spouse (see **2.39**).

3.68 PROVISIONAL LIQUIDATOR

Under s135 the court may appoint a provisional liquidator to a company at any time after the presentation of a winding-up petition and before the making of a winding-up order. The effect of the appointment is to remove control and responsibility for the assets of the company from the directors and to ensure the preservation of the assets until the winding-up order is made or the petition is dismissed.

The application to the court for the appointment of a provisional liquidator may be made by the petitioner, a creditor, a contributory, the company itself, the Secretary of State, or any person who would be able to present a winding-up petition. It must be accompanied by an affidavit showing the following:

1. the grounds on which it is proposed that a provisional liquidator should be appointed;
2. if some person other than the Official Receiver is proposed to be appointed, that the person has consented to act and, to the best of the applicant's belief, is qualified to act as an insolvency practitioner in relation to the company;
3. whether or not the Official Receiver has been informed of the application and, if so, has been furnished with a copy of it;
4. whether to the applicant's knowledge:
    (a) there has been proposed or is in force for the company a voluntary arrangement under Part I of the Act, or
    (b) an administrator or administrative receiver is acting in relation to the company, or
    (c) a liquidator has been appointed for its voluntary winding-up; and
5. the applicant's estimate of the value of the assets in respect of which the provisional liquidator is to be appointed.

The Official Receiver may oppose the application. The court will make an appointment where it considers that there are sufficient reasons for taking control of the assets away from the directors. The appointment will terminate when the court so orders on application of the provisional liquidator or of any of the persons who are able to apply for the appointment of a provisional liquidator.

The provisional liquidator's main role is to safeguard the assets of the company. He has no implied power to realise the company's assets, although he may apply for an order authorising a sale of assets in exceptional circumstances.

The court will generally be reluctant to grant such an order because of the possibility of the subsequent dismissal of the petition.

In certain circumstances the provisional liquidator may apply to the court under s177 for the appointment of a SPECIAL MANAGER to the company to assist him in his functions.

3.69 PROXY

A proxy is a document whereby a creditor or shareholder authorises another person to represent him at a meeting. The proxy may give the proxy holder specific voting instructions (special proxy) or it may permit him to vote at his discretion (general proxy). For more detailed information see VOTING AT s98 CREDITORS' MEETING.

3.70 RECEIVER

Abbreviated title which may be used to describe:
- an ADMINISTRATIVE RECEIVER;
- A RECEIVER UNDER THE LAW OF PROPERTY ACT (1925) (see also FIXED AND FLOATING CHARGES);
- an INTERIM RECEIVER;
- an AGRICULTURAL RECEIVER.

3.71 RECEIVERSHIP UNDER THE LAW OF PROPERTY ACT (1925)

The Law of Property Act 1925 (LPA) provides for the appointment of a receiver in respect of property which is subject to a mortgage or fixed charge. The powers of an LPA receiver are limited, particularly when compared with those of an administrative receiver.

Appointment of LPA receiver

The LPA provides that a mortgagee may appoint a receiver to a property where a power of appointment is expressly contained within the mortgage deed. The deed will usually set out the circumstances in which the power of appointment may be used.

Where no power of appointment is contained within the deed, s101 LPA imposes an implied power which becomes exercisable in the following circumstances:
1. where the mortgagor has been served with a notice demanding payment and the sum has not been paid in full within three months of the notice
2. where there is unpaid interest due under the mortgage of not less than two months
3. where there has been some other breach of the mortgage or the LPA.

The receiver (who does not have to be an insolvency practitioner) must be appointed in writing. Under s109 LPA, he is deemed to be the mortgagee's agent unless the agreement provides to the contrary.

Powers of LPA receiver

Under the LPA itself, a receiver is merely a receiver of rents and income from the property. Unless the mortgage deed provides otherwise, he has no power to take possession of, get in or sell the assets. Nor has he any implied management powers. In practice, a well drawn mortgage deed will usually contain powers of sale for the receiver.

Application of monies by LPA receiver

Under LPA s109, the receiver is required to apply monies recovered in the following order:
1. discharge all rents, rates and taxes in respect of the property;
2. keep down all annual sums and other payments of interest in respect of a prior mortgage;
3. the receiver's commission and any insurance premiums (where directed in writing by the mortgagee to take out insurance);
4. pay interest accruing under the mortgage;
5. pay the mortgagee in respect of the principal debt (if so instructed in writing by the mortgagee).

Since the late 1980s there has been a growing tendency, particularly within the licensed trade, to draw up the mortgage deed to enable an LPA receiver to utilise the chattel assets for the purpose of trade. When combined with an agreement which allows the receiver to continue to trade from the premises, this has the effect of placing the LPA receiver on virtually the same footing as an administrative-receiver.

Not unnaturally, this is causing considerable concern within the insolvency profession, for protectionism apart (as mentioned above an LPA receiver does not need to be an insolvency practitioner) the LPA receiver is not subjected to any of the stringent disciplines which an administrative receiver must observe. As the practice of appointing LPA receivers with combined management powers grows, we can expect to see an increasing demand for a change in the legislation to bring the disciplines for LPA receivers within insolvency legislation.

3.72   RETENTION OF TITLE (ROT)

Retention of Title became firmly established in this country following the decision in *Aluminium Industrie Vaassen BV v Romalpa Aluminium Ltd* [1976] 1 WLR 676, which highlighted the principle of being able to retain title in goods supplied but not paid for.

It is a legal device whereby a supplier of goods, as opposed to services, is able to incorporate a binding clause or clauses into his terms of trade preserving title in the goods until paid for. Thus, he could be in a far stronger position than the ordinary unsecured creditors should his customer commence formal insolvency proceedings.

The principle, however, is not new and has been recognised on the Continent for many years. The Sale of Goods Act 1979 provides that the parties may agree when title in the goods passes to the buyer.

The law relating to ROT is complex and has expanded considerably since the 'Romalpa' Case and if it has caused problems for insolvency office-holders, it has certainly assisted many creditors to improve their position above the ranks of the ordinary unsecured.

Every general practitioner should consider advising his client, where possible, to incorporate a reservation of title clause within his terms of trade. Legal advice is essential and a solicitor should always be consulted to advise. The following detail is intended only as background, to assist in an understanding of the basic principles involved.

Types of clause

There are two main types of ROT clause. A *simple clause* merely reserves the supplier's title for specified goods until those particular goods have been paid for, whereas an *extended clause* may reserve title until all monies owed on all goods supplied under that contract have been paid for ('all monies clause'). Additionally an extended clause may attempt to lay claim to any goods manufactured from the goods supplied or to the proceeds of sale of the goods supplied.

Incorporation

In order to be able to act upon his ROT clause, a supplier must show that its terms have been incorporated into the contract. This involves showing that the clause was brought to the buyer's attention and accepted by the buyer prior to the contract being made. Where, for example, the supplier sends each customer a copy of his terms and conditions of sale and the customer returns a signed copy, it is highly probable that the terms and conditions will have been incorporated. On the other hand, where the first reference to the ROT clause is made on the back of a sales invoice which was sent after the goods were delivered, it is unlikely that the clause will have been incorporated into the contract, although it has been argued successfully that incorporation would be effective for subsequent contracts by virtue of a 'course of dealing'.

The issue can become very complicated however when the supplier has standard terms and conditions incorporating ROT whereas the purchaser has standard terms and conditions specifically excluding ROT from the contract. The court will look at each case on its merits in deciding which set of terms has been incorporated.

Identification

Where a supplier is claiming title to goods it is essential that he be able to identify those goods. Firstly, he must identify the goods as having been supplied by him; where identical goods have been supplied by a number of suppliers, he must show that, on the balance of probability, they were supplied by him. If he cannot do this, his claim will fail.

Secondly, where he has a simple clause it will be necessary for the supplier to identify goods as having been sold under a particular invoice, although where the goods have batch or serial numbers this may not be a problem.

In cases where the goods are being claimed under an all monies clause the supplier does not need to relate the goods to invoices because he is claiming title on all goods supplied until all monies have been paid.

Tracing goods into work-in-progress or finished goods

ROT claims often meet difficulties in cases where the goods supplied were to be used in a manufacturing process. Since this area has been determined entirely by case law, it is best illustrated by reference to leading cases. The decisions of the cases depend upon whether the identity of the goods supplied has been lost in an irreversible process or whether the process may be reversed. In *Borden (UK) Ltd v Scottish Timber Products Ltd* [1979] 3 All ER 961, the Court of Appeal held that where resin was supplied for the purpose of making glue for the manufacture of chipboard, the resin had lost its identity once used since the process was irreversible. This may be contrasted with *Hendy Lennox (Industrial Engines) v Grahame Puttick Ltd [1984] 1WLR 485* where diesel engines were supplied for incorporation into generators. It was held that the incorporation of the engines into the generators could easily be reversed and the engines had not therefore lost their identities.

Tracing into proceeds of sale

Many suppliers incorporate provisions within their ROT clause to enable them to recover proceeds of sale of goods which have been sold-on by the customer. These provisions have however consistently failed to stand up in court.

It would appear from case law that the following must apply in order for the supplier to be able to trace proceeds of sale:
1. There must have been a fiduciary relationship between the supplier and the buyer expressed in the contract.
2. There must have been an obligation on the buyer to store the goods separately, clearly marked as belonging to the supplier.
3. The clause must have stipulated that the goods were sold by the buyer as the agent of the seller and for the supplier's account.

3.73 RE-USE OF COMPANY NAME

See 'PHOENIX' COMPANIES

3.74 SECURED CREDITOR

A secured creditor is a creditor with specific rights over some or all of the debtor's assets which may, for example, take the form of a mortgage or charge.

In the event of the security being sold to repay the outstanding debt, the secured creditor will be paid in priority to any other creditor.

3.75 SET-OFF

Set-off is a complex area of law where legal advice is essential.

In simple terms set-off occurs when one party (the first party) owing money to another (the second party) deducts from the amount due, monies that the second party owes in turn to the first party. Such a position could arise where an individual or company both buys from and sells to, the same customer.

The general rule for a claim for set-off to succeed is that there has to have been 'mutuality of debit and credit'. Thus a claim to set-off would probably fail where (without precedence or contractual agreement) company A sells to company B and company B being a member of a group within which a fellow subsidiary company C is owed money by company A claims to set-off A's debt to C.

This requirement to establish mutuality can be further demonstrated by the problems created following the crystallisation of a FLOATING CHARGE within an administrative receivership. Where set-off is permissible by virtue of transactions entered into before the floating charge crystallised, the debenture holder is obliged to accept the position. Where however set-off is claimed between pre- and post-crystallisation debts, mutuality of dealing will only exist where the two opposing debts arise by virtue of the same contract. This is because crystallisation of the floating charge will <u>equitably</u> assign the <u>pre-receivership debt</u> to the debenture holder making the <u>contracting parties</u> the third party and the bank. The <u>post receivership debt</u> will not be so assigned, making the contracting parties the third party and the company.

3.76 SHADOW DIRECTOR

A shadow director is defined by IA 1986 s251 and CDDA 1986 s22(5) as:

> a person in accordance with whose directions or instructions the directors of the company are accustomed to act (but so that person is not deemed a Shadow Director by reason only that the directors act on advice given by him in a professional capacity).

The concept of 'Shadow Director' is not new; it was an offence over 60 years ago for the name of every director, including a shadow director, not to be stated on all board catalogues, show cards and business letters, of a company registered under CA (see CA 1929 s145).

Nevertheless it is only since the introduction of WRONGFUL TRADING in 1986 that concern has been expressed in a number of quarters, noticeably by the banks, to ensure that they are not caught as shadow directors (and therefore liable to contribute to the company's assets in the event of a claim by a liquidator). Although an action brought by the liquidator in *Re MC Bacon Ltd* [1990] BCC 78 was abandoned after nine days of evidence, Knox J had earlier refused to strike out the claim that the bank had become a 'shadow director', giving a clear indication that *as a matter of law* a bank is capable of conducting itself in such a manner as to become a shadow director. It now however seems unlikely that professional advisers acting strictly wihin their advisory capacity or bankers acting within the normal customer/bank relationship will be successfully challenged by a liquidator as having acted as shadow directors unless they have stepped well outside the normal client relationship.

General practitioners should take note of the exact wording of the definition. To become a shadow director, the propositus must be a person 'in accordance with whose directions or instructions *the directors of the company* are accustomed to act'. This has to mean that the shadow director would be in effect the *managing* director by any name – not simply another director – for 'the directors' collectively constitutes the board of directors.

3.77 SPECIAL MANAGER

Where a company has gone into LIQUIDATION or a PROVISIONAL LIQUIDATOR has been appointed, the court may appoint any person to be the special manager of the business or property of the company under IA 1986 s177.

The application may be made by the liquidator or provisional liquidator in any case where it appears to him that the nature of the business or property of the company, or the interests of the company's creditors or contributories or members generally, require the appointment of another person to manage the company's business or property.

This will often be done where the company's business is of a size or complexity such that the liquidator or provisional liquidator feels that he requires specialised assistance in carrying out his role. There is no requirement that the special manager is an insolvency practitioner and, although normally an accountant, he may be an expert in any field. It should be noted that a special manager may be appointed in a compulsory or voluntary liquidation. The special manager has such powers as are entrusted to him by the court and continue for as long as the court orders. These powers are usually of a limited nature and will not normally include trading unless the company is clearly solvent.

Where the special manager was appointed on the application of a provisional liquidator, his appointment is terminated with the dismissal of the winding-up petition or the discharge of the provisional liquidator without a winding-up order having been made.

Where a liquidator has been appointed he may apply to the court for the discharge of the special manager.

3.78 SOCIETY OF PRACTITIONERS OF INSOLVENCY

The Society of Practitioners of Insolvency (SPI) was founded in 1990 to act as a coordinating body representing the professional interests of insolvency practitioners in the UK. It does not itself issue insolvency licences.

3.79 STATUTORY DEMAND

A statutory demand is a formal demand for the payment of a debt. If a debt (exceeding £750) has not been paid within 21 days of the demand, the debtor is deemed by IA 1986 as unable to pay his debts. A WINDING-UP or BANKRUPTCY PETITION may then be presented.

3.80 SUPERVISOR

A supervisor is an insolvency practitioner appointed by the creditors to supervise an INDIVIDUAL or COMPANY VOLUNTARY ARRANGEMENT.

3.81 TAXATION

Taxation (direct) – corporate insolvency

Taxation is an area where the general practitioner is often able to play an important role, particularly regarding the timing of the insolvency procedure. It is frequently possible to significantly enhance assets available for creditors through good tax planning.

This section seeks to explain the general effect of insolvency upon a company's taxation position and suggest areas where the general practitioner may be able to render assistance.

(a) Administration

The making of an administration order has no effect on a company's direct taxation position. There is no automatic termination of a company's accounting period and corporation tax is still charged on profits. The administrator will carry out his function as agent of the company, with taxation continuing to be assessed on the company.

There would appear to be little scope for the general practitioner to involve himself in specific tax planning in contemplation of an administration order. Any advice he would have given before the order was contemplated is unlikely to vary as a consequence of the order. Once the order has been made the administrator will generally deal with the taxation affairs of the company although there is no reason why the general practitioner should not assist.

Taxation strategy within an administration will normally centre on the use of unrelieved tax losses through the HIVE-DOWN technique which can sometimes preserve losses for a purchaser of the business.

(b) Receivership

The taxation implications following the appointment of a receiver or an administrative receiver are similar to those relating to an administrator with no automatic termination of an accounting period. The opportunities for tax planning are therefore again limited. An administrative receiver will generally take responsibility for dealing with the company's tax affairs although there may be opportunities for the general practitioner to continue an involvement where a fixed-charge receiver has been appointed. Once again unutilised trading losses may be preserved by the use of hive-down.

(c) Liquidation

It is the liquidation of a company which presents additional opportunities for the general practitioner to become involved in tax planning in order to enhance the assets of the company.

—The commencement of the winding-up of a company automatically brings the company's accounting period to an end. A unique feature of an accounting period after the commencement of the winding-up is that it does not end with the cessation of trade.

Utilisation of trading losses

Where a member of a group has been trading at a loss, the general practitioner should consider how the losses may be utilised, which will usually be via 'group relief '.

In cases where the holding company itself is to be wound up, the practitioner should ensure that losses are transferred for group relief purposes as far as possible prior to the commencement of the winding-up, and subsidiaries cease to be members of the group for group relief purposes. This was established in *IRC v Olive Mill Spinners Ltd* (1963) 41 TC 77.

Where the company to be wound up is part of a group but is not the holding company, losses may be surrendered before or after the commencement of winding-up. The agreement of the liquidator is required if the formal surrender is not made prior to the commencement of winding-up and payment may be requested in consideration for the transfer.

Capital gains

Where the company is a group company and has assets on which a chargeable gain will be made on disposal, the practitioner should seek to ensure that the assets be transferred to another group company which has unutilised capital losses.

If the company is not a group company and itself has trading losses within the current accounting period it might be possible to delay liquidation in order to obtain set-off against a capital gain within the same accounting period. However, although this was sometimes encountered as a device to enhance the cash fund in pre-IA 1986 days, the spectre of WRONGFUL TRADING introduced by the IA 1986 coupled with the disappearance of assessable gains following the collapse in the property market, virtually reduces this option to one of text-book theory.

Solvent companies

Where the company which is to be wound up is a subsidiary and is solvent, the practitioner should consider advising that a dividend be paid to its parent prior to the winding up in order to reduce any capital gain arising on the disposal of the shares. No liability for advanced corporation tax will arise where the dividend is paid to other group companies and where there is a valid group income election.

Taxation (direct) – individual insolvency

The general practitioner has much less scope for tax planning in a bankruptcy than in a corporate insolvency. There is however scope for him to continue to work for his individual client after the bankruptcy order has been made. It is important therefore that the main rules concerning the taxation of bankrupts are understood.

(a) Inland Revenue claim

The Inland Revenue will make a claim in the bankruptcy based upon the bankrupt's income for the whole of tax year in which the bankruptcy commenced. The bankrupt will therefore be required to submit a tax return covering all income up to the 5 April following the date of the bankruptcy. If the bankrupt does not submit a return, the trustee will be required to send a certificate giving estimates of his income setting out the allowances to which he appears to be entitled.

No taxation will be deducted from the earnings of the bankrupt for the rest of that tax year, since the Inland Revenue as a creditor is precluded from receiving any payment in respect of its claim.

(b) Capital Gains Tax

Where the trustee makes a disposal of assets and a chargeable gain arises the tax relating to the gain will be assessed on and recoverable from the trustee (Taxation of Chargeable Gains Act 1992 s66). Allowable expenditure will include that incurred by both debtor and trustee, and may include an element of the trustee's remuneration.

Note the vesting of the bankrupt's estate in the trustee does not constitute a disposal of assets for capital gain purposes.

3.82   TRUSTEE IN BANKRUPTCY

Following the making of a BANKRUPTCY ORDER the assets of the debtor vest in the trustee in bankruptcy.

Appointment

Immediately upon the making of a bankruptcy order, the Official Receiver (OR) becomes receiver and manager of the bankrupt's estate (s287). The OR must, as soon as practicable within 12 weeks of the date of the bankruptcy order, decide whether a first meeting of creditors should be called to appoint a trustee (s293).

If he decides not to call the meeting, he becomes trustee as from when he gives notice of his decision to the court. He may however be forced to do so by a request from not less than 25% of creditors (in value) (s294).

The first meeting of creditors may appoint a trustee by a simple majority (in value) of those voting in person or by proxy.

Functions

The principal function of the trustee is to get in, realise and distribute the bankrupt's estate, (s305).

Powers

The powers of the trustee are detailed in s314 and Sch 5. They are extensive and sufficiently wide ranging to permit the trustee to carry out his duties. It should be noted that some powers require the sanction of the creditors' committee or court before they can be exercised.

Control over trustee

The Act contains two main methods by which it may be possible for the creditors or the bankrupt to exercise some control over the trustee:
1   application to court under s303 for an order reversing or modifying any act or decision of the trustee;
2   control by CREDITORS' COMMITTEE.

Removal of the trustee

The trustee may be removed by a simple majority of creditors (in value) voting in person or by proxy at a general meeting of creditors summoned specifically for the purpose. When the trustee is not the OR, the meeting may be requested by 10% of the creditors (in value).

When the OR is trustee, the meeting may only be summoned where one quarter of the creditors request it, where the court directs or when the OR thinks fit.

The trustee may also be removed by order of the court 'on cause shown'.

Remuneration

When the trustee is the OR, his remuneration is on a scale laid down in the Insolvency Regulations 1986. (This is the same scale as used in liquidations: see LIQUIDATOR.)

When the trustee is not the OR, his remuneration is fixed in one of two ways:
1   as a percentage of assets realised or distributed;
2   by reference to the time spent by the trustee and his staff on the case.

The remuneration will be fixed by the creditors' committee (if there is one) or by a general meeting of creditors, who should have regard for:
1   the complexity of the case;
2   the degree of responsibility exercised by the trustee;
3   the effectiveness of the trustee in carrying out his function;
4   the nature and value of the assets.

3.83 UNSECURED CREDITOR

In the strict legal sense, an unsecured creditor is a creditor who holds no security for his debt. However the term is more commonly used to refer to an ordinary creditor who enjoys no preferential rights.

3.84 VALUE ADDED TAX

This section is intended to provide the general practitioner with a brief outline of the VAT implications following the appointment of an administrator, receiver or liquidator to a company. (See also VAT BAD DEBT RELIEF.)

The appointment of an administrator, receiver or liquidator to a company will bring the company's VAT period to an end. The office holder should ensure that the company submits the return for the period up to the day before the date of appointment in order that Customs and Excise may calculate its preferential claim. The VAT (General) Regulations 1985 provide that this return should be submitted within one month of the appointment.

The office holder should also ensure that VAT returns in respect of the post appointment period are completed and returned on time. When the company ceases to make taxable supplies, the office holder should notify Customs and Excise within 30 days and the registration will then be cancelled. Any VAT paid after this date may be recovered on form VAT 427.

3.85 VAT BAD DEBT RELIEF

Prior to 1 April 1991, VAT bad debt relief was available to a supplier only when his customer became formally insolvent. The rules have now changed, enabling a supplier to claim relief from VAT on bad debts without the requirement for his customer to become formally insolvent. Full details of the new scheme are available in a free booklet produced by HM Customs and Excise, *Value Added Tax : Relief from VAT on bad debts*, the major points of which are summarised below.

A supplier may claim relief on VAT for supplies of goods and services made to customers on or after 1 April 1989 for which he had not been paid provided the following conditions are met:
- the VAT has already been accounted for and paid to Customs and Excise;
- the debt has been written off in the supplier's accounts and transferred to a separate bad debt account;
- the debt is over six months old (ie six months from the date of supply);
- in the case of a supply of goods, ownership has passed to the customer.

The creditor must claim for the full amount of his debt in the insolvency (including the VAT element) for dividend purposes. Where payment or part payment is received for a debt after relief has been claimed, the VAT element in the payment must be repaid to Customs and Excise. This will also apply where payment is received from an insurer of the (bad) debt.

3.86 VOTING AT S98 CREDITORS' MEETING

The general practitioner will often be the first to hear from a client who has received notice of a s98 meeting in respect of a debtor company which has gone into

CREDITORS' VOLUNTARY LIQUIDATION. In particular, a client will usually want to know what he has to do in order to be able to vote at the meeting.

In order to be entitled to vote, a creditor must meet the requirements of r 4.67 in respect of:
1   Proof of debt; and
2   Proxy; or
3   be an individual attending and voting in his own name; or
4   as a company utilise the provision of CA 1985 s375.

Proof of debt

A creditor may vote only if a proof of the debt claimed has been lodged and admitted by the chairman for voting purposes at the meeting. No time limit is specified in the IA 1986 or the IR 1986 by which the proof must be submitted, nor is there any restriction on the form of the proof, which must be in writing. A creditor may simply write a note of his name and the amount owed and present it to the chairman prior to the vote being taken. (Note however that this is not the case for the lodgement of proxies – see below.)

The chairman has the power to admit or reject a proof for the purposes of entitlement to vote, although his decision is subject to an appeal to the court by the creditor. If the chairman is in doubt whether to admit or reject a proof, he should mark it as 'objected' and allow the creditor to vote, subject to his vote subsequently being declared invalid if the objection is sustained (r 4.70). The rules for the admission of proofs for voting purposes are the same as for the admission of proofs for dividend purposes (see PROOF OF DEBT for further detail).

Proxy

A person wishing to vote at the meeting must ensure that any requisite proxy has been lodged with the chairman of the meeting by noon on the day preceding the meeting. The chairman may allow a creditor to vote where a proxy was either not lodged or lodged late, but only in exceptional circumstances (r 4.67).

A creditor may list a number of alternative proxy-holders on the form of proxy, in which case the named individuals rank in the order in which they are named (r 8.1(3)). The form of proxy will be sent by the chairman along with the notice of the meeting, and may be used only in relation to that meeting or an adjournment thereof. It must be signed by the creditor or authorised representative (stating the nature of his authorisation) (rr 8.2, 8.3).

Voting directions may be included upon the form. Where no directions are included the proxy holder may vote at his own discretion (r 8.7(5)).

A proxy-holder may not vote in favour of any resolution which would directly or indirectly place him or any associate in a position to receive any remuneration out of the insolvent estate, unless the proxy specifically directs him to vote that way (r 8.6).

It is up to the chairman of the meeting to decide whether or not he will accept facsimilied proxies for voting purposes. (It is the practice of the Official Receiver not to accept facsimilied proxies.) Whatever decision the chairman reaches, he must be consistent in his approach and accept all facsimilied proxies or none at all.

An individual attending and voting in his own name

A partnership will need to complete a proxy in order to be able to vote at the meeting whereas an individual may attend and vote in his own name without having submitted a proxy.

CA 1985 s375

Under this section a company may pass a resolution authorising an individual to attend and vote at the meeting. A copy of the resolution, either sealed by the company or certified by a director or the secretary as a true copy, must be produced to the chairman of the meeting (r 8.7).

This little used section can be of importance to general practitioners advising a creditor client who, for whatever reason, has missed the 'deadline' for submitting a proxy and would otherwise have lost the right to vote at the meeting.

3.87 WALKING POSSESSION

See DISTRESS.

3.88 WINDING-UP ORDER

A winding-up order is made by the court and has the effect of putting a company into COMPULSORY LIQUIDATION which is deemed to have commenced with effect from the date of presentation of the WINDING-UP PETITION.

3.89 WINDING-UP PETITION

See PETITION.

3.90 WINDING-UP RESOLUTION

A winding-up resolution is usually required in order for a company to be wound up voluntarily. (The only exception is where the company's articles contain provision for the company to be wound up on a certain date or on the occurrence of a specified event – IA 1986 s84.) The effect of such a resolution is that the company will cease to carry on its business except so far as is required for its beneficial winding-up. However the corporate state and corporate powers of the company remain until it is dissolved.

Where a resolution is required, the members have a choice under IA 1986 s84 of:

1. a special resolution that the company be wound up voluntarily. This will normally only be passed when the company is solvent; or
2. an extraordinary resolution to the effect that the company cannot by reason of its liabilities continue its business and that it is advisable to wind up.

Members must be given at least 14 days' notice both of an extraordinary general meeting and of any extraordinary resolutions which will be considered therein. For a special resolution, however, 21 days' notice must be given (CA 1985 s378)

Under CA 1985 s 369 the time periods may be reduced where a majority of shareholders holding at least 95% of the voting rights (in a private company at least 90% – CA 1985 s379) agree in writing to accept a shorter notice period.

In order for a special or extraordinary resolution to be passed in a general meeting, at least 75% of the votes cast in person or by proxy must be in favour.

A winding-up resolution must be advertised in the *London Gazette* within 14 days and filed with the registrar within 15 days.

INDEX

Acid test
application of, 3.1
Administration
bank, persuading, 1.165
case study, 1.103
company voluntary arrangement as exit route from, 1.101
contract of employment, effect on, 3.31
creditors' committee, 3.21
creditors' meeting-
    calling, 1.91
    conduct of, 1.92
general practitioner, role of, 1.104
potential of procedure, 1.103
taxation, 3.81
Administration order
advantages of-
    appreciation of, 1.62
    company, to, 1.66
    directors, to, 1.65
    office-holder, to, 1.68
    unsecured creditors, to, 1.67
application for-
    actions against company, staying, 1.81
    consideration by court, 1.79
    documentation filed with, 1.76
    effect of, 1.81, 1.101
    moratorium, imposing, 1.81
    petition, by, 1.73
company voluntary arrangement, extension to include, 1.80
court, made by, 1.101
definition, 1.63
discharge, application for, 1.99
effect of, 1.82
floating charge holder, right to receive notice of petition, 1.70
halfway house, as, 1.101
independent expert's report, 1.75
information given after, 1.94
introduction of, 1.43
likelihood of achieving proposals, 1.79
meaning, 3.2
moratorium, enforcement of, 1.82

Administration order—*contd*
petition-
    application by, 1.73
    appointment of administrative receiver, effect of, 1.72
    directors, presented by, 1.77
    right of floating charge holder to receive, 1.70
    service of, 1.78
    supporting affidavit, 1.77
preferential creditors, position of, 1.69
proposals, which to incorporate, 1.80
purposes of, 1.48, 1.80
reasons for choosing, 1.64
reasons for requesting, 1.74
variation, application for, 1.99
Administrative receiver
administrator's position contrasted, 1.128
appointment-
    acceptance in writing, 1.144
    agent of company, as, 1.125
    bank, by, 1.105
    borrowers, agreement of, 1.122
    floating charge, under, 1.107
    notice of, 1.145
    petition for administration order, effect on, 1.72
    powers and responsibilities of directors following, 1.154
    reasons for, 1.117
    timing, 1.124
    warning signs, 1.118-1.121
choice of, 1.123
co-operation with, 1.134
continuing to trade, 1.112
definition, 3.3
duties-
    abstracts of receipts and payments, filing, 1.152
    certificate of insolvency, issue of, 1.148
    notice of appointment, giving, 1.145
    preferential creditors, paying, 1.150
    principal, 1.135
    proper price for assets, to obtain, 1.137

Administrative receiver—*contd*
  duties—*contd*
    secured creditors, giving notice to, 1.147
    Statement of Affairs, calling for, 1.133, 1.146
    statutory, 1.143-1.153
    unfit directors, reporting on, 1.151
    unsecured creditors, reporting to and convening meeting of, 1.149
    vacating office, on, 1.153
    writing, acceptance of appointment in, 1.144
  duty of care-
    appointee, to, 1.136
    company, to, 1.137
    constructive trustee, as, 1.142
    guarantors, to, 1.139
    preferential and unsecured creditors, to, 1.140
    retention of title-holders, to, 1.141
    secured creditors, to, 1.138
  floating charge holder, right of to appoint, 1.71, 1.81
  introduction of, 1.43, 1.108
  liquidation, effect of, 1.127
  malpractice, 3.53
  meaning, 1.108
  powers-
    company property, getting in, 1.134
    contractual, 1.130
    court, applications to, 1.132
    directions of court, seeking, 1.132
    duty, following, 1.133
    gas, electricity, water or telephone, requiring supply of, 1.134
    office-holder, as, 1.134
    statutory, 1.131
    types of, 1.129
  preparation of Statement of Affairs, payment of costs of, 1.95
  principal, contracting as, 1.126
  sale at undervalue by, 1.138
  statement of affairs, calling for, 1.133, 1.146

Administrative receivership
  advantages of-
    company, to, 1.112
    directors, to, 1.111
  conduct of-
    decision to trade, 1.156
    directors, involvement of, 1.155
    general practitioner, involvement of, 1.157
  contract of employment, effect on, 3.31
  creditors' committee, 3.21
  initial considerations, 1.105
  life after, 1.158
  preferential creditors, position of-
    company in liquidation, 1.114
    company not in liquidation, 1.113
    fixed charge monies, realisation of, 1.116
    liquidation following receivership, 1.115
  property subject to security, disposal of, 1.132
  reasons for choosing, 1.110

Administrator
  administrative receiver's position contrasted, 1.128
  advantage of acting as, 1.68
  appointment-
    banks, reluctance of, 1.62
    nature of, 1.83
  duties-
    acceptance of proposals, following, 1.98
    certificate of insolvency, issue of, 1.100
    conduct of unfit directors, reporting on, 1.96
    creditors, reporting to, 1.100
    discharge or variation of administration order, application for, 1.99
    general, 1.93
    meeting of creditors, calling, 1.91
    principal, 1.90
    prior transactions, investigation of, 1.97
    Statement of Affairs, to call for, 1.95
  duty of care, 1.93
  information after making of order, 1.94
  malpractice, 3.53
  meaning, 3.4
  officer of company, as, 1.84
  officer of court, as, 1.83
  powers of-
    books, papers and records of company, claiming, 1.89
    duty, following, 1.88
    enquiry into affairs of company, carrying out, 1.89
    office holder, as, 1.89
    statutory, 1.85, 1.87
  receiver, requesting vacation of office by, 1.82, 1.87
  remuneration, 3.21

Agricultural receiver
  meaning, 3.5

Anton Piller order
  meaning, 3.6

Assets
  hire-purchase agreement, subject to, 1.12
  lease agreement, subject to, 1.12
  not specifically pledged, 1.14
  pledged, 1.9

Associated persons
  meaning, 3.7

Balance sheet
  historic, advantages of Statement of Affairs over, 1.6

Bank
  administration route, persuading to, 1.165
  administrative receiver-
    appointment of, 1.105
    choice of, 1.123
  borrowing from, 1.106
  fixed charge, assets caught by, 1.13
  floating charge-
    security under, 1.11
    taking, 1.107
  insolvency-
    attitude on, 1.105

Index   191

Bank—*contd*
  insolvency—*contd*
    perception on, 1.106
    operations of, 1.106
    partner, as, 1.168
    preferential creditor, as, 1.10
    rule in *Clayton's Case*, effect of, 3.13
    security, nature of, 1.164
    wages account, insisting on, 3.13
    warning signs from-
      additional security, request for, 1.118
      formal demand for repayment, 1.121
      independent investigating accountant's report, request for, 1.120
      wages account, request to open, 1.119
Bankrupt
  basic standard of living, 2.22
  individual made, situations of, 2.21
  Official Receiver, investigation by, 3.10
  property, vesting of, 2.22
  public examination of, 2.31
  undischarged, restrictions on, 2.32
Bankruptcy
  avoidable option, as, 2.19
  commencement, individual voluntary arrangement delaying, 2.16
  creditors-
    claim, making, 2.36
    conduct of bankruptcy, having say in, 2.38
    dividends, 2.39
    general practitioner advising, 2.35-2.39
    realisations, order of, 2.39
  creditors' committee, 3.21
  discharge-
    application for, 2.33
    automatic, 2.33
    effect of, 2.34
  duration of, 2.33
  general practitioner-
    creditors, advising, 2.35
    role of, 2.20
  home, effect on-
    bankrupt and child, rights of, 2.28
    charge taken on, 2.29
    more than one registered owner, where, 2.26
    no rights of occupation, where, 2.24-2.26
    powers of trustee, 2.23
    rights of occupation, where, 2.27, 2.27
    sole registered owner, bankrupt, as, 2.25
    spouse, rights of, 2.27
  income earned during, 2.30
  insolvency practitioner's report, 3.10
  last resort, as, 2.2
  liabilities, for purposes of avoiding, 2.34
  offences, 3.11
  order, obtaining, 3.10
  petition, 3.10
Book debts
  general assignment, avoidance of, 3.9

Centrebinding
  meaning, 3.12
Client
  conflicts of interest, 1.2
  identification of, 1.2
  separate representation, 1.3
Company name
  re-use of, 3.62
Company voluntary arrangement
  administration, as exit-route from, 1.101
  administration order, extension of, 1.80
  creditors and members-
    meetings, summoning, 1.55
    scheme, bound by, 1.57
  disadvantages of, 1.61
  distribution of proceeds by, 1.80
  flexibility of, 1.59
  individual voluntary arrangement compared, 1.48
  insolvency practitioner, need for supervision by, 1.51
  interim order, calls for, 1.61
  introduction of, 1.43
  liquidation, reversing-out of, 1.45
  majorities required, 1.56
  meaning, 3.16
  medium for reconstruction, importance as, 1.46
  meetings-
    approval by, 1.56
    chairman, report by, 1.58
    decision, challenging, 1.57
    summoning, 1.55
  nominee, 3.57
    directors' report to, 1.53
    meaning, 1.52
  preferential creditors, position of, 1.50
  proposals-
    court, submission to, 1.54
    directors' report to nominee, 1.53
    putting forward, 1.52
  route forward, as, 1.49
  scheme-
    approval of, 1.56
    binding, 1.59
    creditors bound by, 1.57
    effect of, 1.59
  scheme of reconstruction compared, 1.60
  secured creditors, position of, 1.50
  statutory provisions, 1.47
  supervisor, 3.80
  VAT bad debt relief, 1.102
  winding-up petition, risk of, 1.61
Composition
  meaning, 3.17
Connected persons
  meaning, 3.7
Cork Report
  meaning, 3.20
Costs
  realisation, of, 1.22
Creditors
  administrator reporting to, 1.100

Creditors—*contd*
  moratorium granted by-
    advances secured by guarantees or
      collateral, 1.30
    advantages of, 1.26
    agreement to, 1.36
    approaching creditors, 1.35
    consent, obtaining, 1.27
    effect of, 1.26
    fixed charge, advances secured by, 1.31
    floating charge, advances secured by,
      1.32
    insolvency practitioner, involvement of,
      1.33
    issues, 1.29
    likelihood of, 1.169
    meeting, preparation for, 1.34
    personal insolvency, in, 2.8
    partnership insolvency, in, 2.45
    potential benefits of, 1.28
    proposals, 1.29
    scheme of reconstruction, advantage of,
      1.38
  position affecting, identification of, 1.6
  preferential-
    administration, position on, 1.69
    administrative receiver, duty of, 1.140,
      1.150
    administrative receivership, position on,
      1.113-1.116
    bank as, 1.10
    company voluntary arrangement,
      position on, 1.50
    list of, 1.15
    meaning, 3.65
  secured-
    administrative receiver, duty of, 1.138
    company voluntary arrangement,
      position on, 1.50
    disposal of property, notice of order for,
      1.147
    meaning, 3.74
  unsecured, 1.16
    administration order, advantages of, 1.67
    administrative receiver, duty of, 1.140
    administrative receiver reporting to and
      convening
      meeting of, 1.149
    meaning, 3.83
Creditors' committee
  generally, 3.21
Creditors' meeting
  voting at, 3.86
Creditors' voluntary liquidation
  creditors' meeting, voting at, 3.86
  general practitioner, continuing role of,
    1.162
  last resort, as, 1.160
  liquidator, 3.52
    choice of, 1.161
    joint appointments, 1.161
  overview, 3.22
Crown
  set-off, 3.23

Debenture
  meaning, 3.24
Debts
  inability to pay, 1.1
  interest on, 3.47
  preferential, 3.66
  proof of, 3.67
Deed of arrangement
  generally, 2.9
  meaning, 3.26
Directors
  administration order, advantages of, 1.65
  administrative receivership-
    advantages of, 1.111
    involvement in, 1.155
  appointment of administrative receiver,
    powers and
    responsibilities following, 1.154
  company, conflict with, 1.2
  corporate insolvency, personal position on,
    1.171
  disqualification-
    fraudulent trading, following, 1.178, 3.15
    order, obtaining, 3.15
    statutory provisions, 3.15
    wrongful trading award, following,
      1.187, 3.15
  guarantees, advances secured by, 1.30
  malpractice, 3.53
  misfeasance, 3.56
  pitfalls facing, 3.63
  preferences, 1.170
  separate representation, 1.3
  shadow, 3.76
  undischarged bankrupt as, 2.32
  unfit, 3.15
    administrative receiver reporting on,
      1.151
    report on, 1.96
  wrongful trading, consequences of, 1.183
Disclaimer
  liquidator, by, 3.27
Dissolution
  company, of, 3.28
Distress
  meaning, 3.30

Employees
  claims on insolvency, 1.20
  insolvency, effect of, 3.31
Extortionate credit transactions
  setting aside, 3.33

Fixed charge
  advances secured by, 1.31
  agricultural, 3.5
  assets caught by, 1.13
  effect of, 3.34
Floating charge
  administrative receiver appointed under,
    1.107
  advances secured by, 1.32
  agricultural, 3.5
  avoidance, 3.8

Index 193

Floating charges—contd
bank's security under, 1.11
crystallisation before appointment of receiver, 1.115
debenture incorporating, 3.3
definition, 1.115
effect of, 3.34
holder-
  petition for administration order, right to receive, 1.70
  receiver, right to appoint, 1.71, 1.81
limited, debenture granting, 1.82
registration, 1.109
rule in *Clayton's Case*, effect of, 3.13
unpledged assets subject to, 1.10

Fraudulent trading
advice on, 1.171
court, powers of, 1.173
criminal offence, as, 1.176
definition, 1.172
dishonest intent, proof of, 1.174
disqualification following, 1.178, 3.15
insolvency, test of, 1.1
knowing party, establishment of, 1.177
orders, 1.173
parties at risk, 1.175
wrongful trading compared, 1.188
wrongful trading, effect of introduction of, 1.179

General practitioner
administration, role in, 1.104
administrative receivership, involvement in, 1.157
bankruptcy, role in-
  bankrupt, advising, 2.20-2.34
  creditors, advising, 2.35-2.39
creditors' voluntary liquidation, role in, 1.162
individual voluntary arrangement, role in-
  creditor, guiding, 2.13-2.17
  debtor, guiding, 2.12
insolvency practitioner distinguished, 1.5
partnership insolvency, role in-
  conflicts of interest, avoiding, 2.42
  financial affairs, ascertaining state of, 2.43
  involvement of, 2.41
  options, considering, 2.44-2.48
personal insolvency, initial involvement in, 2.4

Going concern
meaning, 3.36

Guarantor
acting as, 3.37

Hire-purchase
assets subject to, 1.12
consolidation clause, 1.12

Hive-down
meaning, 3.38

Individual voluntary arrangement
commencement of bankruptcy, delaying, 2.16

Individual voluntary arrangement—contd
company voluntary arrangement compared, 1.48
creditors' meeting, 2.11
general practitioner-
  creditor, guiding, 2.13-2.17
  debtor, guiding, 2.12
interim order, 3.45
  application for, 2.11
meaning, 2.10
modifications, suggestion of, 2.17
nominee, 3.57
outline procedure, 2.11
procedure, 3.39
proposal-
  financial implications in, 2.14
  making, 2.11
  reasons for believing, 2.15
refusal to sanction, 2.19
setting up, 2.18
supervisor, 3.80
unscrupulous debtor, 2.16

Insolvency
Centrebinding, 3.12
debts, inability to pay, 1.1
definition, 1.1
inter-relation of routes, 1.44
leased assets, recovery of, 1.167
legislation, 3.40
partnership. *See* PARTNERSHIP INSOLVENCY
personal. *See* PERSONAL INSOLVENCY
potential distraint, dealing with, 1.166
recommendations on, 1.189
right to distrain, 3.30
Rules, 3.42
strategic planning-
  bank, position of, 1.164, 1.65
  creditors' reaction, anticipating, 1.163
taxation, 3.81

Insolvency practitioner
authorisation, 3.41
company voluntary arrangement, supervision of, 1.51
debtor, report on, 3.10
definition, 3.41
ethics, 3.32
general practitioner distinguished, 1.5
informal general moratorium, involvement in, 1.33
nominee, 3.57
professional conduct, 3.32
qualification, 3.41
receipt of instructions, steps on, 1.4
scheme of reconstruction, supervision of, 1.39, 1.41
security, 3.41
separate representation by, 1.3
Society of, 3.78
Statement of Affairs, preparation of, 1.6

Interest
debts, on, 3.47

Lease
assets subject to, 1.12

Lease—*contd*
  original tenant liability, 3.60
Leased assets
  recovery of, 1.167
Lien
  insolvency office-holder, enforceability against, 3.49
Liquidation
  administrative receiver, effect on, 1.127
  alternatives to, 1.25
  contract of employment, effect on, 3.31
  creditors' committee, 3.21
  creditors' voluntary. *See* CREDITORS' VOLUNTARY LIQUIDATION
  enforced, 1.159
  forms of, 3.50
  insolvent, 3.43
  matters requiring attention before, 1.170
  procedure, 3.50
  reversing out of, 1.45
  taxation, 3.81
Liquidator
  creditors' voluntary winding-up, in, 3.22
  disclaimer by, 3.27
  functions of, 3.52
  malpractice, 3.53
  meaning, 3.52
  powers, 3.52
  provisional, 3.68
  removal, 3.52
  remuneration, 3.52
  resignation, 3.52

'Mareva' Injunction
  effect of, 3.54
Members
  overall deficiency, inclusion in, 1.17
Members' voluntary liquidation
  insolvency, test of, 1.1
  insolvent, not, 1.160
  liquidator, 3.52
  procedure, 3.43, 3.55

Official Receiver
  bankrupt, investigation by, 3.10
  functions of, 3.58
  liquidator, as, 3.52
  meaning, 3.58
Original tenant liability
  concept of, 3.60

Partnership insolvency
  approach to, 2.40
  creditors-
    formal arrangement with, 2.46
    informal moratorium, agreeing to, 2.45
  general practitioner-
    conflicts of interest, avoiding, 2.42
    financial affairs, ascertaining state of, 2.43
    involvement of, 2.41
    options, considering, 2.44–2.48
  Insolvent Partnership Order, 2.47, 3.44
    revised, 2.48
  involvement of director in, 3.15

Partnership insolvency—*contd*
  options in, 2.44
  partners, personal bankruptcy of-
    winding-up of firm, with, 2.47
    winding-up of firm, without, 2.47
  partnership, winding-up, 2.47
  rules as to, 2.40
  statutory provisions, 2.40
Personal insolvency
  appropriate option, selecting, 2.7
  client, dealing with, 2.1
  current and future cash flow, review of, 2.6
  deed of arrangement, 2.9
  disclaimer in, 3.27
  general practitioner, initial involvement of, 2.4
  individual voluntary arrangement. *See* INDIVIDUAL VOLUNTARY ARRANGEMENT
  moratorium, creditors agreeing to, 2.8
  situations of, 2.3
  Statement of Affairs, preparation of, 2.5
  taxation, 3.81
  thinking positively, 2.2
Petition
  meaning, 3.61
Phoenix companies
  meaning, 3.62
Plant and machinery
  fixed charge, under, 1.13
Preferences
  meaning, 3.64
Property
  receivership under Law of Property Act, 3.71
Proxy
  meaning, 3.69

Receiver
  interim, 3.46
  Law of Property Act, 3.71
  meaning, 3.70
Retention of title
  holders-
    duty of care to, 1.141
    process of, 3.72

Scheme of reconstruction
  company voluntary arrangement compared, 1.60
  framework for, 1.37
  implementation of, 1.41
  informal arrangement, advantage over, 1.38
  insolvency practitioner, need for supervision by, 1.39, 1.41
  majorities-
    obtaining, 1.42
    required, 1.40
Set-off
  Crown, 3.23
  rules for, 3.75
Special manager
  meaning, 3.77

Statement of Affairs
  administrative receiver calling for, 1.133, 1.146
  administrator calling for, 1.95
  analysis of, 1.23
  bases of valuation-
    book values, 1.18
    cessation, 1.18
    comparison of, 1.19
    going concern, 1.18
  compulsory winding-up, in, 3.18
  creditors' voluntary winding-up, in, 3.22
  figures, build-up of, 1.7
  format of, 1.8
  historic Balance Sheet, advantages over, 1.6
  insolvency, position of, 1.1
  personal insolvency, in, 2.5
  preparation of, 1.6
    costs of, 1.95
  side by side, preparation of, 1.19
Statutory demand
  meaning, 3.79
Surplus and Deficiency Account
  construction of, 1.24

Taxation
  insolvency, in, 3.81
Transactions at undervalue
  meaning, 3.64
Transfer of undertakings
  employees' rights, protection of, 3.31
Trustee in bankruptcy
  disclaimer by, 3.27
  generally, 3.82
  property vesting in, 2.22

Unfair dismissal
  award for, 3.31

Value added tax
  bad debt relief, 1.21, 1.48, 1.102, 1.148, 3.85
  claims, elements of, 1.21
  generally, 3.84

Wages account
  bank requesting opening of, 1.119, 3.13
Winding up
  compulsory, 3.18
  court, by, petition, 3.18
  order, 3.88
  resolution, 3.90
Wrongful trading
  advice on, 1.171
  award-
    application of, 1.186
    assessing, 1.185
    compensatory, 1.184
    disqualification following, 1.187, 3.15
    liquidator, paid to, 1.186
  defence, 1.182
  definition, 1.181
  directors-
    duties of, 1.184
    practical consequences for, 1.183
  fraudulent trading-
    compared, 1.188
    effect of introduction on, 1.179
  insolvency, test of, 1.1
  interpretation of law, 1.184
  new law, need for, 1.180